Achieving Moral Health

Achieving Moral Health

{ AN EXERCISE PLAN
FOR YOUR CONSCIENCE }

Charles M. Shelton, Ph.D.

A Crossroad Book
The Crossroad Publishing Company
New York

The Crossroad Publishing Company
481 Eighth Avenue, New York, NY 10001

Printed in the United States of America

Library of Congress Cataloging-in-Publication Data
Shelton, Charles M.
    Achieving moral health : an exercise plan for your conscience /
Charles M. Shelton.
        p. cm.
    Includes bibliographical references.
    ISBN 0-8245-1868-3 (alk. paper)
    1. Conscience. I. Title.
BJ1471.S54 2000
170 – dc21

                                        00-008880

1   2   3   4   5   6   7   8   9   10   06   05   04   03   02   01   00

For Mom and Dad,
my first teachers of conscience,
and
for my students,
whose questions, comments, and behavior
help to keep my conscience
open, challenged, and (I hope) healthy

CONTENTS

FOREWORD

In my first job out of college, as a telecommunications engineer, I observed right away that there seemed to be two kinds of behavior in the workplace: that which displayed a conscience, and that which did not. The latter type of behavior was a source of constant irritation to its practitioners' co-workers. It included making falsified measurements and data, taking credit for others' work, padding expense reports, playing hooky from work, stealing competitors' ideas, scheduling useless meetings in exotic places... and so on. Generally speaking, the people who practiced these behaviors had more trouble in their work relationships — *and in their personal relationships* as well. You've seen these behaviors in your workplace, too.

On the other hand, conscience-driven behaviors were always a breath of fresh air. They involved such attributes as working hard, caring about customers and co-workers, generally being fair, and challenging "group think" whenever it stretched the limits of propriety. This included not being afraid to say "Wait a minute!" when a committee was about to compromise integrity for short-term gain. People who consistently practiced conscience-driven behavior had more friends at work, enjoyed better personal lives, and usually, over time, reaped more rewards at work. They are the ones I remember most fondly — as you do. But I also observed that many people appeared to be conscience-driven in some instances and "conscience-free" in others. They'd insist on honest advertising, yet cheat on their expense accounts. Or they would devote endless hours to public service projects, yet ignore the needs of their families or co-workers.

Why were their behaviors so compartmentalized?

9

Are mine?

Are yours?

How many of our daily stresses, work problems, relationship issues — and even health problems — arise from these inconsistencies?

And how can each of us go about examining — and changing — our behavior so it will lead to more satisfying careers and personal lives? Too few have asked this question, and even fewer in modern times have attempted to answer it in a practical way. We owe a huge debt of gratitude to Dr. Charles Shelton for tackling this vital, yet difficult, subject, and for compiling the thoughts, examples, and exercises he has assembled in this book. Reading it will, indeed, be good for your conscience.

But what is conscience, anyway?

In this era of guaranteed, unlimited "self-esteem" for everyone, it might surprise some people to know that conscience involves the capacity *to feel guilt:* to be embarrassed by our actions or uncomfortable with our thoughts. If that's the case, why would anyone *want* a conscience? To have a satisfying life, that's why. Dr. Shelton tells us how to turn our negative feelings into positive ones by examining and morally choosing our decisions and actions. He also helps us to understand that conscience is a combination of feelings and forces, and that it easily succumbs to the demands and stresses we face in our everyday lives. As Dr. Shelton teaches us, "What appears simple calls for continual reflection, discipline, and effort." Indeed. As my career continued, I discovered that it wasn't always easy to categorize behaviors or to identify the moral high ground between two or more choices. What if you had to choose between maintaining an aging factory in a small town whose economy depended on your business or meeting your obligation to keep prices low, profits growing, and the company (and its jobs) alive?

What if two equally valuable employees were having a turf war or personality conflict and stubbornly refused to cooperate on a project that was vital to the business?

What if the demands of your job required you to spend too much time away from your family?

What if your career goals were in conflict with your health?

Dr. Shelton provides guidelines to help each of us make the right decision for every situation — and for ourselves.

As I moved into leadership positions, I realized that I could actually influence behaviors in the workplace. When someone asked the conscience-driven question, "Why are there no women or minority persons in management?" the "conscience-free" response was "Don't rock the boat." But my own conscience echoed the question: "Why *don't* we ...?" And while the immediate answer was, "Because cultural biases created unequal opportunity," the longer-term answer had to be: "Here's what I'm going to do about it." For leaders, this kind of situation is an opportunity to demonstrate — and teach — moral behavior. I made the unpopular decision to require managers' participation in gender- and racial-awareness workshops, to ban company-paid memberships in organizations that discriminated, and to make senior managers' bonuses contingent on improving the diversity of their teams. In the beginning, resistance was high. Over time, what had been a source of contention became a source of pride among all managers and employees, not to mention a better workplace and a more competitive company, ready to deal in today's international marketplace. Leaders face similar opportunities every day. But it's often difficult to know how to evaluate the moral choices that face us and to examine the feelings those choices involve. This book is an outstanding resource for every corporate and organizational leader who faces such dilemmas.

But moral health is not just a workplace issue. It is a home, school, club, church, and neighborhood issue, as well. In my roles as spouse, parent (and, recently, grandparent), organization member, and citizen, I have faced a steady progression of questions, challenges, and choices that would have been, and will be, made easier by using the exercises in this book.

Although my parents have passed on, I could not accept this forum without acknowledging their contributions to my moral health. I learned about conscience the old-fashioned way: by being told what kinds of behavior were right, what kinds were wrong, and that the latter came with great parental disapproval. My father was a judge, both at the courthouse and at the dinner table. My mother was a teacher, both in the classroom and in the living room. I am thankful, every day, for the example they provided me, the eyebrows they raised at me, and the punishments they dispensed to me — as well as praise for good behavior. They were patterns for me in my own parenting, and I know that many readers will relate to this belated appreciation of a parent, grandparent, youth-group leader, or other role model. We should be thankful for all such teachers, as well as for Dr. Shelton.

Finally, a timely quote, a personal point of view, and a timeless recommendation: in her syndicated newspaper column, Mona Charen observed recently, "There is no question that low self-esteem is associated with much pathology. But that insight has been ridden into the ground in modern America, to the point where building strong self-esteem has become a substitute for serious moral reasoning and self-examination." In my view, true self-esteem comes from knowing yourself, your limitations, and your ability to handle difficult times — not from the idea that "you're worthy no matter what you do" — because what you do is who you are.

Self-esteem also comes from having a moral "base," from asking, as Dr. Shelton suggests: "Given the realities of my personal and/or professional life, what human qualities must I attend to in order to insure that I make the best possible moral decisions?"

In the pages of this book, you will find how to inventory those realities, how to identify and develop those qualities, and how to make those decisions.

You will learn a great deal from this book — about yourself, about choices, and about achieving true success at work and real satisfaction in life.

Read on...and let your conscience be your guide!

RICHARD D. McCORMICK
Chairman Emeritus, U S WEST, Inc.
President, U.S. Council for International Business
Vice-President and President-elect, International Chamber of Commerce

ACKNOWLEDGMENTS

I am most grateful to Regis University for granting me a sabbatical year that allowed the time to put my thoughts to pen. The university's campus, with its library and faculty, provided a delightful and stimulating environment to think through my thoughts on the meaning of conscience and how it functions in our everyday lives. In particular, I am most grateful to John Ridgway, a faculty colleague, who not only read the entire manuscript but offered invaluable comments throughout the writing process.

I would appreciate your comments and thoughts on the various aspects of moral health and conscience as they are presented in this book. I can be contacted through e-mail at: cshelton@regis.edu or through the Department of Psychology at Regis University.

Acknowledgment is gratefully give for permission to quote from the following:

Isaiah Berlin, "On the Pursuit of the Ideal," *New York Review of Books,* March 17, 1988. Reprinted with permission from the *New York Review of Books.* Copyright © 1988NYREV, Inc.

Robert Coles, "Gatsby in the B School," October 25, 1987. Copyright © 1987 by the New York Times Co. Reprinted by permission.

Thomas F. Green, "The Formation of Conscience in an Age of Technology," *American Journal of Education,* November 1985, p. 23. Reprinted by permission of the University of Chicago Press.

Sports Illustrated: "Sportsmen of the Year," by Gary Smith, December 21, 1998, copyright © 1998, Time Inc.; "The Big Hero of Littleton," by Rick Riley, May 3, 1999, copyright © 1999, Time Inc.; "Goodbye, Sweetness," by Don Yaeger, November 8, 1999, copyright © 1999, Time Inc. All rights reserved.

"American Opinion: A Quarterly Survey of Politics, Economics, and Values," December 13, 1996, republished with permission of the *Wall Street Journal, Western Edition.*

James Q. Wilson, *The Moral Sense,* copyright © 1993 by James Q. Wilson. Reprinted with permission of The Free Press, a Division of Simon & Schuster, Inc.

Achieving Moral Health

{ Introduction }

HUMANITY'S UNIQUE ATTRIBUTE

═══════════
═══════════

Always do right; this will gratify
some people and astonish the rest.
— MARK TWAIN

Focusing on health is an American pastime. An enormous amount of energy and resources is invested in research and programs to alleviate physical suffering and emotional disorders. Sadly, this noble goal has the unintended consequence of restricting health's meaning to its physical and mental domains. But there is another area that is especially worthy of consideration: the moral realm. More specifically, humanity's most cherished attribute — our capacity to evaluate and make moral decisions — deserves the title "moral health." On a positive note, the subject of morality now receives greater media coverage than in previous decades. However, all too often such reporting merely reflects reaction to and increasing concern about our nation's moral decline. "Moral health" is a novel concept, not so readily recognized as the more familiar "physical health" and "mental health." I have written this book to raise public consciousness regarding this aspect of health and claim for it a status comparable to other domains.

The very phrase "moral health" strikes us as unusual. No doubt it is the word "moral" rather than "health" that captures our attention. Harvard psychologist Jerome Kagan reminds us that one of the "seductive ideas" driving the discipline of psychology is the erroneous assumption that human beings are motivated solely by pleasure.[1] In contrast to this belief, Kagan makes the

17

point that "unlike any other animal, humans continually judge the moral implications of their wishes, behaviors, and feelings."[2] In other words, contrary to popular opinion and against the pronouncements of some that pleasure seeking is the driving force behind everyday behavior, humans are capable of organizing their lives, actions, and goals around noble ideas. Moreover, the ability to evaluate personal behavior in a specific situation and subsequently to label actions "good" or "bad" is beyond the capacity of any other species. Animals have emotions, and some species closely related to humans possess limited forms of self-awareness and empathy.[3] However, the word "moral" involves such sophisticated mental complexity that its application outside of human endeavors is meaningless. Indeed, we reserve the words "moral" and "immoral" solely for evaluations applied to ourselves or other human beings.

To explore this point more fully, consider what human qualities are required in order to make an ethical judgment. Think of several instances when you have applied the label "right or wrong," "good or bad," or "moral or immoral" to your own or someone else's behavior. Though we normally do not reflect upon the underlying capabilities needed to make such judgments, in reality, many attributes are required, including:

1. an awareness of your own as well as another's thoughts, intentions, and feelings;

2. a willingness to take personal responsibility for your actions and the corresponding expectation that others do likewise;

3. an awareness of and judgment about what can and cannot be done within a given situation;

4. belief in a set of moral principles that guide behavior and enable evaluation of your own as well as others' actions;

5. the ability to feel guilt as a consequence of your actions.

The above list could easily be expanded. There is no evidence that creatures other than humans possess such a complex set of attributes. For example, I have often asked colleagues or students,

"Have you ever seen a guilty rat?" or "What moral principles does a monkey consciously reflect upon to shape and guide its life to become a more ethical monkey?" This "moral sense" or "moral motive" has been labeled in various ways. I prefer the word "conscience" to describe this most defining feature of our humanity. Whether religious or atheistic, liberal or conservative, pessimistic or optimistic, committed to someone or something or searching for such commitment or at the moment content with aimless wandering, we are first and above all human beings who make judgments of conscience.

Conscience's roots are evident even in very young children. Parents are able to foster their children's moral growth without the highly focused drills and study time that accompany the learning of subjects such as spelling, writing, and math. Helping children develop a good conscience is far from an effortless task; nonetheless, children are natural moralists. Even two- and three-year-olds become upset and apply terms such as "good" and "bad" to specific people and events. "By the second year of life, children compare their behavior to standards of goodness and badness, including standards of competent performance, and so the habit of self-evaluation is acquired early and is pervasive."[4] Indeed, a "striking" aspect of the child's moral sense is that it surfaces even "before the child has acquired much in the way of language."[5] As children continue to develop, this labeling takes on an increasingly moral tone as they internalize moral rules and develop a complex sense of empathy. Not surprisingly, such moral growth is enhanced by a nurturing family climate that both teaches moral responsibility and displays caring behavior toward others. "In conscience formation, the psychological bond between parents and children becomes moralized — immediately for parents, and gradually for children."[6]

Unfortunately, although the capacity for conscience is a uniquely human attribute, it does not follow that all children grow to be adults with well-functioning consciences. Nonetheless, knowing we possess such profound capacity offers both challenges and hope.[7] "Only people with relatively clear consciences are capable of distinguishing good and evil with clarity; and only people who are capable of distinguishing between good and evil with clarity are capable of making sound decisions."[8] In essence, this book is about the conscience of any person. But no person exists as an isolated entity. Just as we never truly can appreciate conscience unless we view the person, so too we can never adequately understand the person unless we acquire insight into his or her culture.

Conscience and Culture

We have witnessed rapid change in American culture over the past few decades. We hear discussions or read about "culture wars" and increasingly polarized opinions surrounding a number of controversial issues. One camp (I'll use the phrase "establishment critics" to describe it) focuses on the lack of traditional values among youth as well as, at times, their baby boomer parents. Establishment critics are wary of our increasingly psychologically minded culture. American culture is awash in psychological themes. Finding self-fulfillment through relationships, achieving self-actualization, and adopting trendy value stances under the mantle of "political correctness" are particularly disturbing to establishment critics. Excessive self-focus and rampant individualism most certainly loom large across our cultural landscape. Left unchecked, excessive individualism "flattens and narrows our lives, makes them poorer in meaning, and less concerned with others or society."[9] As the pages ahead demonstrate, I am in sympathy with many establishment critics' concerns. Nonetheless, the critique itself is at times excessive. Over the past several generations, particularly since the end of World War II, our country has undergone many positive changes. For one, increased opportunities for education, particularly higher education, have helped many people acquire not only basic necessities but also the means to live fairly comfortable lives with considerable leisure time. Also, as a nation we have grown increasingly aware of discrimination and bias. The passage of civil rights legislation as well as laws that protect the rights of the disabled are just a few examples of America's social progress. Of course, there is much to criticize in

American culture, even beyond what establishment critics might decry. Poverty still exists, with women and minorities its major victims. Racism and sexism are alive and well in the workplace. Nonetheless, we must acknowledge in the light of any critique the positive changes that have occurred.

Equally important, the culture in which we live is the only culture we have. I doubt many establishment critics desire to turn the clock back to the early post–World War II era. To do so would negate the technological advances (along with the comfort they produce — just consider computer or medical advances) and the ethical sensitivities (a national consciousness that segregation is wrong or the legal recognition that all citizens enjoy certain rights such as privacy) that have come about over the last half of the previous century.

The legal and social changes transforming American culture over these decades blend with Americans' growing acceptance of psychologically minded themes such as self-fulfillment. One effect of these cultural shifts is the promotion of individual self-expression and the corresponding belief that one is free to think, feel, and act (with some limitations of course) as one desires. In other words, the growing ethos that appeals to more and more people is the goal (and increasingly "felt" as the right) to become an *authentic self.* Today many Americans assume that achieving authenticity is a worthy life-objective. Additionally, the very notion of "becoming more authentic" spawns a wide supporting cast of perspectives that include: (1) a belief in subjectivity: "my experience" is the sole arbiter for making moral decisions; (2) the notion that all viewpoints are equally valid; and (3) the idea that individual entitlement takes priority over community obligations. Of course, not everyone accepts such thinking, and qualifications must be placed on the above views. For example, "individual entitlement" does not mean one is free to disregard with impunity the laws of society or community standards. Such an extreme position would lead to anarchy and chaos. Nonetheless, the trend toward subjectivity, the intellectual equality of ideas, and individual self-expression is so common today, especially among the young (and frequently their baby boomer parents), that the legitimacy of the drive to realize one's authentic self has become deeply and irrevocably interweaved within the nation's cultural fabric. Because this focus on authenticity is often accepted as a cultural norm, we fail to recognize how truly dramatic this cultural transformation is when compared with the two decades immediately following World War II. (This point is raised again when we compare the hierarchical and relational models; see p. 142.) Establishment critics make valid criticisms of this cultural shift when it leads to a self-absorption or an indulgence that demonstrates little if any consideration for the welfare of others. But, again, we cannot avoid the reality that it is the *only* culture we have.

Here we have a dilemma. What to do? One answer of course is to adopt wholeheartedly either one or the other end of the spectrum. On the one hand, we can embrace the establishment critics' views and make sweeping indictments that predict moral disaster. On the other hand, we can align ourselves with those individuals who champion an authenticity that features individualism and self-indulgence. *Are we left with choosing between the extremes of indicting culture or going along with it?* To choose the former is to invite continual alienation that drains us psychically. Few people are capable of waging ongoing war with the culture and at the same time sustaining the energy and focus needed to live a morally healthy life as envisioned in these pages. This is one reason that alienated individuals frequently seek support through association with like-minded individuals. But another concern must also be noted. Condemning the culture represents a biased, simplistic viewpoint whose sole message is negative. Surely, a morally healthy life embraces more than constant censures and denunciations.

At the same time, to adopt the viewpoint that moral health is achieved by embracing uncritically the notion that "I" must trust only my experience and fashion a life that seeks to express only what "I" hold to be most authentic leads nowhere. Uncritically endorsing such a viewpoint endangers the cherished notions of commitment, fidelity, community, and self-sacrifice. Within this mind-set, we disconnect ourselves from the very roots on which the moral life depends. In the long run, such a position bends to the excesses that render moral living shallow and superficial. So, again, the question needs to be asked: Since a person achieves moral health only *within a culture,* what stance toward culture offers the most promise for attaining moral health? I believe that instead of dismissing the authentic self, we should acknowledge its value. Most certainly, being an individual, having freedom, experiencing fulfillment, and expressing one's desires are valued ends. In other words, being authentic is a good we truly can seek. But the *truly authentic person possesses a moral quality: his or her conscience.* As envisioned within these pages, conscience serves to ground authenticity in the good, just as it corrects its excesses. It amends errant steps toward authenticity and remedies misguided assumptions about its meaning. Thus I maintain that we can seek and acquire authenticity. We should relish the opportunities that go with being an authentic human being. We should even be appreciative that we live in a culture that holds the search for authenticity in such high esteem. But because we exist not only as persons in a culture but as *persons of conscience in a culture,* seeking opportunities that promote our authenticity makes sense only when due consideration is given to the moral dimension inherent in such a search. Put differently, conscience provides each person's authentic search with an irreducible moral quality. The functioning of healthy conscience grounds the authentic quest in a way that insures it remains true to what is most noble about humanity: the reality that we are moral beings.

I propose that we forsake the blanket censuring of American culture. At the same time, I reject expressions of authenticity whose primary purpose appears mere self-absorption or self-serving ways of relating that ignore both others' needs and the wider community. I believe a middle ground is possible. As explained in the pages ahead, the uniquely human attribute of conscience allows our striving for authenticity to flourish, while keeping us faithful to the truest meaning of being human.[10]

The Most Critical Question

What is the "most critical question" we could ask ourselves? Assume, for example, that you are a parent, a coach, or a teacher —

in a role allowing you to influence the lives of youth. Now ask yourself: *If I could wish for one thing for all the children under my care or direction what would I ask for?* Obviously you want young people under your care to feel loved. Yet other worthy answers abound: self-esteem, trust, faith, problem solving ability, communication skills, are just a few of many worthy responses. But just as this question proves difficult, it provides opportunity for insight. It forces us to consider what is most essential for the child's good. Every time I ponder this question my answer remains the same. I would want every child under my care to have, above all, a *healthy functioning conscience.* Young people increasingly confront adult-like decisions at younger and younger ages. More and more children and early adolescents (ten-to-fifteen-year-olds) encounter opportunities for sexual relationships and drug use. "Should I have sex now or wait?" and "Should I try drugs?" are life-threatening issues today. A well-functioning conscience provides young people their sturdiest ally for dealing with such temptation. In fact, conscience is the *only* resource any child, adolescent, or adult will *always* have available for resolving moral issues and dilemmas.

The urgency surrounding the need to nurture every child's and adolescent's conscience becomes all the more compelling when considering the sheer number of young people making up the current youth generation. "Generation Y" numbers more than fifty million children and adolescents under fifteen years of age, and in only a few short years this teenage population will check in at thirty million. As a result, this generation's impact will be enormous well into the twenty-first century. In the moral realm this means, of course, that our nation's moral character rests in large measure on the decisions these adults of tomorrow make.

Living a Moral Life

Every day numerous opportunities exist to test our moral compass (or perhaps to dust it off!). Moral health involves everything: the attitudes we hold, the decisions we make, the personal life history we sort out (and come to terms with), and the future we plan.

Place yourself in each of the six following situations:

- My income tax is due. Should I report all my taxable income?

- I make a career move and take a sales position for a company specializing in making software for managing corporate accounts and information flow. After my sales training concludes I am given a targeted monthly sales quota on which I earn a commission. As I call upon potential customers and demonstrate a new product I realize all the glitches have not been worked out and conclude that the software has been rushed to market too quickly in order to get a leg up on the competition. I am troubled by the product's failure to meet specific standards and sometimes question whether customers I serve need this advanced software. At the same time, I know all too well that failure to promote enthusiastically this new product will diminish my sales and lower my income. I am married with two children, and my paycheck is essential to make ends meet. What should I do?

- As a company manager in charge of long-term planning for corporate growth I rely on the continuing presence of a knowledgeable organizational consultant for needed advice. This consultant requests that because of the illness of a family member she cut in half her consulting time. Should I honor her request?

- I enjoy team sports. I'm also married and have a demanding job. Given these commitments, should I join the team?

- A friend's behavior concerns me. I know bringing up the behavior would be awkward and most likely painful for both of us. Should I bring my concern to her attention?

- In the office I find myself increasingly spending time browsing the Internet, surfing the web, and e-mailing jokes and personal notes to friends and relatives. I realize I am using work time for personal rather than company business. At times, I worry about this "virtual morality" issue, yet I see many of my colleagues doing the same thing. During work hours should I cut back my use of the computer for personal enjoyment?[11]

We can pick out the moral issue of honesty central to the first case. But some situations described above would stimulate a lively discussion among most adults. Every situation described above relates to moral health. Why? Because whatever decision we make influences both our ability and our desire to be good sons or daughters, good brothers or sisters, good parents, good friends, good spouses, and good colleagues. In one way or another, all the above situations invite us to confront what it means to live daily a *good* life. We know that for our muscles to maintain their form, we must choose to stay physically active. The same principle applies if we wish to become morally fit. We must develop an exercise plan for our moral lives; otherwise, moral fitness declines, leaving us morally weak and infirm.

At times such moral exercise requires considerable effort because many situations lack a clear moral solution. Take the example of whether to join a sports team while married and employed. On the surface no right answer is evident. Some no doubt would subscribe to the position that no clear moral issues are at stake. But examine the situation more closely. On the one hand, joining the team might offer time for relaxation, or a chance for rediscovering fond memories from youth, or an opportunity to reconnect with old friends. All of these consequences are worthwhile. Moreover, feeling relaxed, experiencing joy, and relating to friends provide avenues that energize moral fitness. On the other hand, being a team member demands time and energy. If I join the team, will the quality of my life as a spouse, parent, or business associate suffer? These are moral questions precisely because they pose the fundamental issue of how we experience goodness in the cherished roles that define our lives.

Morality in the Trenches: The World of Work and Relationship

We best understand the link between our human actions and their moral significance when examining the two commitments that provide our lives their most valued meaning: working and loving. Let's take work first. Unfortunately, the principles of business ethics often are viewed as irrelevant to corporate leaders precisely because they are applied as absolute moral principles to extraordinarily complex situations with numerous entangled (and often competing) relationships.

To say that the struggle to be a moral person in the business world is challenging and complex is not to say that we should view moral concerns as irrelevant to the world of business. Like all endeavors, work issues influence our lives as moral people because the very nature of our work raises serious questions as to who we are, who we are becoming, and who we desire to be. It leads us to ask: "How do you balance your business life and your home life? How do you resist the temptation to become callous and selfish? How do you hold to moral and religious values in the face of all sorts of challenges at work? What happens to people, emotionally and spiritually, when they compromise with certain important principles — start down the road of rationalizations and self-justifications?"[12]

The world of work invites these soul-searching moral questions. But the issues we encounter within our relationships provide an equally rich source for moral reflection. Consider for a moment life as an adult son or daughter, a friend, a spouse, or a parent. Think of the tangled, competing interests and time commitments these roles entail and the demands each requires. What type of person do we become when a cherished relationship proves burdensome? At what point do negative feelings such as anger, hurt, disappointment, or the mere stress of trying to be so many things to so many people undermine the good intentions and desires we have for friends and family? In short, all aspects of our relational lives, like our work lives, are threaded and interwoven with moral concerns.

Becoming, being, and growing morally fit incorporates all we do. Moral health depends not just upon the major decisions we make but also includes the ordinary, everyday decisions that occupy our work lives and relationships.

Surprisingly, moral health is rather easily defined (though not so easily achieved!). In essence, moral health requires having a healthy functioning conscience. In one sense it seems so simple!

Having a good conscience? "Sure," we say. But what appears simple calls for continuous reflection, discipline, and effort.

My work as a therapist and teacher confirms the observation that from childhood on we never escape recurring questions surrounding the moral meaning of our actions. Parents scrutinize personal behaviors, always wondering how their actions influence their children. Children, on the other hand, seek the approval of authority figures, yet inevitably begin to shape and finally sculpt a set of moral beliefs they call their own. Older adults reflect back on many decades of experiences while striving to construct a personal narrative that produces enduring peace, healing, and contentment.

Most psychologists describe our attention to moral meaning as essential for healthy functioning. No matter what our beliefs, attitudes, worldviews, or (for many) religious leanings, there is no dismissing the fact that virtually all of us strive to see ourselves as ethical.[13] A common assumption in psychology is the single observation that "humans will resort to all means of self-deception to fortify their view of themselves as moral."[14] Even groups we regard as removed from the moral mainstream subscribe to some type of ethical code. The gang member caught violating the gang's code usually receives from other gang members a response that is swift and brutal.

Rarely does a week pass by that a national magazine or television show fails to publicize some story or issue provoking reader or viewer concern about our country's moral fiber. Many are dismayed by the publicity surrounding a number of well-publicized school shootings and other acts of random violence. However, our national moral discussion lacks something absolutely essential if it is to prove productive. We speak too little of the need to acknowledge the simple, yet essential, point that being ethical requires that we be persons of conscience. To talk about values or morality without focusing on conscience is like discussing an upcoming vacation without considering how we will get to our destination. Like the method of transportation we choose, conscience serves as the means for achieving the moral health we desire. And this is the rub. We spend so much time talking about values, beliefs, and right actions but neglect the human being, whose conscience must adhere to and is the source for living out beliefs and right actions.

Introducing Conscience

What is conscience? Ponder for a moment each of the following real-life situations:

- The headline reads: "Boy, 5, Is Killed for Refusing to Steal Candy."[15] What went on in this child's mind that led him to refuse to steal candy when pressured by older children?

- "Tormented by pangs of conscience, I hesitated and thought a number of times that I should stop. But I couldn't go against orders."[16] These words are reported to have been spoken by Ikuo Hayashi, a doctor who was a member of the Aum Shinrikyo sect that carried out the gas attack on the Tokyo subway. What is our initial impression when reading such words?

- The now retired United States Senator Mark Hatfield cast the deciding vote that defeated legislation championed by younger senators from his own party. Angered over his decision, some junior senators wished to strip him of his chairmanship of the Senate Appropriations Committee. Hatfield, dismayed over this turn of events, stated, "I said what I would do from the beginning. I at no time got any indication that I was going to be chastised or disciplined for voting my conscience."[17] In the end, Hatfield retained his chairmanship of the committee and was praised by senior senators for sticking to his principles.

- Most gruesome and horrific is the statement made by one of the most notorious political leaders of the late twentieth century. The Cambodian dictator Pol Pot, whose policies led to the slaughter of millions of Cambodians, stated shortly before his death, "Even now, and you can look at me: am I a savage person? My conscience is clear."[18]

- How do we make sense of the actions of Brian Stewart, a thirty-two-year-old Missouri man convicted of injecting AIDS-tainted blood into his infant son? His motive, said prosecutors, was to avoid paying child support.[19]

- Finally, how do we explain the actions of someone who drags a man to death by tying him to the back of a truck?[20]

All of these examples beg further questions. But each in its own way fascinates, drawing us to reflect and wonder about the moral decisions people make and how conscience functions. With this in mind, let us say for now that conscience is our moral center; it grounds our humanness in moral ways. To invoke a currently popular phrase, conscience serves as our "moral compass," providing the guidance for all that we do.

Conscience nurtures, from a moral perspective, the worlds of work and relationship. Most concretely, conscience exists as our moral core, telling us how we "ought" to act in our cherished relationships as friends, parents, spouses, siblings, and colleagues. Conscience is the guidepost for believing, feeling, and acting within these treasured roles.

In a similar vein, conscience lies at the foundation for work and career decisions. Yet work is increasingly driven by spiraling knowledge bases and specialized skills. From the perspective of moral health, such trends pose potential problems. A businessman focuses on finance, a lawyer restricts her practice to copyright law, a teacher specializes in instructing emotionally disabled children. These specialized flows of information, though understandable (and often even necessary), encourage a narrowing perspective that desensitizes us to the moral issues that surround complex, intertangled relationships and situations. The lawyer specializing in copyright law, for example, might be technically quite proficient in the fine points of the law and its application, but such law's reach and impact go beyond ownership and royalties. It involves access to information, reader choices, quality of knowledge, and questions of fairness — all of which carry potential moral weight. Specialization often makes grasping the wider moral picture more difficult.

In order to increase moral sensitivity and resolve ethical issues occurring in work settings, professional organizations publish
"codes of ethics," and academic institutions develop specific
courses addressing ethical issues that future career professionals
might encounter (e.g., business or medical ethics). Such efforts are
vital, yet also incomplete. I grow increasingly concerned about the
all too common assumption that morality is "out there" in a professional code that "I" simply follow and apply or that morality
is contained in an academic course whose content "I" am expected to learn. This approach neglects the fundamental reality
that *people* rather than codes initiate, apply, and carry out moral
choices. A code of ethics or a course on ethics too often ignores
the person making the moral decision. As a result, half the moral
equation remains unsolved or ignored. Too often we are left with
an *ethics-without-people approach to morality.*[21]

Today's corporations are so concerned about instilling an ethical
climate in the workplace that management resorts to approaches
like implementing ethical codes, establishing ethics offices within
the company, and hiring managers whose MBA transcripts include
courses in business ethics. Unfortunately, promoting an ethical
environment must compete with corporate climates characterized
by pressures to succeed, loyalty to the company, and cumbersome
layers of bureaucratic decision making. As a result, despite the
noble goals of American businesses, there exist far too many ethical lapses and moral failures. Yet corporations are more likely to be
profitable and thrive when they develop a reputation for honesty
and integrity. In the long run, being good really does pay off![22]
Most importantly, the simplest way in the business world to insure
a reputation for honesty is to hire men and women of good conscience.[23] Furthermore, in the real world of business relationships
and everyday job settings, when ethical issues arise, the typical
employee is inclined to look to how his or her boss handles such
problems rather than refer to a code of ethics.[24] As a consequence, a
corporate head might well look no further than the closest mirror if
he or she is puzzled to learn about ethical lapses among employees.

Corporate America must be willing to rediscover the *person* in
business ethics, and this requires that priority be given to sup-

porting and promoting the development of conscience among employees, supervisors, managers, and corporate CEOs. Robert Coles fondly quotes Paul Tillich's saying that "morality for ordinary people is not the result of reading books and writing papers, as we're doing. Morality is not a *subject;* it is a life put to the test in dozens of moments."[25] Unless we consider this latter half of the equation — this "life" and its innumerable "moments" — then the moral ideals we desire suffer the fate of an important theory never applied, essential skills never tested, or helpful tools never used.

Books and articles on morality most commonly promote specific moral principles or champion specific courses of action. What has not been addressed adequately, however, is the focus on the person who daily encounters numerous moral choices. Let's formulate this issue as a question: *Given the realities of my personal and/or professional life, what human qualities must I attend to in order to insure that I make the best possible moral decisions?* Failing to give attention to these "qualities" renders conscience increasingly ineffective or even impaired. No matter how noble or well-intended our beliefs or how intensely they are held, without adequate human functioning, we undermine conscience and, inevitably, moral health.

In the chapters that follow I explore what every person must do to make his or her conscience function well. Each chapter offers exercises or discussion questions to promote the self-awareness necessary to sustain moral health. My hope is that by reading these pages you come to a deeper understanding of how your conscience functions. Inevitably such an undertaking cannot help but lead to a deepening realization of the joys and struggles that go with being both human and moral.

WHY CONSCIENCE?

═══════════

I merely had come to see honor and conscience as a psycho-logical necessity, as the sine qua non of a stable identity. If you did not adhere to your conscience, if there was nothing that in some way absolutely limited your conduct in life, then who were you, I asked myself? What were you?

— PATRICK GLYNN

Our Lives as Moral Persons

As a psychologist I share many moments with people struggling with personal issues and relationship conflicts. What is striking about so many clients is the underlying (and often undetected) moral issue so vital for their eventual healing. Underneath the hurt, felt inadequacy, or conflicted state there exists for most clients an unspoken wish: the desire to be the good person, spouse, parent, friend, or co-worker. My clients often perceive themselves as having failed to live the ideal they desire (the "good") in a relationship or realize that a significant person in their life has failed to live this ideal (quite often both are true). As a consequence they struggle to resolve acute feelings of anger, guilt, and sadness.

Working in therapy with a troubled adolescent boy became the basis for developing and eventually holding firmly to the belief that most people have within themselves *an unspoken desire for goodness.* His mother requested that I see him after several thefts had led to legal problems. As I earned Sean's[1] trust, he shared the linger-ing self-defeating feelings that arose from his parents' divorce and his father's abrupt exit from home. These negative feelings trig-

33

gered growing friction with his mom, building barriers with his siblings, and increasing withdrawal from his friends. Though he knew stealing was wrong, Sean continued to steal. He was angry at his dad for leaving him, angry at his mother for what he (for the most part mistakenly) perceived as encouraging his dad's departure, and angry at himself for both his conflicted feelings and his wrongful behavior. As therapy progressed, I asked Sean to consider a "hypothesis." I said that deep down inside he most certainly loved his parents, and I wondered aloud if the real issue was "your desire for your parents and for you." Sean responded with a quizzical look. I continued gently: "I wonder, Sean, if the real issue for you is admitting the desire you have to be good. In other words, you really want to be good and you want others you love to be good, too. You want your dad to be a good dad and you want to be a good son. Your dad's leaving causes you hurt and anger. Your own angry feelings have gotten the best of you. They have gotten you into trouble and made you feel down on yourself — making you feel you're not a good son." I paused as Sean considered my words. Then with an empathic tone I cautiously continued: "It must be really hard not being able to have what you really desire for yourself and others — having a loving family where everyone shows they care for everyone else."

Sean's facial expression changed. He broke into tears. What was happening? I believe this powerful emotional undercurrent reflecting his desires both for himself and for his parents surfaced, breaking through the imposing barrier his negative feelings had erected. Even though he struggled with intense hurt and immense anger, Sean was able to tap into a deeper part of himself — a part more fundamental than the negative emotions holding him hostage.

As I interpret his experience, his tears reflected a core desire to be a "good" son who had "good" parents. In short, Sean's reaction to my statement reflected an unspoken desire for goodness that is absolutely central to who we are as human beings. Over time and working together, we were able to make this "felt" desire more conscious and focused. Helping Sean develop awareness of the good he desired enabled him to feel his moral worth — a felt sense of goodness that served as a foundation for his taking responsibility for his behavior, for being realistic about his home-life situation, and, subsequently, for the motivation to work in therapy to develop concrete and practical coping strategies for the future. This example provides a glimpse into the power that moral health offers each of us. When we are morally healthy, we recognize our desires for goodness along with the self-pride that goes with living out such desires. When we are morally fit, we take personal responsibility for who and what we are. As I look back on my time with Sean, I realize that the therapy I used was an invitation to Sean to experience a healthier conscience. In Sean's case, a healthy conscience provided the source for his healing. Truly, Sean had begun to glimpse what it meant to be an authentic human being and to enjoy some measure of personal fulfillment.

Conscience: A Brief Look at History

Where does the word "conscience" come from? The Greek word *syneidesis* translates to the Latin word *conscientia,* hence the word "conscience." In the popular mind, conscience has traditionally been associated with Freud's notion of the "superego." Freud believed two human tendencies influence the moral life: the need to idealize (idealization) and the need to prohibit (prohibition).[2] Unfortunately, over time conscience became associated exclusively with prohibition and punishment. In popular terms, we view the superego (conscience) as an internal parent lacking compassion for moral failure and personal shortcomings. This distortion of conscience is, I suspect, a major reason why it is so little talked about today. After all, who wants to spend time discussing something we understand and feel as solely self-critical and punishing? Fortunately, scholars who appreciate aspects of Freud's thinking have moved beyond his limited perspective and offer a broader view of moral functioning. Modern revisions of Freud's theory emphasize the qualities of early relationships with caregivers as well as personality development throughout the life span.[3]

Not surprisingly, most individuals in academic psychology have abandoned Freud's perspective on morality. For many psychologists today, the study of moral psychology consists of exploring how individuals assign value to certain moral ideas. The two principles receiving the most attention have been the principle of justice and the principle of care. The debate over whether justice or care best represents morality has been joined (and overshadowed) by a larger issue: do men and women understand morality from similar or different perspectives? Psychologists favoring the justice school of thought believe women and men view morality in similar ways. For these psychologists, morality is composed of an "ethics of justice," and those individuals expressing the most sophisticated reasoning about justice are the most morally mature.

In contrast, other psychologists view women's experience, particularly their experiences as caregivers and being culturally pressured to assume certain social roles, as leading them to view morality as more associated with asking, "How do I care?" (as opposed to the male view, which focuses more on the "just" thing to do). Psychologists supporting this view maintain that, overall, women more than men tend to give priority to the relational aspects of morality.

Which view best expresses morality's meaning: an "ethics of justice" or an "ethics of care"? Along with many others, I think the most sensible answer to this question is that both are important and that we must view morality as consisting of both justice and care. I venture to say that most people would find room for both justice and care in their definitions of morality. Depending on the issue at hand, one or the other of these perspectives might dominate the discussion.

Moreover, what remains essential is the need for justice and care to inform each other; when making moral decisions we need the aid of both perspectives. Think for a moment what morality would be if it was simply being just. Lacking a perspective of care, would not such morality render judgments all too frequently harsh, cold, and calculating? Think what a judge, boss, supervisor, or parent would be like if every decision was based on a justice perspective that lacked compassion? On the other hand, does not a morality equated solely with care also fall short? If what is right were always equated with showing care, would we not soon become biased, shortsighted, and self-absorbed? For example, public officials could become so engrossed in the needs of the homeless that they failed to realize the fair (just) demands of other public concerns (e.g., crime prevention, school funding).

No doubt there is at times a tension between the demands of justice and the demands of care. A good case in point is the juvenile justice system where youth must be held accountable for their deeds (justice), yet offered opportunities that encourage maturity and growth (care). The rub between justice and care is found easily in our own lives too. Is there any spouse who has not struggled with the dilemma of trying to decide when to challenge her spouse's hurtful comments and attitudes (justice) and when to ignore such shortcomings because of his personal limitations or background (care)? Moreover, one of the most compelling events aiding a child's moral growth is the struggle to resolve successfully the tension between laying claim to legitimate rights in relationships with friends (justice) while simultaneously developing a sufficient level of empathy that sustains a disposition for sharing, cooperating, and self-giving (care).

Finally, other psychologists find that the study of emotional development, particularly experiences such as the growth of empathy, allows the most productive avenue for understanding human moral growth. In addition, some scholars who argue for this view focus on the role of what have become known as moral emotions (e.g., compassion or guilt) and emphasize how we come to display specific altruistic behaviors. Scholars sympathetic to this point of view give priority to what makes up a moral self or a moral personality.[4]

Moral Entropy

It does not take much convincing to acknowledge that for whatever reason each of us fails to sustain a consistently high level of moral health for any length of time. Those with religious leanings often interpret this failure as rooted in "original sin," while others frequently are inclined to point to the "existential condition" to which we are fated. Regardless of the explanation, a reasonable conclusion on which we can agree (and for which there is considerable data in each of our lives) is, simply, that we are human. Achieving an exemplary level of moral growth and development requires a level of motivation and vigilance we can only hope to approximate. Though we can certainly imagine ourselves as relatively morally healthy beings, there is a vast difference between "imagining" ourselves as morally virtuous and "consistently living out" ideals that reflect a high level of moral rectitude. Stated simply, being human means living with our limitations, which often serve as invitations for moral setbacks or failures.

"Moral entropy" refers to the habits, downfalls, disappointments, slips, and failures that undermine our strivings for moral fitness. Borrowed from physics, the term "entropy" refers to the inevitable tendency of virtually everything to break down. Moral entropy refers to our recurring slide toward moral laxity.

The topic of moral failure is a vast one. By suggesting the phrase "moral entropy" I do not wish to brush over or dismiss lightly this darker side of our human experience and our national moral infirmity with its ugly facts of crime, hypocrisy, and personal suffering. When viewed from the wider perspective of moral dysfunction, the phrase "moral entropy" appears too trendy. The phrase neglects the wrenching pain, personal turmoil, and seething anger surrounding senseless acts of violence, countless instances of personal deceit, and innumerable other events that drain our personal as well as national moral resolve. A nine-year-old child is savagely beaten, raped, and left for dead. A pizza delivery boy is murdered for the apparent thrill of it. "Moral entropy" can never convey the horror of these unspeakable acts. In the conclusion (see p. 210) we explore more closely this darker feature of human nature. Nonetheless, we cannot introduce a discussion of healthy conscience or its malfunctioning without at least calling attention to our everyday moral lapses.

The Moral Climate Today

The current forecast for our nation's moral climate indicates stormy conditions and rough seas. If the nation has a moral compass, many would consider it on the blink. Consider the following. The homicide rate for ten-to-fourteen-year-olds has doubled. At the same time, these children were the victims of assault more than any other age group. One of every four adolescents reports being assaulted or abused in the previous year. Two-thirds of eighth-grade students report that they have tried alcohol.[5] A survey by the Josephson Institute of Ethics of nearly seven thousand high school and college students shows alarming rates at which youth report lying, cheating, and stealing.[6] Dishonesty has become so widespread on college campuses that only a minority of undergraduates refrain from cheating. In addition, this climate of dishonesty poses ever-increasing challenges as "electronic plagiarism" tempts students to acquire papers on the Internet.[7]

Youth are hardly the country's only cause for concern. Nearly half of the science graduate students and faculty stated in a national survey that they are aware of misconduct by scientists, and one-third of the faculty stated they had direct knowledge of students who plagiarized or falsified data.[8] Perhaps one of the most distressing signs of moral failure is the widespread publicity surrounding charges of boundary violations by clergy, educators, and health care professionals. Even if the number of professionals who engage in such misconduct is not large, the very fact that such basic (and sacred) trust — the care of the vulnerable by professional caregivers — is violated at all results in deep outrage. Further, though Americans report confidence and optimism about their future, they worry about the nation's values.[9] "Americans," according to one survey, "are more upset about values than at any time in modern history."[10] A staggering 78 percent noted that the "state of moral values in this country" was "very weak" or "somewhat weak," while 75 percent report that in their view "moral values" in the country have declined over the past twenty-five years.

Americans seem poised to ask searching questions regarding morality's role in public and private life. Psychologist Thomas Lickona notes that "there is a hunger for morality in the land. ... People really do want to create a society where they can count on their neighbors to be decent human beings. The schools can't ignore them and the families know they can't do it alone."[11] Recently, a national newsmagazine's survey reported "moral concerns" was second only to crime as the nation's most serious problem. Needless to say, crime itself involves numerous moral issues.[12] Another major poll reported that 76 percent of Americans view the country as in a state of moral decline.[13] In a similar vein, a weekly magazine featured a major story focusing on how Americans were "fed up" with problem-plagued social behaviors such as excessive drinking and teen pregnancy; the magazine chronicled recent American history and the journey leading to the "Return to Shame" (though I would prefer the word "guilt" rather than "shame").[14] Reflecting such survey trends, one social philosopher comments that "the nation's return to this discussion [of morality] is one of the decisive events of the last twenty years."[15]

Educational leaders, likewise, are increasingly inclined to address issues of morality. Schools are beginning to take seriously their role in moral education. Around the country growing numbers of school districts focus on educationally related ethical themes such as "character education," "values education," and "common morality." An increasingly popular workshop offered today for elementary and secondary school teachers is "character education." Currently America's institutions of higher education annually offer eleven thousand courses in areas of applied ethics over a wide variety of disciplines (e.g., business ethics, health care ethics, etc.). Reflecting morality's central role in today's public dialogue, former Harvard president Derek Bok remarks that "nothing is more likely to produce cynicism, especially among those taking courses in practical ethics, as a realization that the very institution that offers such classes shows little concern for living up to its own moral obligations."[16]

Why Is Conscience So Important Today?

Like many psychologists, I find academic psychology's spirited debates about the nature of morality to be energizing.[17] Nonetheless, academic psychology must never lose sight of its primary purpose, which remains discovering ways to offer knowledge that benefits people's everyday lives. Given this perspective, I find the debates that preoccupy academics, though necessary, all too frequently removed from people's daily struggles and concerns. Psychology has not been as helpful as it could be in enabling people to understand and improve their moral lives. Moreover, conscience rarely appears as an item for discussion among academic psychologists.[18]

Sadly, by ignoring the study of conscience, psychology has abandoned the most essential quality humans have for making everyday moral decisions! But let's not bemoan this fact. Rather, let's redirect our energies to viewing *why* conscience is fundamental for living a moral life.

Personal Conscience Is Vital for a Free Society

First of all, we live in a free yet dangerous moral climate. The fruits of democracy depend upon a citizenry of virtuous people — individuals who are knowledgeable, fair, and open to the free exchange of ideas based on mutual respect. The eminent jurist and historian John Noonan has argued persuasively that an essential rationale for setting forth the First Amendment was the belief in the sacredness of personal conscience. This belief, as advocated by James Madison, resulted in a uniquely American experiment — the free exercise of religion — which, in time, became America's gift to the world.[19]

Embedded in the public discussion taking place in a democratic society, ideally, is an assumption of trust in governmental structures and public officials. It is probably not an exaggeration to say that nothing would contribute more to resolving alienation and mistrust felt by so many voters today as the personal commitment of each and every citizen to be a person of conscience. If voters formed their opinions about political and social issues with an awareness of themselves as men and women of conscience, we could predict with confidence a rise in voter turnouts. Of course, these observations point to an ideal state of affairs. Nonetheless, no one would disagree that if all public officials and citizens strove on a daily basis to recall that they were *persons of conscience,* then virtue in politics would show a dramatic rise.

Increasingly Complex Moral Decisions Await Us

Second, in this new century we confront increasingly complex ethical decisions having profound human and moral consequences. Nowhere is this truer than in the field of health care technology. For instance, with every passing year more and more people are part of four-generation families that include children, parents, grandparents, and great-grandparents. As advances in health care allow people to live longer, increasing pressures are placed on family members to assume caregiver roles for older family members. How do family members decide how much time, effort, and money to provide those needing assistance? Increasingly, family members struggle in their roles as "good" children, brothers and sisters, parents, and grandparents as they negotiate among themselves in search of the "right" decision for their elderly kin. Furthermore, growing numbers of parents find themselves squeezed by the extended adolescence and dependency of their own children at the very time they begin to assist infirm parents. Many adult children grapple with the demands of being parents to their aging parents. In addition, large numbers of grandparents support (both emotionally and financially) their grandchildren, especially when the grandchild's family is chaotic or overwhelmed. As another sign of this intergenerational support, more and more adult children and their parents look for ways to assist isolated great-grandparents. All of these intertwined family relationships pose ethical issues and questions.

The growing "right to die" movement adds further complications. Who makes such decisions? Is this question acceptable for people to consider in their twilight years? What about those lacking financial resources? Will there be subtle pressures placed on the sick and infirm to terminate their lives? Or consider an aging family member whose illness is draining family resources. Might there be a temptation subtly to "hint" that ending one's life might be the most noble thing? Scary? Most certainly!

Numerous Other Ethical Issues Directly Related to Health Care Confront Us

1. As more expensive *drug treatments* become available, how do we decide who receives the new (and most expensive) medications? We already see this concern with newer generations of drug treatments to fight the AIDS virus. The use of medications for mental illness pose other complex situations. Increasingly, mind-influencing drugs are used with children and adolescents. The use of Ritalin to treat some distracted and overly restless children, has increased dramatically in the past five years.[20] As children more frequently become the focus of such drug interventions, what criteria do we use to decide when to use them?

2. Rapid expansion of in-vitro fertilization has led to the storage of *frozen human embryos.* Should this practice be continued? What regulations should govern the storage of these embryos?

3. As medical science continues its advancement, *genetic engineering* will play an increasing role in fighting disease as well as offering lifestyle choices.[21] Examples of moral issues include creating "designer babies," using knowledge of genetic profiles to manufacture specific drugs, exploring what rights government and insurance companies have to information about one's genetic make-up, and creating methods to forestall aging.

4. Biotechnology has paved the way for the rapidly expanding field of *regenerative medicine,* which holds promise for regrowing various body tissues such as cartilage, ligaments, tendons, bones, and blood cells. Will the poor as well as the rich have access to these new medical procedures? What are the moral issues involved in using living cells or tissues to treat diseases and genetic disorders?

As the health care issues ushered in by twenty-first century medicine grow increasingly complex, resolving such debates to everyone's satisfaction in a pluralistic culture such as ours will remain elusive. Nonetheless, few will deny that, overall, the "best" ethical choices will be made when people approach such decisions with the awareness that they are men and women of conscience.

Conscience Is Linked to Our Emotions

Emotional health and moral health are intimately linked. Conscience growth interweaves with the growing pains, the emotional struggles, and the everyday stressors that make up our daily lives. The businessman pressured from the demands of work, the woman agonizing over a broken relationship, the couple contemplating divorce, the adolescent attempting to deal with acute pangs of loneliness, or the parent worried about both her children and her aging parents are more than likely, because of the stress experienced and personal feelings involved, to find their consciences sorely taxed, if not overwhelmed. Painful feelings, troubled relationships, and difficult life situations absorb us, leaving less resolve to live up to the moral ideals we cherish. Consider, for example, a time when you experienced significant stress. During this period were you as attentive as usual to the needs and situations of those you loved? As the next chapter points out, an increasingly stress-filled life overloads and derails the workings of conscience. In sum, conscience *always* functions within the confines of our humanity and is vulnerable to the personal pains, struggles, and worries that are part of human living.

An Awareness of Conscience Is Vital for Our Increasingly Pluralistic Culture

A fifth reason to champion conscience arises from growing cultural diversity. Achieving a moral consensus in America is more difficult than ever before, and on some issues (such as abortion) the nation will never come to a moral truce acceptable to all sides.[22] Yet, if we view conscience as inseparable from our humanity, conscience has the potential for being a unifying force that offers the opportunity for those with highly opposed and partisan perspectives to converse *with civility*. My hunch is that if two people differing on an issue perceived the other as a "person of conscience" as reflected in a statement such as "my conscience leads me to this position, yet I can acknowledge your conscience leads you to a different conclusion," then the shrill and hostile tone surrounding current moral debates would lessen considerably. Would we be such a conflict-ridden and divided country on such volatile issues as abortion and affirmative action if we understood that those who differ from us are men and women of conscience — moral beings like us with ethical sensitivities that deserve respect? Only if we redirect our focus and consider our common moral heritage as men and women of conscience can we hope to temper the hostile and judgmental tones that engulf today's public discussions.

Being Aware of Conscience Means Becoming More Aware of Ourselves as Moral Beings

A final reason for focusing on conscience is that it leads each of us to a deeper awareness of our own lives as moral beings. Though we are often not conscious of its presence, morality penetrates virtually all human endeavors. As James O. Wilson puts it,

> The daily discourse of ordinary people is filled with oblique references to morality. We talk constantly about being or not being decent, nice, or dependable; about having or not having a good character; about friendship, loyalty, and moderation or fickleness, insincerity, and addiction. When we overhear these conversations or read about these topics in magazines and novels, we sometimes say that people are preoccupied with personal relationships: the problems of mother and child, of wife and husband, of lovers, friends, and co-workers. This preoccupation is not simply about relationships, however; much of it is about what those relationships ought to be. This preoccupation, like the adjectives with which we express it — loyal, kind, or nice; disloyal, selfish, or rude — is with the language of morality, even though we often disguise it in the language of personality.[23]

I genuinely believe that most people are good people who desire to live ethical lives. A major obstacle to living the moral life lies in our failure to sustain *ongoing awareness* of our lives as moral beings. Our moral resolve falters because we neglect to take the time to foster a conscious sense of ourselves as moral beings, just as we fail to invest time and energy in pursuits that improve our physical fitness. Most of us are content, with occasional second guesses, to live the lives we have always lived. The challenge is to *alter* this inertia and assume responsibility for increasing self-knowledge of *who we are as moral persons* and what this moral sense requires of us.

To link conscience and consciousness raising try the following reflection. Take a moment and put this book aside. Close your eyes and say quietly and slowly to yourself, "My conscience," or the phrase "I am a person of conscience." Slowly repeat these words several times as you absorb their meaning. If you do this very simple exercise several times a day over a few days, I believe you will have a different perspective on life than you do now. Why? We discover the reason when we reflect on conscience's meaning. Upon reflection, we come to view conscience as signifying something beyond its definition. As a word, "conscience" attracts us. The word "conscience" could be described as an *Urwort*. An *Urwort* is best translated from the German as a "source" or "primordial" word. An *Urwort* evokes a profound meaning that conveys a unity of depth, purpose, and mystery about humanity. When I say "my conscience," I am saying that at this moment in time I am a moral being. Yet this moral quality simultaneously embraces a mystery still taking shape. I am, in other words, in some ways defined, yet still needing to be formed. As time passes I more readily view conscience as the moral center of my life, rooted in my self-identity, and understood through my unique life history.

Psychologist Dan McAdams notes that human beings are "like all other persons, like some other persons, and like no other persons."[24] More than most human qualities, conscience expresses this fact well. Every person possesses a conscience (whether healthy, ill-functioning, or grossly impaired), and this attribute more than any other serves as the distinctive and common bond that links humanity ("all other persons"). Given this common heritage, humanity does indeed exist as a moral community that expresses horror and outrage when it is made aware of serial killings, the human carnage from a terrorist bomb, the rape and savage murder of a young child, the abandoned body of a one-day-old infant, or the callous disregard for human dignity in the predatory sexual assault on a child by her classmates. At the same time, the learning and life experience each of us undergoes affords conscience a link with other persons who share similar beliefs and heritages ("some other persons"). Our attachments naturally lead us to form common bonds with some others (e.g., family upbringing, neighborhood environments, or similar faith commitments) and forge in the process similar beliefs. Finally, the very fact of our existence as beings with unique life histories calls us to be morally responsible for our own actions ("no other persons"). In the final analysis, to say that I am a person of conscience is to acknowledge that I must take personal responsibility for who I am and what I do, while simultaneously making the commitment to abide by those cherished moral principles that guide my behaviors.

Finally, fostering awareness of *ourselves as moral beings* who share a common humanity makes excellent "psychological" sense. As the noted psychologist Albert Bandura points out:

> Psychological research tends to emphasize how easy it is to get good people to perform cruel deeds through dehumanization and other self-exonerative means.... What is rarely noted is the striking evidence that most people refuse to behave cruelly, even with strong authoritarian commands, toward people who are humanized.... The affirmation of common humanity can bring out the best in others.[25]

OUR DEFINITION OF CONSCIENCE

1. Reflect for a moment on how you define conscience. Say your definition aloud to yourself or write it down.

2. Generally speaking, when you make important life decisions, what role does your conscience exercise in helping you come to a decision? Take an important life decision you have made with regard to a relationship or a work concern. What role did your conscience play in helping you arrive at your decision?

3. Take a piece of plain white paper and a pencil or pen. Now *draw* your conscience. What do you draw? What is it about your drawing that you find most meaningful? If possible, share your drawing with a trusted friend and explain your drawing to him or her. Ask your friend to comment on your explanation.[26] I have found that most people, when asked to draw their conscience, respond with a perplexed, quizzical look. I believe this response reflects a bias most of us learned through school. We are so trained to respond through rational analysis and reflection that a statement asking us to "draw our conscience" meets with puzzlement. We are unaccustomed to tapping into the more emotion-based aspects of our experience, which inevitably convey highly prized forms of personal meaning.

4. As you reflect on your life, what areas (family, relationships, work) do you believe are most vulnerable to moral entropy?

5. Take a personal moral concern you struggle with. State the "ideal" way you would like to respond to this concern. In everyday life how do you find yourself responding? How does your definition of conscience (as you defined it above) help you deal with your moral concern?

If you answered question 1 above, you have your own definition of conscience. Now I invite you to consider mine: *Conscience is best understood as decisions or judgments based on an internal sense of oughtness (how I should live or what I must do) that is the result of a life history that incorporates who I am, who I am becoming, and who I desire to be.* Before reviewing the dimensions that make up conscience, we need briefly to explore this definition.

Oughtness: This definition allows us to link conscience to a course of right action ("oughtness"). This understanding reflects a traditional notion of conscience. That is, conscience's purpose makes clear "right and wrong," "dos and don'ts," "good and bad," "moral and immoral." This traditional notion is absolutely correct as far as it goes, but it narrows and shortchanges conscience's mysterious richness. If I limit conscience to right and wrong, then I ignore its link to the personal meanings and emotional connections that make up my life history.

We must also distinguish between the "oughtness" we refer to above and the "oughts," "shoulds," and "have tos" we find so common in everyday speech. At times, we find ourselves evaluating our behavior by such statements as "I should..." or "I must..." More often than not, such absolutist messages reflect the excessive demands, unrealistic expectations, or unforgiving judgments we place upon ourselves. These statements originate from our life histories and often are a major source for depressed feelings, anxious moods, and personal distress. Over the years these statements are etched into our thinking patterns, becoming integral parts of the self-evaluations we make. In most instances, we fail to live up to the absolute demands of these statements and thereby fall victim to feelings of guilt, anxiety, or sadness.

Therapy interventions have been developed to help people become aware of and correct these rigid, demanding ways of viewing the self and others.[27] As much as possible, those whose lives are burdened and weighed down by such "shoulds" and "oughts" need to take whatever corrective steps they can to alleviate such rigid thinking patterns. Having said this, I find disturbing the blanket condemnation of "shoulds" by some of my peers in the mental health field. Sometimes when we say "I should" or "I must," we are reflecting not some distorted or dysfunctional thinking pattern. On the contrary, we are revealing the depths of our personal integrity and such self-statements are conscious messages (and reminders) that we take seriously the calling of conscience to live our lives dedicated to cherished ideals. These "shoulds," "musts," and "have tos" that flow from personal integrity are statements of conscience. "I must confront a colleague at work about her behavior" can be a statement of one's conscience, as can "I have to be with a friend this evening because of the hurt he is feeling." These statements reflect the good life I strive to uphold. We must be careful to avoid a blanket condemnation of "ought" statements.

Who I am: Every decision we make is rooted in "who I am" at this moment in time. Yet we remind ourselves that this "present" in which we feel, think, and act is influenced by our current situation as well as by our life histories that over the years have shaped for us preferred ways of feeling, thinking, and acting. The mental aspects of these preferences are often labeled "schemas" whereas the actions we carry out are termed "scripts." Situations we find ourselves in activate certain schemas (ways we interpret and view other people and situations) as well as scripts (the actions we take). For example, close friends or married couples, because of their shared life histories, gradually develop specific interpretations (schemas) about one another and behave accordingly (scripts). When we wonder what is "wrong" with our friend, we are actually saying that her behavior (script) is different from the script we have grown accustomed to and that her new behavior does not quite fit our view (schema) of her. Schemas and scripts are a natural part of any relationship; otherwise every time someone said or did something, we would have to take the time to figure out the other's behavior and its meaning. In effect, schemas and scripts conserve psychic energy. The cumulative effect of the schemas and scripts we develop in our life histories, the choices and decisions interwoven throughout those years, and the situations in which we currently find ourselves come together to fashion for each of us an identity: "who I am" at this moment in time. Central to this identity are the specific ideals, beliefs, and valued roles that provide our lives with meaning and that have been shaped by the forces discussed above.

Who I am becoming: Conscience is dynamic, not static. In other words, our decisions lead us down a distinctive path. Based on the decisions we currently make, the journey leads ideally to challenge, growth, and insight — all of which become feedback that invites us to a deepening sense of "who I am." As we continue this journey with its innumerable decisions, we sometimes find ourselves making fundamental choices involving our deepest desires as to what type of lives we should live.

Who I desire to be: Traditional notions of conscience fail to acknowledge that conscience reflects a moral vision, a horizon that portrays our cherished ideals, our deepest aspirations that we craft into enduring commitments. When we take the notion of conscience seriously, we are always implying a future that is yet to be. Moreover, when scanning the decisions of our lives, we come to realize that over this period we have grown more aware of our hearts' deepest desires and have gained insights into which choices bring us closer to those desires while acknowledging those decisions that have led us astray. Over time, as we are brought closer by our choosing to the fulfillment of who we desire to be, we normally come to view the future as a hopeful one, and we assume responsibility for our lives, our choices, and our ongoing journeys. Eventually, given the perspective explored above, we come to understand how conscience is the hallmark of those who are truly wise.

The Dimensions of Conscience

As a psychologist I have always been fascinated by the human factors that influence how people make moral decisions. As a way to introduce the multidimensional side of conscience, I will share a story from my own life.

In 1975 I was completing my master's degree and at the same time living in a college residence hall as a dormitory counselor. This living situation provided numerous opportunities for discussions with undergraduates. I became intrigued by a phenomenon I perceived over and over again in these students. Their questions about right and wrong and how to treat themselves and others were closely linked to their personal struggles and the developmental issues with which they wrestled.

The memories of these conversations stayed with me as I continued my professional training and accepted a job as a secondary school teacher. What I discovered at the high school level were adolescents struggling with the same moral concerns as college undergraduates, only at a more rudimentary level. One incident in particular proved a catalyst both for my own thinking and for targeting my future area of study. I was teaching a course in sociology to seniors. One day the class engaged in a lively discussion regarding social class and upward mobility. One senior (I will call him Tom) made a rather forceful argument that people could achieve anything they wanted and the only thing standing in their way was their level of motivation. In contrast to Tom's argument for rugged individualism, another student, Jim, vigorously disagreed. Jim maintained that achieving success was not that simple. On the contrary, he pointed out that there exist many sources of discrimination and obstacles in society that frequently prevent people from achieving their life goals.

Interestingly, the backgrounds of these students were revealing. Tom's background was upper middle class. His father was a successful businessman, and Tom had been given many opportunities over the years. Jim's background, in contrast, was quite different. He came from a family of limited means, and his father faced periodic unemployment. The point I wish to make of course is how the background of each student helped shape his personal view of life. Jim had seen and experienced numerous hurdles and obstacles in his quest to achieve success. Because of his experience, he was capable of empathizing with those burdened by troubled life situations. Tom, on the other hand, had not experienced such roadblocks. His life had been shielded from the sufferings Jim had endured, thereby giving him only limited opportunities to empathize with others' plights. It was not that Tom lacked compassion or sensitivity; indeed, I knew him to be a caring and sensitive adolescent. Yet he lacked Jim's range of experiences.

After school that day I pondered this lively class discussion. I recall writing down on a piece of paper and circling the word "empathy." What stood out for me was the role empathy had in influencing the moral judgments these adolescents made. I began to wonder about empathy's role in shaping our moral experience and to consider what other experiences shape our moral judgments of self and others. Having made the decision to pursue graduate work in psychology, I made a promise to myself to have as a future goal the study of the personal attributes that contribute to making us moral persons.

As the years of research and study continued, I began to formulate a theory of conscience that was true to human experience while remaining sensitive to Tillich's observation that morality "is a life put to the test in dozens of moments." My training in clinical psychology afforded me the opportunity to appreciate the many facets of human experience that nourish or impair the functioning of conscience. Over and over I observed in myself and others, whether clients, colleagues, or friends, that troubled feelings, stressful events, and negative thinking frustrated and all too often sabotaged conscience's functioning. Frequently, people's personal distress or dissatisfaction with life prevented them from living out the ideals they cherished and blocked their becoming the people they desired to be. Further, one simple truth stood out over and over again: Attaining moral health parallels the essential steps required to achieve physical or emotional health. All three forms of health take concerted effort, disciplined focus, and hard work.

After examining the psychological literature on moral psychology, studying everyday human behavior through personal interactions and observations, and working with clients in psychotherapy, I concluded that conscience consists of seven dimensions. Here we will briefly examine each of these dimensions. In the chapters ahead we will provide a more detailed look at each dimension, its contribution to a healthy conscience, and steps the reader can take to strengthen each dimension in order to foster a well-functioning conscience.

Psychic Energy: Our psychic energy constitutes the psychological resources we need to function in everyday life. From another perspective, psychic energy is the psychological fuel required for healthy and adaptive functioning. Psychic energy allows us to attend to everyday concerns and adjust or alter our goals as we encounter new demands and challenges.

Defenses: Defenses are psychological processes we employ to protect our self-esteem and to avoid undue anxiety or other negative feelings.

Empathy: Empathy refers to the capacity to feel the pains, hurts, and joys of others as if they were our own.

Guilt: Feelings of regret or remorse (self-devaluation) after doing something wrong constitute a "healthy" experience of guilt.

Idealization: Idealization serves as the foundation for what we term "positive morality." It focuses on aspirations and ideals — what we aspire to be rather than what we should or should not do.

Self-esteem: This experience refers to our capacity for adequate self-appreciation.

Moral beliefs: These are the moral principles and statements that guide our lives. Examples might include the Golden Rule (do to others as you would have them do to you) or moral statements as found in the Ten Commandments. However, the moral beliefs we subscribe to are, ideally, not just intellectual statements. They are vibrant beliefs that convey who we are and what we stand for, just as they call us to live them responsibly in our daily lives.

More specifically, to the extent that each one of these dimensions functions well, then our consciences function well. As we might expect, it is unlikely that all dimensions of our conscience function at optimum levels in all situations. In all likelihood, some dimensions are more advanced than others. When all dimensions work reasonably well together, they nurture the well-formed and well-functioning conscience.

These seven dimensions form an *interactive* rather than a linear process (i.e., we do not first acquire psychic energy, then defenses, etc.). Each dimension interacts with the others while providing its own significant contribution to conscience's healthy development. The diagram on the following page represents the interactional nature of a healthy conscience. It reflects how each dimension influences other dimensions as well as contributing to the overall functioning of conscience. For example, empathy nourishes a caring, sensitive conscience and idealization fosters hopefulness about what we decide just as it nurtures an overall moral vision.

Conscience and Human Experience

A multidimensional, interactional approach to conscience addresses the very nature of our moral experience, which involves the intricate interplay of *cognition* (thinking), *emotion* (feeling), and *the capacity for meaning-making* (meaning). When we say to someone, "It's been my experience that ... " we are expressing our experience to others as thinking, feeling, and meaning-making creatures. For our purposes we can define each of these aspects of experience as follows. Thinking (cognition) refers to how we

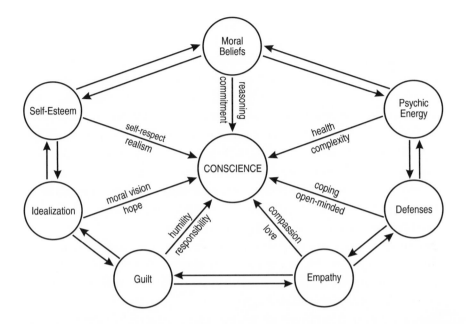

take in, store, retrieve, and analyze information that the senses gather from our environment. This aspect of experience is best understood through verbal, conscious statements we make that reflect how we are aware of and interpret ourselves, others, and the world around us. Feeling (emotion) is best understood as an aroused state of varying degrees of intensity that encourages specific types of responses.[28] For example, when we feel happy, we are apt to respond with a smile. A more intense state of ecstatic joy might lead us to laugh aloud and hug someone. We recognize the importance of thoughts and feelings, though for many defining cognition and emotion is in all probability a new venture.

But what about our capacity for meaning-making? The word "meaning" is not easily understood. As used here, meaning refers to those people, objects, events, and activities to which we assign value.[29] The quality and depth of human intellectual and emotional expression along with the capacity for language make human beings unique in their meaning-making capacity. Meaning-making is most apparent in what we choose, choices that frequently involve a wide spectrum of preferences. For instance, we might have an opinion about a food or sports team that reveals one or another preference. For some people, a certain food or sports team might reflect a loyalty of great intensity. Yet, even the most rabid chocolate lover or sports fan (perhaps with some rare exceptions) fails to place such loyalty on a par with career, spiritual beliefs, or cherished friends. Even highly vocalized opinions pale when compared to certain other preferences that we hold dear.

We are always acting on such preferences; it is in the very nature of our humanness to parcel out and allot varying degrees of preference that create priorities among people, events, ideas, causes, situations, and things. At birth such preferences are relatively simple as the infant gropes for a nourishing object or the soothing of touch. But as adults the preferences we have and the meanings they evoke take on at times extraordinary complexity and commitment. Such preferences are value-evoking — highly prized forms of meaning — for they reflect the deepest desires of our hearts. Ask someone to name and then discuss the significance of a lifelong friendship. Ask a parent to describe the satisfaction of observing his or her child's fascination with discovering new aspects of the environment or the mastery of a new task. Human beings cannot help but be meaning-makers. Discovering and constructing meaning is as integral to human beings as breathing, eating, and drinking. "Humans," as the philosopher Jonathan Lear notes, "are inherently makers and interpreters of meaning. It is meaning — ideas, desires, beliefs — which causes humans to do the interesting things they do."[30] Language in particular provides flexibility to our meaning-making capability because it allows us to generate and convey a diverse array of images, symbols, and highly nuanced forms of expressions.

Be Wary of Being Too Rational

For conscience to function well it must tap into our lives as thinking, feeling, and meaning-making creatures. I suspect that one reason we have abandoned the discussion of conscience is that over the years it has not been presented in a way that relates fully to people's actual experience. For the most part, when we think of the word "conscience," we call to mind "dos and don'ts" — statements that tell us what to do and not to do. Viewing conscience in this manner reflects a highly rational (cognitive) approach, which strongly favors the thinking aspect of personal experience but gives little attention to its emotional and meaning-making aspects. There exists nothing inherently wrong with this viewpoint as long as we acknowledge its limits and incompleteness. Healthy conscience functioning requires that *reasoning* supports our principles and beliefs. But is it enough to say that such moral beliefs and the guidelines and prohibitions they entail constitute conscience?

To broaden our focus, we need to consider the following question: Why is the discussion of conscience functioning so heavily tied to reason while emotion and personal meaning are summarily ignored? Several reasons surface. For one, most people writing about morality and the moral life are academics. As such, there exists a natural bias toward viewing conscience as merely a thinking enterprise. Fortunately, several disciplines are placing more emphasis on emotion research. In the integration of emotions with the moral life psychologists and moral philosophers are increasingly finding common ground.[31]

I suspect that for many academic writers and scholars, writing about emotion and morality is like flirting with the irrational. Emotion is understood as an inferior experience because of its perceived irrationality. Emotions are typically associated with the darker side of human nature. "One reason many scholars have preferred to base morality on logic, rather than on feeling, is that most Western philosophers have assumed human nature to be basically selfish, cruel and deceitful."[32] A wide body of psychological research contradicts this view, however, and explores the positive role that emotions contribute to the moral life. More and more frequently subjects such as "altruism" and "moral emotions" find coverage in psychological literature.[33]

Finally, I think some academic writers genuinely believe that emotions don't really add anything of substance to a moral argument. If you want to know the "right" thing to do, then simply commit yourself to reasoned reflection and discussion, arrive at a conclusion on the right course of action and commit yourself to such action. If it were only that easy! I can recall innumerable occasions with clients when their emotions and unacknowledged motivations led to behaviors that contributed to shame and guilt. At times they were at a loss to explain their actions. Invariably they knew that they were in the wrong and could recite numerous rational reasons why they should never have behaved as they did. Yet, they did act this way. Simply stated, their troubled emotions, their unmet needs, and their unacknowledged motives eclipsed the moral principles they held dear.

Bringing Emotion Back into the Discussion

This bias favoring the cognitive aspect of our experience is woefully misguided. In no way do I mean by this that rational reflection is unimportant. On the contrary, reasoning is essential for conscience functioning and the moral life. We cannot simply "feel" what is right. To rely only on feelings as the basis for our moral lives renders us directionless. The choices that flow from conscience must signify some purposeful life-direction that incorporates the demands of intellectual rigor and rational reflection. Furthermore, in our moral decision making we are often confronted with competing courses of action. Adequate choosing among alternatives requires a wise, reflective stance. Thus a teacher who believes she must confront a colleague's questionable actions might have a "gut" feeling that her colleague's behavior is inappropriate. Even so, when discussing the problem with another colleague or supervisor, the teacher must be able to express clearly the merits of the moral issues at stake and principles she believes are being violated as well as give an accurate rendering of her colleague's actions. Otherwise, her evaluation of her colleague becomes truly (and only) subjective and in all likelihood holds little persuasive power.

Further, I am not maintaining that emotions become the sole arbiters of what is moral. Emotions most certainly can lead to moral blindness. Think back to a time when you were intensely angry toward someone you cared about. What did these feelings lead you to say or do? Did you later regret your statements or actions? At a minimum, even if your feelings did not lead you to say or do anything you later regretted, your intense anger more than likely led you to form an unfavorable view of the person or to overemphasize the person's negative qualities. With such anger, were you really able to perceive the other's point of view and examine fairly all other factors related to the situation that triggered your anger?

Notwithstanding these cautions, the moral life in general, and conscience in particular, is severely shortchanged if emotion has no significant role. Feelings convey significant information about the moral life and our own moral stances. As psychiatrist Robert Jay Lifton notes, the word "emotion" is derived from the Latin word *emovere*, which means "to move out, stir up, excite."[34] The intensity of our feelings communicates deeply felt concerns. Emotions inform both ourselves and others. "Emotions form the prime material in the exploration of an individual's concern."[35] Thus emotions frequently convey an *evaluation*. For example, if a friend's remark hurts you, your anger can reflect, among other things, the value you give to this relationship and your friend. In other words, you are angry precisely because of the friendship's significance. Summarizing this train of thought, psychologist Norma Haan writes that "emotions accompany and enrich understandings, and they convey far more authentic information about a person's position in a dispute than any well-articulated thoughts. In ordinary circumstances, emotions instruct and energize action."[36]

At the same time, the fragile nature of emotion's role in the moral life bears repeating. "In situations of great moral costs, emotions can overwhelm and disorganize cognitive evaluation."[37] Our emotional displays, in other words, present a double-edged sword. On the one hand, they provide knowledge and meaning regarding our moral concerns; on the other hand, they also have the potential to distort and bias our moral responses.

To understand the interplay of thinking and feeling in the moral life, ask yourself whom you admire as "moral heroes." Make a list of these people. Most likely, the individuals you list are women and men of deep moral conviction who believe strongly and resolutely in certain moral principles. At the same time, in all likelihood these heroes profess an allegiance to principles with a conviction that is both passionate and compassionate. Martin Luther King and

Mother Teresa are two moral heroes who exemplify this blending of reason and emotion.

Emotion's relationship to the moral life must also be considered in light of the potential dysfunction that might occur. As a college professor and clinician I am increasingly concerned about the destabilizing effect that dysfunctional backgrounds are having on healthy young adult development. More and more students that arrive on college campuses today come from home backgrounds containing significant levels of psychological distress. Divorce, family conflict, addiction issues, and lack of healthy relationships or role models are increasingly part of many students' life histories. Accumulating evidence shows that such backgrounds are taking a toll on young people.[38]

For example, large numbers of students who attend college struggle with residual feelings from family breakups and divorce. Though many have weathered the situation well and have discovered in their hurt a new strength, for others this is not the case. Some students find it difficult to make relationship commitments. For others there are continual struggles with anger and negative feelings. Trust, too, is often an issue. Yet how can our moral lives develop adequately, not to mention flourish, when we are preoccupied with hurt and mistrust? The lingering effects of difficult family backgrounds — psychic pain, chronic loneliness, and poor self-image — complicate how young adults understand ethical issues and arrive at moral decisions. Some young people compromise their moral lives to ease the pangs of loneliness or distract themselves from negative feelings. Excessive use of alcohol or other drugs, a compulsion to gamble, and involvement in unhealthy relationships are just some examples of behaviors college students use to cope with the personal pains they feel.

Though my example is the young adult population, we need not limit ourselves to this age group. Think of the struggling parent who is attempting to be a "good" parent and treat his children with fairness and affection while being severely taxed by the possibility of a job lay-off or the worry of having to take care of two aging parents. Or consider a saleswoman who tries to respond honestly to her clients and relate to her colleagues with integrity, yet in the workplace finds herself sexually harassed by her supervisor as she tries to meet demanding sales quotas.

To review the interplay of the cognitive, the emotional, and the meaning-making aspects of conscience, consider the following questions:

1. List the characteristics you associate with being a moral person. Which of the characteristics you have listed do you associate with thinking? With feeling? With personal meaning-making?

2. What are the dangers of viewing conscience as solely a cognitive experience? As solely an emotional experience?

3. Take the drawing you made in the first exercise. What features in your drawing do you associate with thinking? With emotion? Could you explain to someone else how your drawing conveys what is most meaningful to you?

{ Dimension One }

PSYCHIC ENERGY

Have you noticed how active your mind is? In the span of an hour or two a wide ranging stream of ideas and impressions intrudes into consciousness. Sometimes these thoughts are anticipated, for example, when we intentionally try to solve a problem or deliberate over an important matter. But at other times our thoughts are simply "there" — bursting into awareness. Both examples reveal our awareness of the world around us. Today we find this external world a balancing act requiring us to negotiate among the competing interests of family, friends, work, and personal time. When we are spread too thin, dissatisfaction seeps into our lives, with chronic stress, burn out, and exhaustion as the result. Over the last few years employee surveys have shown increasing concern about excessive workloads as many people struggle with the burdens arising from family demands and personal needs.[1] In one recent survey, roughly three out of every four working men and women found undue stress in their attempts to find balance between home and work.[2] This sense of an overload goes beyond the adult workforce. The middle-class segment of school-age Generation Y has more material advantages, choices to make, and activities to engage in than any previous generation in American history. As one headline summed up, "At Age Five, Reading, Writing and Rushing."[3] Teens in these early years of the twenty-first century feel the pressure too. Numerous forms of technology are at their disposal, and with a strong economy and the need for workers many youth perceive the looming message: You've been given everything, so be successful and don't make mistakes![4]

The blurring of boundaries between our private lives and the de-

62

mands of world and work continue to accelerate. On the one hand, personal computers, fax machines, cellular phones, and beepers contribute to efficiency and productivity. On the other hand, this technology intrudes into our lives, shredding personal boundaries. How do the pressures and obligations of everyday living influence our moral health? Here we will explore this question by examining the first dimension of conscience: psychic energy.

What Is Psychic Energy?

What is psychic energy? We can't calculate it. We aren't able to point to an area of the brain and say, "There it is." But we can observe it. To get at its meaning ask yourself the following three questions:

1. What thoughts preoccupy you?

2. What do you spend your time doing?

3. What are the things that usually attract your attention?

Psychic energy is the means we use to engage our world. It is our internal resource that allows us to function as thinking, feeling, and acting beings.[5]

Consider the following questions that can further help us to get at the meaning of psychic energy:

1. Give a definition of an adult. Now place the word "healthy" before the word "adult." In your view, does the word "healthy" alter for you the meaning of adulthood? List five specific behaviors you typically expect of "healthy adults."

2. What do you *feel* when you are alone? That is, when you have moments of solitude, what feelings usually surface?

3. What do you do when you are alone?

4. What do you *relish* in your life? What provides your life true enjoyment?

5. Recall yesterday. In that twenty-four-hour period, how often did you take time to consider what you were "grateful" for?

Recall the past week. In that seven-day period, how frequently did you take the time to consider what you were grateful for?

6. As you view yourself at this point in time, are you becoming the person you truly *desire* to be? If not, what do you need to begin doing now in order to fulfill this desire?

Psychic energy is the source for our conscious experiences of everyday life. And such experiences are quality ones to the degree they reflect healthy, mature behavior. "Health" and "maturity" are words we often hear, but rarely do we reflect on their meanings.

The Quality of Life

When Freud was asked what made an emotionally healthy human being, he responded simply, *lieben und arbeiten* (to love and to work). Freud was certainly right to note that health meant commitment to others and productive labors, but might other qualities also be necessary? For one, being healthy includes the capacity for finding contentment through solitary pursuits, "to feel comfortable alone, usually by developing a rich and fulfilling inner life."[6]

In addition, healthy people self-evaluate. If we combine all four elements, then health (some might prefer the term "emotional health") is defined as a fourfold process: *Being healthy is an ongoing process of (1) committing, (2) producing, (3) enriching, and (4) evaluating.* When we invest wholeheartedly our psychic energy in this fourfold process, we are doing what is required to live fully human *and* moral lives.

Living an emotionally healthy life not only offers the opportunity for greater life satisfaction; it also serves as a critical component for moral living. *Living a moral life goes hand in hand with living a healthy human life.* Yet how many people take the time to link consciously their everyday thoughts, feelings, and behavior with moral living? For too many of us, morality is something out there that I "do" part-time when confronting a moral issue. Thus, stealing from an employer is a moral issue. Or how

I treat a friend, a spouse, a colleague, a child, likewise has moral consequences. But achieving moral health is more than making choices. To achieve moral fitness I must probe the ebb and flow of my daily life. Its quality — how I structure it, what I attend to, what I invest in — is intricately tied to being the moral person I strive to be, and having the healthy functioning conscience I desire to have.

The Need for Solitude

Take a simple but essential experience like finding time for reflection. For human beings, asking questions is as natural as walking or eating. We are naturally inquisitive and wonder about the course of daily events. We wonder why someone wins the lottery or why that particular person was involved in a tragic accident. As we gain more life experience (usually through work and relationships), we are provided opportunities to sort out our experiences and look for meanings — the patterns and purposes of our lives. Frequently, our questions are as simple as "Where am I going?" or "Am I really happy?" or "Am I doing what I want to do with my life?" It is in our nature to try and understand our *unique* role in the world.

> *Reflection equals a location*
> *plus a period of time*
> *plus good questions.*

Ask yourself what settings or places provide the best opportunity for reflective questioning? Perhaps when driving or flying or walking. Or perhaps we are most likely to reflect when listening to music, reading a certain book, praying, or pondering our thoughts after a fruitful exchange with a friend. Take a moment and *identify* specific settings that nourish your ability to reflect on your life.

Meaningful reflection also requires a time commitment. One of the casualties of modern living is the decline of solitude. Mass media and advertising deliver the message that human happiness exists solely in the enjoyment of relationships. The experience of being alone, on the other hand, is frequently portrayed as a deficient, needy state. Naturally, relationships remain one of the most significant sources for personal fulfillment. Even so, the sacrifice of solitude is particularly regrettable because solitude is a vital catalyst for creativity and a source for healing during periods of loss.[7] Further, it provides a period for rejuvenating personal resources and deepening self-understanding.[8]

Unfortunately, too often we surrender our time to false solitudes. For example, television, video, the Internet, and computers most certainly offer entertainment and educational benefits, enormous opportunities for increasing knowledge and personal enjoyment. Nonetheless, as with any technologies we must reflect critically on their usage. How many Americans, disgruntled and tired after a long work day, find themselves "vegging out" in front of a television screen? Such "down time" is understandable, at times even necessary, but if it is the primary source for rejuvenation, then optimal moral, emotional, and physical health is at risk. Regrettably, many adopt the false assumption that being solitary is having solitude. Thus we erroneously equate solitude with solitary play of the newest video game or surfing the net. Using a similar line of reasoning, quality communication is mistakenly equated with Internet usage. Ironically, frequent use of the Internet, even to communicate with others on-line, has been linked to an overall decline in psychological and social well-being.[9]

Advances in technology also pose the danger of eroding personal standards. All too frequently, people and events viewed on television are portrayed as so glamorous, adventurous, or ideal that the viewer's own internal standard of realistic accomplishment or satisfaction becomes distorted. Seeping into consciousness for many youth (and even adults) is an unrealistic desire for "something more" or a feeling of "deprivation" about their own condition or state when compared with what they view on the screen. Over time, such distortion leads to a corroding self-alienation. A continual challenge is maintaining a realistic attitude about what is possible in our relationships and weathering disappointments when they do occur.

To summarize, when instances of solitude and fruitful reflection are infrequent or chronic dissatisfaction with life takes root, we become distracted from using our psychic energy in ways that promote moral health. When schedules are so full that we fail to carve out regular time for serious or even playful reflection, then moral fitness declines.

The Need for Adequate Sleep

Though modern living diminishes time for solitude, a more immediate issue is the toll taken by sleep deprivation. Over the past century Americans' sleep time has steadily declined. On any given morning tens of millions of Americans struggle with the consequences of inadequate rest. Lack of sleep is commonly associated with car accidents and other tragedies, and some experts are so alarmed by the sleep shortage that they label it one of the country's major health problems. In order to enjoy leisure, to function at work, and to be available for relationships, Americans are cutting back in the only area they can — sleep![10]

How rested are you? How do you relate to people when you are tired? What is the quality of the decisions you make? Weariness triggers irritability, impatience, and distraction. Personally speaking, when I am not rested, I find that I am not the teacher I desire to be. When I am tired, it becomes more difficult to listen and really hear students' questions and concerns. Call to mind the significant roles in your life (e.g., spouse, parent, friend, colleague, student) and consider how fatigue undermines your goal to achieve moral health. How many spouses or friends fail to initiate a critical conversation that would challenge and enrich their personal lives and relationships because they find themselves too weary to summon the needed energy? How much reflection has been lost, books not read, and vital discussions abandoned because of insufficient sleep?

Most readers are aware that solitude and sleep are vital for healthy living. But they also have a critical role in nourishing our moral lives. Work, family life, care of parents, commuting time, and personal obligations sometimes make solitary reflection and sufficient sleep seem like luxuries. Busy schedules are often rigid schedules that do not allow for the introduction of new pursuits (even ones as beneficial as sleep and solitude). We must resist what work and family columnist Sue Shellenbarger labels "the tomorrow trap," that is, always postponing until a future date some valued activity or significant behavior. With such a mind-set some critical desires might never be fulfilled.[11] You need not answer every question asked in this chapter or completely redo your schedule in an attempt to find time for solitude. The important point is: *do something today!* Perhaps you might only set aside five minutes each weekend to think over a question asked above or to probe the thoughts your reading generates. Fine. It's a start. The important point is to introduce small shifts that become part of your regular routine in the weeks and months ahead. Begin where you can. Establish a beachhead and build on it. Small steps taken now are the source for later momentum.

Is Chaos Good for Your Moral Health?

A very popular theory making the rounds in business and academic circles is chaos theory. The complexity of chaos theory is beyond us here (and I might add to a great degree beyond this writer); nonetheless, one aspect of the theory is helpful to our discussion. Chaos theory tells us that at a set point in time, the appearance of even scant differences can lead to highly divergent, unpredictable outcomes. For example, we might mix several chemicals and, given certain conditions, know some type of chemical reaction will take place. However, we are often unable to predict precisely what the final outcome will be. As various factors (such as heat) interact with the chemicals the ensuing chemical breakdown triggers instability (chaos) and even random movement of substances that eventually combine to achieve a certain order or pattern. From this chaos an identified outcome emerges, but what that exact outcome will be remains elusive. "This unpredictability occurs because it is typical for infinitely small differences in the starting conditions to lead to a very large and qualitatively different outcomes."[12] The eventual effects of small or even faint factors have come to be known as the "butterfly effect." The ever so slight increase in wind velocity stemming from just a butterfly's wings might generate significant (though unpredictable) effects on weather patterns in distant geographic areas at some future date.

Because biological, social, and organizational systems are inter-active and dynamic — thus producing complex, diverse out-comes — researchers increasingly turn to chaos theory as a way to understand their functioning. A major point of the theory — the unpredictability of some future events — proves useful for understanding the role of active reflective questioning in promot-ing moral health. All of us have benefited from the caring advice of others and often their advice includes asking about our mo-tives or behaviors. Recall the various adults, whether instructors or staff, affiliated with the educational institutions you attended during your high school or college years. Recall a coach, super-visor, or boss who took an interest in you. Or reflect on your relationships with special people in your life such as close friends.

The numerous intersecting relationships you've experienced with others over these years have included pivotal conversations. A teacher's question sparks an interest that grows. A friend's view-point widens your perspective. A coach's firm yet caring correction forms the basis for future achievement. A parent's comment makes you reconsider your feelings. Somehow in some way such en-counters engaged you, focused your thinking, and became the wellspring for positive growth. Like the movement of the but-terfly's wings, an adult's interaction with you might have been fleeting — a couple of minutes, perhaps only a few moments in which a few words were exchanged. Yet it *made a difference.* Slowly at first, but inevitably, it began to influence your self-understanding or perspective. More than likely, in ways not even known to you, other aspects of your life were altered. As you con-tinued to grow, your newly acquired understanding blended with your experience and opened new avenues of insight that led you in unexplored directions. You could not predict the outcome or the shape this growth eventually took. Yet it happened. You are a better person as a result of what happened in those brief moments long ago.

In a similar vein, investing your psychic energy *now* in self-inquiry as well as the other positive behaviors highlighted in this chapter form the basis for positive (though unpredictable) growth. Even if the investment is only for a few moments with one question, *do it* — invest the psychic energy! The slight ripples now can offer significant moral health benefits later.

A word of caution: as you take self-inquiry seriously, some of your feelings and thoughts might prove troubling. You might have to reconsider some assumptions or live with contradiction as you explore various issues. In other words, your own mental state might show some disorder or chaos! Describing the relationship between creativity and chaos, columnist Thomas Petzinger remarked that the experience of some chaos, as long as it is not too severe, can be viewed as a positive sign. "People recognize this in everyday life: A slightly messy office is a productive one; rollicking families are happy; economies flourish under scant regulation. The edge of chaos, but not chaos itself."[13] It makes sense for our moral health, too. When we reflect on our moral fitness we should not hesitate to encourage reassessment of our life assumptions, personal attitudes, and everyday behaviors.

The Effects of Suffering

Disappointment, failure, and emotional hurt are all experiences we might include under the mantle of "suffering." We all aspire to be well-integrated, healthy individuals. But as one prominent psychologist observes, human beings find it difficult to maintain mental health on a consistent basis.[14] Every new experience we encounter intersects with our life history. But our personal histories or the demands of a situation (or both) frequently create roadblocks that derail our good intentions or compromise our ideals. For every promise we make to live better lives there exists an almost infinite number of potential factors that undo or sidetrack our good intentions. Take a common example. Your extended family comes together for a holiday celebration. Over the years the irritating behavior of your uncle has made your relationship with him a rocky one (Factor 1: your life history). You promise yourself that this holiday you will refrain from making any comments that upset or cause division within the family. Unfortunately, at your parents' home (Factor 2: the situation) your uncle's rude comments (Factor 3: a problem family member) eventually prove unbearable, triggering from you a cynical comment that soon widens into a heated exchange drawing in other family members (Factor 4: other family members' behavior). On your way home with your family you feel terrible for responding to your uncle as you did (Factor 5: your self-reproach). Both our life histories and specific situations have the potential for sabotaging our good intentions.

Even the healthiest and most mature individuals experience disappointment, encounter failure, and find life, at times, burdensome. Suffering is part of each of our lives. But we know suffering can be a springboard to deeper insight and greater maturity. The key, of course, is not to go looking for suffering (which some people do!) but to acquire those behaviors and attitudes that help us to lead productive lives and cope successfully with disappointment, hurt, and failure when they occur. For example, a person comes to the point in her life where she admits her powerlessness over alcohol. Addiction undermines moral health, not to mention emotional and physical health. But once her alcoholism is honestly acknowledged and confronted (that is, her psychic energy is put to good use by investing it in ongoing recovery), her admission strengthens her moral health. In turn, the meaningful commitment she makes to aid others suffering from the same illness allows her to live more fully the moral life she desires.

Consider the parent who stays up nearly the entire night to comfort her sick child and who has an 8:30 a.m. sales meeting for which she must be alert and attentive. Or the friend who though tired from a busy work week willingly gives up a weekend to help a friend move furniture into his new house. The positive feelings that significant relationships generate lead us to assume burdens and make personal sacrifices that range from minor inconveniences (going to the store) to heroic actions (faithfully caring for a parent or spouse with Alzheimer's).

The moral entropy and psychological flaws that underlie our daily struggles pose constant roadblocks as we journey to become men and women of good conscience. Such infirmities, and the suffering they bring, are part and parcel of being human. There is a final cost that goes with moral fitness. G. K. Chesterton once remarked that "a person must be certain of his morality for the simple reason that he has to suffer for it."[15] Persons taking their moral fitness seriously at some point "suffer for it." Taking morality seriously will inevitably "demand something." A morally healthy person acknowledges and *understands* this stark but unsettling truth.

Psychic Energy's Limits

Deciding upon a specific course of action, spending time with a particular person, or reading a certain book necessarily means that another option, another person, or another book do not have our attention and focus. We can attend only to so many matters and invest in a limited number of people and activities. But keep in mind that we write our future history *now*. The decisions we make currently often determine the course of our actions for years to come. How we invest psychic energy has a cumulative effect. If we use it wisely, that is, investing it in healthy relationships and personal goals that foster maturity, then we can achieve contentment. If the decisions we make (marriage, career, or personal pursuits) are poor choices, then the cumulative effect of those decisions grows increasingly burdensome.

Most people's happiness rests somewhere between complete contentment and onerous burden. All of us can acknowledge times we wasted psychic energy through ill-advised choices. As the years pass, we sometimes feel the need to make life changes by redirecting psychic energy to pursuits that appear to promise greater contentment and peace. Many psychologists seriously question whether the "midlife crisis" truly exists.[16] Regardless of the merits of the debate, a hopeful perspective views midlife changes as a reasonable attempt to correct previous life decisions by redirecting or refocusing psychic energy in ways that promise greater contentment. Changing a job, making a geographic move, or altering a relationship is best viewed as a corrective measure to refocus psychic energy and begin anew. Many times these corrections prove beneficial and afford new opportunities for personal growth and health. Of course, some adults (whether in young, middle, or later adulthood) make changes that prove in the long run disruptive and at times disastrous for their personal lives. Further, we experience anxious moments and even heartache when poor decision making involves family members, friends, or others we care about.

It might be helpful to think of the path from young adulthood (twenty to forty) to middle adulthood (forty to sixty-five) like playing a "personal stock market." Most of us have the opportunity in young adulthood to invest psychic energy wisely in pursuits and relationships that contribute to our happiness, health, maturity, and goodness. This initial investment serves as a source for "interest," eventually contributing to even further growth through our middle and later adult years. Fortunately, many young adults have at their disposal a generous admixture of supportive relationships, personal talents and motivations, and some luck that helps insure an adequate return on the psychic energy they invest.

Relate psychic energy to your life by practicing the following exercise:

1. Designate a decade of your life. Take this time span and list three life decisions that you consider wise investments of your psychic energy.

2. Imagine someone you know disputing the "wise" decisions you list. What reasons can you offer for designating your decisions as wise?

3. What criteria do you use to evaluate whether a decision has been made wisely?

4. How has each of the decisions you listed influenced your moral health?

5. Now list three life decisions from the same decade in which you made poor use of your psychic energy. What leads you to conclude that each of these decisions was a poor choice? How has each of these decisions influenced your moral health?

The sooner we make wise investments the better. The old adages we heard while growing up — "Choose friends wisely," "Watch the company you keep," "Think seriously about your career choice" — were good advice that made sense. Unfortunately, too many young people whose lives lack supportive environments or a sympathetic adult ear squander psychic energy. Without the interest and feedback of caring adults, youth are denied the necessary counsel that makes wise choices possible. In addition, the personal and emotional struggles that occupy many young people distract them from the focus and attention needed to acquire important skills. I have personally witnessed undergraduates struggling with painful feelings and emotional hurts arising from troubled family backgrounds. Unless instructors or residence hall staff provided special attention to them and unless they utilized resources available from the Counseling Center, troubled young adults often wasted psychic energy on distracting pursuits (e.g., excessive partying) and eventually left school.

Active Reflective Questioning

The key to moral growth is *dialogue* with self and others. Questions stimulate us to reconsider how we handle a problem or to entertain a fresh perspective on an issue. Often people make the erroneous assumption that when they encounter dilemmas or difficult problems, they must have "the" answer. Often, however, a more fruitful approach is to invest psychic energy in formulating the "right question." It is the *question* that triggers the right answer.

Take an employee contemplating a career change. Though naturally thoughts will turn to specific work opportunities (Should I take this job offer?), an essential question to ask before accepting any offer is: What do I really like doing? Moreover, an often conflicted and emotionally charged dilemma arises when a loved one is near death and family members must make a decision about what medical procedures to permit that might prolong the relative's life. Though family members understandably agonize over their choices, clarity often arises when the question is asked: "What was his wish about prolonging life by medical interventions?" The question that addresses the loved one's wishes is integral to any moral decision.

Active reflective questioning probes nonconscious and untested assumptions. It challenges habits to which we have grown all too accustomed. Such assumptions and habits are often the roadblocks that limit productive use of our psychic energy.

Even with all the brain's potential, humans are notorious for being simply creatures of habit. Frequently we adopt an autopilot mode, spending our days conforming to daily schedules. When we add to this routine-prone existence the overload factor arising from too many activities and too little time, then our lives become stuck in routine and reaction. Not surprisingly, too much mindless routine and stressful reaction undermines moral fitness. Active reflective questioning dislodges autopilot consciousness. As psychologist Mihaly Csikszentmihalyi so wisely observes, the key to personal development and happiness is winning daily the struggle to maintain control of personal consciousness.[17]

The struggle for consciousness is an unending battle we wage daily. To the degree we prevent consciousness from gravitating to the autopilot mode of routine and reaction and instead create an awareness for ourselves through active reflective questioning, we notch a victory for moral health.

The outline below contains topic areas for active reflective questioning. Go rapidly through the list until you find a question of interest. For now, ignore the rest. Just sit for a minute or two with the question you chose. Jot down a thought or share your answer with a friend. Keep probing your thoughts. Reconsider your answer at a future moment. Later, allow another question to engage you. Keep inquiring, keep answering, keep thinking. Keep *engaging* yourself. This engagement is the fundamental first step for increasing moral fitness. You need not address every question or even a majority of them. But do take time today and over the next few days or weeks to consider some of them.

Relationships

- Who are my close friends? Name them or list them on a sheet of paper.

- What do I find most significant in each of these friendships?

- How healthy is each of these friendships?

- Do I engage with this friend in some unhealthy behaviors (e.g., gossiping, cynicism, blaming others, excessive drinking)?

- Are there aspects of this friendship I wish to change? Why?

- What personal needs of mine does this friendship most satisfy? Are we both aware of our own and the other's needs? Would I describe the "needs" I have as appropriate?

Sense of Humor

- How do I use humor in my life?

- Does my humor make me a more loving person in my relationships?

- Are there unhealthy aspects to my humor? For example, do I use humor to be cynical or hurtful to others?

Meaningful Work

- What work activities do I find most satisfying? Why?

- Do I have a hobby?

- Do my activities enhance my creative side?

- Am I able to create distance (boundaries) from my work?

- Do I play? How?

The Future

- Who do I hope to be in five years? Ten years? (Note: This question addresses not what you want to do, but who you want to *be* as a person.) What must I begin to do *now* to become this person?

- Am I motivated to begin taking these steps? Why? Why not?

- What issues and concerns demand more of my attention over the next few years?

Integrity

- What are my desires? What are my deepest desires?

- How would I define my "personal integrity"?

- Which of my behaviors are most threatening to my integrity?

Spirituality

- How do I describe my spirituality?

- How do I nourish my spirituality? Through meditation? Prayer?

- What are the ways my spirituality contributes to my moral fitness?

- What is the *quality* of my solitude?

Don't try to do too much too soon. But *do something*. Do ask yourself a question. Do start reflecting. Establish a beachhead upon which you can build. The wise investment you make now will appreciate considerably and generate sizeable benefits in the years to come.

Friendship

Of all the topics and human activities that fall under the category of psychic energy, I propose three as likely to offer the most direct path to the goal of moral fitness: (1) sustaining friendships, (2) achieving emotional regulation, and (3) creating a life project. These three uses of psychic energy can enhance moral fitness, and when these life experiences are absent, we stifle our growth both morally and humanly.

Significant social relationships form the essential ingredient for building trust and meaningful bonding among people. With the exception of family ties, friendship remains the most significant bond people have for insuring emotional connection and trust. Human beings are social animals requiring meaningful interchange. Unfortunately, in modern life a wide variety of factors converge to form roadblocks to building friendships. Suburbanization and geographic mobility separate people from families, friends, and colleagues. Packed schedules leave little time for relaxing visits and quality discussion. Technology and telecommunications encourage private, self-absorbed endeavors such as viewing cable television or surfing the Internet. To be fair, we must again acknowledge technology's role in enhancing communication. Many of us have access to faxes, cellular phones, and e-mail. At times, these devices are vital means of communication. Nonetheless, without the opportunity for spontaneous give-and-take (which includes the nonverbal cues of voice tone, facial expression, and body gestures that friends interpret so well) through face-to-face interchange, emotional connection and the personal meaning it offers can prove difficult to sustain.

From the perspective of human psychology, friendship more than any other experience is essential for moral health. Call to mind someone who lacks healthy friendships, and I guarantee that you have identified someone with poor moral health. This statement is a bold one, yet without friendship the moral life falters.

Close your eyes! Sit back, relax, and engage in the following exercise. Ask yourself: Which people in my life mean most to me? Review briefly your life history and ask yourself which friends you have most appreciated and valued. Take the time to name each of these people. What do you say to each? With each one what do you feel? How much gratitude do you feel for each relationship? Now choose one of the friends you recalled and imagine your life *without* this friend. Suppose you had never met this person. Without this friend what would your life be like today? Would you feel less complex? Less complete?

Intimacy

In its most general sense, intimacy refers to the mutual sharing of thoughts and feelings in an atmosphere of trust. To have intimacy means we connect with another through an emotional bond that furthers wholeness and complexity, both in oneself and in the other.[18] Thus when we enjoy friendship's intimacy we experience ourselves as more connected, more enriched, and more complex.

From another perspective, we might approach the value of friendship by asking ourselves: What is the opposite of friendship's intimacy? Most people, I think, would respond "loneliness." Loneliness is a growing problem in modern cultures. Speaking as a clinician, I would say that the word "hunger" best captures the lonely state. Unless they are satisfied, hunger pangs eventually distract us from everything else. Food becomes an obsession preoccupying us totally. Loneliness is a similar state. Over time loneliness proves more and more distressing. In order to relieve this distress people resort to any number of escapist behaviors. These range from innocent and recurring distractions to relentless, compulsion-driven activities like overeating, workaholism, or compulsive sexual behavior. In some instances, the unhealthy behavior is linked to a biological constitution leading to alcoholism or other form of substance abuse or dependence. Sadly, the friendless state deprives us emotionally of the intimacy needed for satisfying, enriching lives.

Intimacy in one form or another is a popular theme in modern life. The vast array of bookstore titles devoted to relationships and their dysfunction provides ample evidence that more and more people define their life satisfaction in terms of their interpersonal relationships.

Adolescence

No group is more preoccupied with relationships than adolescents. Healthy adolescent friendship insures productive use of youth's psychic energy. Try this exercise. Think back to the years twelve through eighteen. Remember a friend, a pal, a confidant, a buddy during that period of your life. What did you say to one another? What did you do together? How did you feel toward him or her? In all likelihood, building this friendship helped cement a foundation for your moral health. Consider for a moment the positive experiences this relationship promoted. This friendship gave you feelings of significance, thereby bolstering self-esteem. The everyday give-and-take of this friendship enabled you to learn the meaning of trust. Through self-disclosure you were made aware that you were not alone in having the feelings you had; others, too, felt the loneliness, moodiness, excitement, and joy you experienced. Mutually shared feelings were confirming moments, for they soothed self-doubts and defused personal anxieties. Even though you did not consider them to be such at the time, ethical questions also surfaced. Should you keep a confidence or share what your friend revealed? You took time to consider when relating to this friend what behaviors were and were not appropriate. How should I behave? How should I respond? How should I care? What is fair? In short, the relationship became a "mutual lesson plan" for learning how to negotiate conflicts, handle tensions, and weather disappointments. Given all this relationship offered you, we could conclude that this friendship served as an "apprenticeship" on how to be a moral person.[19]

Though you and your friend were not aware of it at the time, you both accepted the adventure of constructing an *integrity* for your relationship. As you grew more comfortable in the relationship, you just "knew" there were some behaviors allowed (actions displaying loyalty and support) and others clearly forbidden (mean-spirited comments and betrayal of trust). Failure to live up to this unwritten code proved embarrassing and provoked guilt. This "budding" integrity became the foundation for your later relationships. From these early friendships you learned that trusting another feels good; living up to the ideals of friendship through loyalty, fairness, and care permitted a measure of self-pride while affirming your developing value system. The nitty-gritty aspects of friendship — savoring ideals, building trust, resolving conflicts fairly — all became the signposts guiding you down the road to moral fitness.

Consider once more the friendships of your youth. Only this time by way of contrast substitute an image of yourself as a member of a gang. Take a moment to speculate, in light of all that is stated above, about what the state of your moral health might be today if these gang ties had been the primary relationships of your teen years.

From the time of young adulthood (roughly eighteen onward), the best way to promote moral health is to build healthy friendships. More than any other resource, friendship is a catalyst for critically reflecting on our attitudes, assumptions, and behaviors. By its very nature of mutual interchange, friendship periodically spawns conflicts and compromises that encourage the working out of ethical values and the exploration of previously untested assumptions. A basic ingredient of friendship is trust and its requirement to honor confidences. The results of healthy friendship are self-knowledge and greater openness to others. A friend's opinion is valued, and, though not always agreed with, our friend's comments and suggestions are seriously considered because of the friendship's history and the respect it elicits. At a minimum, the comments of a friend broaden our personal views and encourage us to stretch our interpretations, thus scrutinizing more closely our behaviors. Such reconsiderations can forge new understandings of life and provide numerous opportunities for self-insight.

Yet more and more today the word "friend" is carelessly used and sloppily defined. So many relationships we define as friendships are in reality loosely connected relationships that are more properly understood as acquaintances — bonds of familiarity existing between people centered around their situations (e.g., members of an organization) or activities (e.g., workers laboring on a project). In contrast to this more casual relationship, friendship requires a certain degree of emotional connection. Naturally, we feel closer to some friends than others. As a consequence, we distinguish among friends with adjectives such as "close," "best," "dear," and "trusted," while labeling others simply as "friends." The functions and benefits that friends provide vary according to the talents and interests of ourselves and our friends. Thus one friend is a marvelous companion whose hobby or recreational interests are similar to our own, while we turn to another friend when we desire serious conversation. Combining such diversity with varying levels of emotional depth allows for the possibility of an extensive network of friendships.

A good way to understand friendship is to explore mutual experiences shared by friends. Although there is no universally agreed-upon definition of friendship, friendship offers a set of common experiences that enrich each friend's life. These common experiences make up friendship's *domains*. Few friendships embrace all of them, since allotting the necessary time and psychic energy to any one friend proves difficult as we try to juggle numerous commitments. This all-consuming focus is most often found in adolescent friendships, which encourage intense psychic investments. As you reflect on the list below and the questions posed, you can see that mutual participation by friends in a number of domains contributes substantially to sustaining emotional connection and moral fitness. Try to answer each of the questions. Call to mind friends that fit comfortably in each domain.

The Domains of Friendship

1. *Family Background.* These friends know something of my family of origin. Perhaps they have visited my home, know some of my siblings, or have just heard me talk about my childhood and adolescent years. These friends have some understanding of why I am the way I am — how my strengths and talents as well as various limitations and weaknesses emerged from my family history. Perhaps I have periodically shared with them some information from my childhood that few others know.

- Which of my friends have some understanding of my family history?

2. *Current Life Situation.* These friends know what is going on in my life here and now, my joys and struggles in living everyday life. They know what I worry about and what occupies my time.

- Which friends are most familiar with my current situation?

3. *Personal Desires.* These friends know about my desires and life goals. As I share with them these desires, they are willing to offer encouragement, clarification, and, when necessary, challenge.

- Which friends do I turn to when I need to share future plans, dreams, goals?

4. *Negative Feelings.* With these friends I am more willing to talk through negative feelings or doubts about a wide range of issues. With certain friends I feel "safe" in sharing feelings and concerns.

- Which friends do I trust enough to openly share my negative feelings?

5. *Wishing the Good of the Other.* I genuinely wish the good for my friends. If the "good" means I experience some personal pain or discomfort (e.g., undergoing long separation or coping with troubled feelings), I am willing to endure such distress if it is in the best interest of my friend.

- Do my actions and attitudes convey to my friends a genuine desire for what is best for them?

6. *Challenge.* More so than is true of other relationships (e.g., acquaintances), I am willing to intrude into my friends' lives. I am more comfortable (as are my friends) when we do this with one another, since our shared life history generates the trust that allows for such mutual intrusion.

- How comfortable am I with lovingly challenging as well as accepting challenge from my friends?

7. *Silence.* Just as we know what to say to our friends, we also know what not to say. All of us at one time or another said something inappropriate on some social occasion. For example, we offer comments about some person or issue that we would have discreetly refrained from bringing up if we had known better the people in the group. With a friend, on the other hand, we have a sense of when to refrain from raising a certain issue or concern. Friendship rests in part in each friend's awareness of what need not be mentioned. This assurance provides each friend a sense of safety and even relief.

- Do I have an intuitive sense of what not to say as well as what to say in various friendships?

8. *Positive Feelings.* Certain friends stir within us feelings of joy and gratitude that prove tremendously satisfying. When we think of positive moments in our lives, specific friendships naturally surface as essential ingredients for producing such positive feelings. With these friends we can laugh and play.

- Which of my friendships leave me feeling more grateful about my life?

9. *Nurturing Solitude.* Experiences with certain friends spill over into other areas of my life. These friendships enrich my solitude, for they lead me to be more self-aware and creative about my life and desires. In turn, these insights lead me back to the friendship in order that I might share such insights and so enrich the relationship.

- Can I articulate how I have changed as a result of a specific friendship?

10. *Disclosing Personal Intimacies.* These friends are familiar with my life history and know things about me that are reserved for a select few. Intimacies might include sharing deeply felt desires, personal traumas, or notable achievements or failures.

- Do I know my friend well or are there areas we avoid discussing?

11. *Priorities.* Good friends are priorities in my life. To the extent possible, I try to give time to my friends, which includes communicating or doing things together. (In this instance, e-mail offers some benefits, though only rarely might it fulfill what the physical presence of the other person offers.)

- Which friendships in my life are valued priorities?

If we all had friendships that allowed us to invest in many of the above domains, think of the advancement that would take place not only in individual but also in national moral health!

Nonetheless, our psychic energy is limited. Though we are called to show appropriate respect to all, we are not called to universal intimacy. Emotional connection with some people means limiting connection with others. We need boundaries, not only in our relationships but also in the number of relationships. (The chapter on empathy examines the role of boundaries in fostering moral health.) Though every person requires emotional connection, the number of such connections varies considerably. Furthermore, though we may remain open to new relationships, with advancing years people frequently prefer to deepen already existing relationships rather than continually seeking new ones.[20]

Regulating Our Emotions

Newborns display a distinctive style in their interactions with the world (what psychologists label temperament). Some babies are soothed easily, whereas others require from parents enormous effort and time to remain calm. As infants or toddlers encounter the world, gradually venturing out to explore it, their emotional style reacts to their surroundings (parental responses, specific location, availability of desired objects). Through the interaction of surroundings and emotional display children develop their distinctive responses most broadly identified as "personality." Every child's personality is unique because it blends together various active/passive behaviors, negative/positive moods, consistent/inconsistent actions, responding/withdrawing tendencies, and content/discontented reactions that constitute the child's unique approach to her world.

The temperamental tendencies of early age and the events encountered in our life histories, such as treatment by parents, cultural background, and relationship experiences, blend together with personal triumphs and successes as well as disappointments and failures to forge a distinct personality expressing "Who I am."[21] When we ask a friend "What's wrong?" or wonder about our child's behavior or find a colleague's actions strange, we are reacting to what we perceive as the other person's personality being at odds with what we have come to expect.

A fundamental building block making up personality and its display is the strength and intensity of emotional expression. Recall that emotion comes from the Latin word *emovere,* which includes the notion of movement or action.[22] Emotions encourage us toward a goal. They play a central role in helping us understand our motivations. Emotions are integral to the richness and complexity we experience. Without emotions "our once-colorful world would be bleached a drab gray. We'd drift along aimlessly, under slack sails, bereft of the impulses that motivate and direct our everyday pursuits."[23] A life in which emotion is infrequently felt is both barren and dull.

Emotions reflect a core sense of what we term "the self." Recall a time when a friend presented to you a variety of compelling reasons to convince you of the correctness of her position. You listened patiently and understood and even appreciated her arguments. Even so, when she was finished making her case, your response was "I understand what you're saying, but I still feel...." We have all had such experiences. No doubt there were reasons for your holding a contrary position to your friend. However, your reasons also reflected some sort of intuition, some level of felt intensity surrounding your hunch. You stayed with your informed hunch because you experienced it as more honestly reflecting your sense of the truth. In this instance we might say your emotion was more "you" than any thought or logical conclusion you could have reached.

More than most experiences, emotions can be double-edged swords. On the one hand, our feelings provide for the most serene contentment and joy. On the other hand, they have potential for creating extraordinary depths of paralyzing despair. The primary goal of emotional regulation is the satisfactory negotiation of positive and negative feelings. Health and happiness are in large measure determined by our capacity to generate and maintain positive emotions, while acknowledging and regulating negative emotions when they occur in order that they not strangle or sabotage growth and happiness.

Skills necessary for regulating emotions are acquired gradually. Infants display very general reactions such as crying; but signaling behaviors such as gazing and smiling at parents demonstrate that even at an early stage young children find ways to regulate their emotions. Crawling, walking, and language development soon follow as the child shows increasing capacity for monitoring feelings and demonstrating likes and dislikes. Steady intellectual development and growing language skills serve to make the child more self-aware and goal-seeking. At the same time, the child acquires internalized rules and understandings as to what is expected in a wide variety of social situations. Encouraging parents provide instruction on proper emotional displays. Other authority figures and peers provide further feedback by their own emotional expressions.[24] With adulthood, "emotion regulation is no longer simply desirable, it is absolutely necessary for daily functioning."[25]

We all know people whose emotions get the best of them. Amy's tone of voice communicates the rage consuming her, whereas Ramon's guilt causes continuing distress. Even if we don't identify with either of these emotional states, we can all recall times in our lives when the intensity of our feelings overrode even our best intentions. Not surprisingly, such emotional experiences have the potential to sabotage moral health. Negative feelings — anger, sadness, fear, jealousy, and envy — are more often than not pathways for emotional turmoil. When negative emotions are experienced too intensely or are prolonged, they diminish moral health. Intense emotions absorb psychic energy, thereby leading us to lose perspective on our goals and the mature behaviors necessary for accomplishing the priorities we set.

Is Self-Disclosure Always Healthy?

One trend noted by many is society's increasing identification as a confessional culture — a climate that permits and even encourages uncensored expressions about personal hurts, faults, angers, and injustices.[26] No force in society fosters this belief more than television talk shows, where every weekday all-too-eager guests divulge anything and everything about their private lives and personal sufferings. Frequently the conversation is flooded with anger and distress as guests pour out every possible hurt and disappointment. At times such televised catharsis is best described as a tell-all confessional.

Paralleling this trend is an upsurge in people's willingness to self-disclose. While it is certainly healthy to have relationships in which confidences are shared and acknowledged and negative feelings are worked through constructively, revealing too much, too fast, to too many, especially about personal intimacies, poses threats to

Used by permission of Cartoon Features Syndicate.

moral health. Indiscriminate self-disclosure undermines the very boundaries that make intimacy possible. Friendship involves freely conversing about personal information to which others are not privy. Disclosing too much to too many blurs the boundaries between trusted friends and other relationships. If there are excessively large numbers of people with whom we share personal intimacies, we run the risk of diluting friendship's meaning because privileged confidence is integral to any definition of close friendship. Friendship is sacred in part because of the trust friends feel that allows for privileged sharing of personal intimacies. Unless there is a discipline to limit such disclosure, the opportunity for trust evaporates, which reduces all relationships to a least common denominator.

Regulating emotion also helps us resist the temptation to squander psychic energy. When we overreact to upsetting events, disappointments, or unexpected situations, then, inevitably, less energy exists for other worthwhile pursuits. Fortunately, one of the distinguishing marks of middle age is the gradually growing capability to temper emotional reactions and the anxious uncertainty of earlier years. As we enter middle age, physiological changes in the brain contribute to this growing sense of calm. Anxiety disorders, for example, are more likely to occur in early rather than middle adulthood.[27] Our life experience fosters a growing sense of mastery and confidence as we go about our daily tasks. For example, most adult children agree that parents' treatment of the last born in the family was less strict than that of the first child. Because their parents are more comfortable in their roles, later-born children usually find themselves with more freedom, often to the chagrin of their older brothers or sisters.

Nonetheless, even though we might become more skilled at certain tasks and develop a broader perspective that lessens our anxiety, nearly all of us encounter situations that trigger inappropriate or intense emotional reactions. For example, one definition (though fortunately not the only one) of a family is an emotionally connected group of people who know how to push each other's buttons! To recall an earlier example, family members come to holiday gatherings or family reunions to celebrate and socialize, but we also bring our previous histories with other family members to these events. Even an innocent comment or benign facial expression by one family member, if interpreted wrongly, can be the trigger point for intense discussion or heated exchange. Other potential trouble spots include a colleague's or neighbor's behavior that we judge offensive. The irritant need not even be a person. An unexpected traffic jam that makes us late for an appointment, a sudden rainstorm that cancels an eagerly anticipated event, or discovery of a flaw in a recently purchased item all have the potential for causing emotional firestorms. What we frequently fail to consider is how the hassles, irritants, and problems we encounter take their toll on our moral health. Often it is not any one irritant but the *accumulation* of irritants over a period of time that proves upsetting.[28]

The Negativity Bias

We need to regulate our emotions because of the human bias to focus more on negative than positive experiences. Though it may be uncomfortable to acknowledge, human beings possess a negative bias that remains remarkably resilient and difficult to overcome. Research consistently demonstrates that people are more aware of others' negative attributes or failed outcomes than of their positive features and personal successes.[29] For example, you plan a surprise party for a close friend. What could go right? Well, the "surprise" could work and everyone present has a good time! Now ask yourself: What could go wrong? Well, your close friend could find out about the party. Maybe not all the people you invite show up. Maybe you'll be called away because of a family crisis. What if you get sick? Or perhaps your close friend must suddenly leave town because of an emergency. What if something is wrong with the food? What if your camera doesn't work? And there is even more you can worry about if you give yourself permission! The Y2K scare with its dire warnings of economic disruption might have demonstrated a negativity bias on a grand scale.

Why are negative perceptions in such abundance? For one reason, when we think about what "might happen," the numbers favor the negative. "Considering all the possible things to think about, the negative possibilities always outnumber the positive ones."[30] More than likely at one point in human history such negative bias proved adaptive. With our early ancestors two tendencies — one positive and one negative — increased chances for survival. Love, empathy, and loyalty enabled individuals to form emotional bonds. The struggle for survival in the harsh, brutal, and hostile surroundings our ancient ancestors faced was winnable because of the mutual protection and support that group membership provided. On the other hand, survival was also fostered by fear, envy, jealousy, and anger — negative feelings that encouraged ongoing vigilance. Rapid responses to intruders or to a threatening situation increased chances of survival for individual group members.

Today we live in a technologically sophisticated society whose social norms require conduct that is both civil and nonaggressive. Yet, even though it no longer is appropriate to display or act on intense negative feelings, no one would deny their continued presence. Thus, if we are envious, fearful, or angry toward someone, we are expected to refrain from physical aggression or verbal abuse. Though social customs and norms require such restraint, our negative bias remains. (Perhaps being passive-aggressive toward someone is our modern way of carrying on the negative feelings of ancient ancestors.) When acutely felt for a short period of time (one could react very negatively to the unexpected cutting remark of a close friend) or chronically felt over a prolonged period (spouses in a difficult marriage might be hardened from even considering what it means to be a "good" spouse), our negative emotional states make us prone to distractions and emotional upset. As a consequence, our good intentions are eclipsed. Simply recall a time when you were intensely angry, fearful, or sad. How would you describe your moral resolve? Your motivation to be good? Fortunately, the struggle between our negative tendencies and the desire to feel and think positively about ourselves and the world around us is winnable. But it takes *effort*.

Regulating Anger

When it comes to weakening moral health, no emotion is apt to prove more deadly than anger. Just as anger undermines physical and emotional health, it also takes a toll on our moral fitness. We can't avoid anger. It goes with being human. In fact, in some situations anger serves as a moral emotion. Anger in response to witnessing an injustice might well be positive. It communicates our desire for fairness. For example, viewing a television program that displays the bodies of murdered children triggers intense emotional reaction. Multiple emotions surface — sadness, shock, disgust. The visual images assault our moral sensitivities, which in turn invite anger or outrage.

At the same time, we need to acknowledge that anger can undermine our moral health in a variety of ways. For one, it derails our good intentions. If our anger is intense, it can become all-consuming, blinding us to its consequences both for ourselves and for others. A mental illness known as borderline personality disorder fits this description well. With little prompting the anger of the borderline personality turns to uncontrollable rage.

Second, when highjacked by the emotion of anger, we tend to

think in "I-you" terms. We are more inclined to do battle than to engage in dialogue. The goal is to win at the expense of the other rather than creatively work to find just, satisfactory outcomes, that is, win-win solutions.

Third, when we are angry with someone, our perceptions are easily distorted. It is as if we put on a pair of "biased" glasses that allow only the negative qualities of the other to come into view. Thus, we interpret every motive, gesture, and behavior as suspect or self-serving. We slip into blanket condemnation of whatever the other person thinks or does.[31]

In some instances, being angry is not really an issue of much concern, especially when the anger is briefly felt over an issue of little importance. But how we deal with and express our anger is *always* a moral concern because it involves how we express "goodness" in our relationships with others. In sum, anger is impossible to avoid, but what we become as a result of experiencing anger matters immensely.

Because anger is such a universal aspect of our experience, psychologists offer helpful strategies and skills for sorting out and constructively dealing with this feeling.[32] My reflections focus on ways to insure anger does not undermine moral health.

1. It can be helpful to probe periodically questions such as: "What angers me?" or "Is there anything that I am angry about that needs my attention?"

2. Because customs, social values, and experiences in our life histories at times send the message that anger is "bad" and should be avoided, we might not be aware of its intensity. This lack of awareness receives reinforcement from the avoidance strategies we employ. Because anger often results from hurts and disappointments, we frequently employ sophisticated ways to keep such negative feeling from self-awareness. As a consequence, we should not rely exclusively on our own answers to the two questions posed above. Check with a friend or someone you respect. Inquire how that person views your behavior and the feelings you communicate.

3. When we are angry with someone, it can be helpful to place ourselves in the other person's position. Ask yourself: "Where was she coming from?" or "What was she experiencing when this happened?" or "Do I really see and understand her point of view?" Always have as a goal the desire to understand the other person's perspective. An intense emotion can blind us when we attempt to interpret another's situation.

4. Be honest. It usually takes two to tangle! Ask yourself: "What part do I play in the hurt, disappointment, or misunderstanding that is taking place?" Try to be as accurate as possible when describing exactly what happened, and acknowledge that your own subjectivity might distort the situation. If your feelings are so intense that you can neither take the perspective of the other nor entertain the possibility that you bear some responsibility, then you have an obligation to be very careful about how you express your anger. Feelings of such intensity, if expressed openly not only might cause enormous hurt to someone else, but also might damage your own reputation.

5. When you are angry, ask yourself: "What's causing my hurt?" "What expectation is not being fulfilled?" and "Am I being wronged in some way?" Anger is frequently a *symptom* of feeling hurt ("I am disappointed," "I am being offended," or "I was treated unfairly"). Coming to terms with the fact that you are hurting and examining your expectations of the person or situation that triggered it are essential. Be aware of what you expected from the person or situation, and then ask yourself whether such expectations were realistic. When we admit our hurt and are able to understand it as the root of our anger, we are on the road to coping constructively with this disruptive feeling.

6. Ask yourself: "What do I do when I am angry?" "What type of person do I become when I'm angry?" Assess what your integrity means to you personally. How do you reconcile the intensity and depth of your anger with your desire for integrity? Do lingering feelings of anger and the accompanying

resentment they breed prevent you from becoming the person you truly desire to be?

7. Even if most of the misunderstanding is not yours, do you still consciously desire to be a person of integrity? Can you still resist the cynicism and bitterness that so often accompany anger? Everyone gets angry, and there exist legitimate reasons for doing so. From the standpoint of moral health, what is essential is how we allow anger to influence our behavior and attitudes.

Human beings are all too often held captive by negative emotions. Embedded deep within our natures is the tendency for positive emotions to vanish quickly while negative ones linger. Our joy might be intense, but soon the intensity vanishes, whereas fear is a burden some bear for a lifetime. Anger can consume us for weeks, months, or even years. Depressed and anxious feelings likewise can be sources for endless distress. As a result of the imbalance in the staying power between positive and negative feelings, there seems to be in our human makeup, psychologist Nico Frijda observes, a natural tendency for emotional distress. A prolonged or enduring state of happiness, as a consequence, is often elusive and can never be taken for granted. Still, human beings are resilient and have within them the power to rectify this imbalance between positive and negative feelings. "Happiness seems possible," says Frijda, "and it can be understood theoretically. However, note that it does not come naturally, by itself. It takes effort."[33]

Life Project

A productive use of psychic energy, especially for our moral health, is developing a life project. The importance of a life project will be treated more fully below, where we examine its critical role for idealization (see p. 177).

A life project offers us purpose and meaning. It configures our life history, personality, and interests in a way that enables us to say, "I have made a difference."

If we desire moral maturity, then it is incumbent upon us to maximize opportunities that foster our moral growth. As noted previously, one casualty flowing from our all too hectic lives is ethical awareness. People do have moral and ethical standards: the problem is we spend too little time thinking about them. On any typical day the pressures of juggled schedules, the surprises of unplanned events, and our desires to be "present" in our relationships leave us distracted and depleted (one need only imagine the parent who after a busy day caring for the children attempts to be present to his spouse). It is not that we are morally insensitive, but often we are just so distracted or tired we simply fail to recognize the moral issues at stake.

Being overly committed and rushed is increasingly commonplace today. Sadly, how many valued relationships never realize their fullest potential because one or both parties fail to come to terms with their lack of self-awareness over disappointments, hurts, and problems simply because they feel pressured, rushed, or always on the move? Suppose you want to lose weight. Though you begin to watch your diet more carefully, you know an exercise program combined with reasonable weight-watching offer the best opportunity for shedding those unwanted pounds. Of course, beginning an exercise program takes motivation and effort. A similar course of action must be envisioned if we wish to increase our moral awareness. An excellent place to begin is a *focused* activity that increases moral sensitivity.

The Daily Moral Inventory

One opportunity to increase our moral sensitivity is the Daily Moral Inventory (DMI). The goal of the DMI is not to create some dramatic moral conversion to right principles. After all, most of us already have what it takes to be "good" or "morally fit," but we can always use some exercise! Using the DMI can take as little as five minutes (alter it in any way that suits your needs). The first thing you need to focus on is when to do it and where to do it.

Is there a particular part of the day when you feel most reflective? You might want to experiment until you find a time that suits you best. Early morning after rising? A short break at midday?

Evening or right before retiring when you have the opportunity to get some distance from the day's events? The goal is to find a suitable routine. You want to get in the *habit* of doing the DMI, just as you develop the habit of exercising. And this takes *effort*. The DMI's essential steps are as follows:

I. Recall That You Are a Moral Person

It is helpful to have a phrase that helps maintain your focus. We have already pointed out the benefits of recalling to mind simply the phrase "my conscience" or "I am a person of conscience." Other statements that might prove helpful are "I am a moral person," or "I have a moral purpose," or "I am a good person." Whatever expression you choose, take a few moments and "be" with it by slowly repeating it several times to yourself. Breathe slowly, repeating the expression in the quiet location you have chosen. Focus on a key word such as "conscience," "moral," or "good." Repeat this word several times and note any feelings or thoughts that occur.

After a few moments ask yourself:

- Do I detect any difference in myself after repeating this phrase or word?

- By saying the phrase and reflecting on it, how do I now understand myself?

- How might reflecting on the words alter my self-definition?

II. Spend a Few Moments Being Grateful

Though you have probably not thought about it, feeling gratitude is enticing. The complexity of this emotion makes it a uniquely human experience. Though just about everyone has felt grateful for something, little consideration is given to understanding the meaning of this powerful human emotion. In its most general sense, gratitude can be defined as an experience in which we feel a sense of appreciation for something. This "something" might be material or spiritual, a thing or a person, an event or a personal perspective. Experiences of gratitude elicit positive feelings such as contentment or joy. When we feel grateful, we evaluate our lives as gifted.

- Close your eyes and call to mind something for which you are grateful. Spend some moments imaging what comes to mind — an object, a person, an event.

- Pay particular attention to what you feel.

- After a minute open your eyes. What are you feeling? Having posed this question to numerous people, I have found the most common emotional state reported is joy mixed with serenity and peace.

Recall that gratitude involves "something." Many people report that they feel "gifted." How are you likely to respond when receiving a gift? Most people are happy and feel a sense of appreciation. Recall such a moment in your own life. Many people feel that they want to give something back — to reach out and offer something in return. In other words, once gifted, there is the natural inclination to respond generously. This response has important consequences for living a moral life. Moral people demonstrate generosity by giving back, reaching out, and sharing with others. In an in-depth study of individuals whose lives demonstrated a high degree of moral commitment, psychologists Anne Colby and William Damon note that "many of our exemplars express their positivity as a deep gratitude for the satisfaction they get from their work."[34]

Gratitude is an essential ingredient for healthy living. It plays a powerful role in helping us deal with the hassles and disappointments of daily life. Controlling emotional irritation before it becomes unduly upsetting or crippling is critical for physical and mental health. One of the best ways to deal constructively with such negative experiences is making the effort to be grateful. And it does take effort. Gratitude, in many instances, does not come naturally. It contests for awareness on a daily basis with competing feelings and in the process is easily shunted aside. When was the last time you felt a deep sense of gratitude?

When we feel grateful, we have the sense that something "special" exists in and for our lives. Gratitude is a powerful antidote to negativity. It offers a protective buffer from the hurts and frustrations that preoccupy us. Try the following exercise.

- Take a moment and close your eyes. Think of an event or a situation that made you really angry. Become aware of your upset.

- Open your eyes for a few moments. Now close them again, but this time image in your mind something for which you are grateful. It could be a person, a situation, or an attribute you possess. Just *be* with this person, situation, or trait for a few moments. Focus on the gratitude you feel. Now open your eyes. What are you feeling?

Chances are the anger you felt previously with its upset and irritation has diminished significantly. It is true. Gratitude works!

A final benefit of gratitude is its power to ease the way for making more honest self-evaluations. When we feel grateful, we can more readily admit our shortcomings and faults. Chronic irritation or ongoing frustration hinders self-honesty. All too often we are absorbed in difficult feelings that draw us away from honest self-examination. When we feel grateful, we often experience a condition that is best described as a "surplus of goodwill." These spillover positive feelings foster self-honesty and critical reflection on the problem areas of our lives.

In sum, the advantages of gratitude are threefold.

1. Gratitude encourages our reaching out to others.

2. Gratitude offers a sturdy buffer to the irritants and negative feelings that make up daily life.

3. When feeling grateful we are more willing to examine our lives honestly.

Having briefly explored the benefits of gratitude, let's now incorporate them into the DMI. After acknowledging yourself as a good and moral person, go through your day and call to mind several things for which you are grateful. These recollections can be about significant people or events or simply the ordinary situations that we so often take for granted.

In this phase of the DMI it is important to be as concrete as possible. It is often helpful to think of the day's positive events as "gifts." Thus, a wide spectrum of events becomes available. Note, however, that you don't have to run through the entire list. Pick out one or two items as focal points for your reflection. Gratitude-in-depth is as important as gratitude-by-the-numbers. Some examples:

The everyday —

- The scent of the air or a fragrance that has caught my fancy.
- The taste of coffee or the texture of a specific food.
- Nature's colors or a certain scene that attracts me.
- The recognition of an idea or the use of my creative energies.

Important people —

- Someone who gave me some time or went out of his or her way for me.
- A person I love and have deep affection for.
- A man or woman who offered me guidance and counsel.
- A friend who....

My life —

- A strength or talent (e.g., health, intelligence, a personal trait).
- A feeling.
- An insight that came to me.
- An experience.

Periodically updating our "gratitude" list sustains the feeling of gratitude, keeping fresh its focus while expanding our awareness of why we are grateful.

III. Examine How You Lived a Moral Life Today

In Part III of the DMI we evaluate the day's events. Scan your day and note the moral ups and downs. What went right for you? What disappointed you? In what ways were you not the person you desired to be?

Consider the cherished roles in your life: friend, spouse, parent, daughter or son, work colleague, volunteer, coach, or some other. Think of concrete instances in any of these roles in which you were not the "good" person you desired to be. In considering your shortcomings or failures, pay particular attention to:

- Your feelings: Name the feelings you experienced.

- Your behavior: What did I do?

- Your attitude: What was I thinking?

Spend some moments in sorrow for your misdeeds. Perhaps you might wish to say to yourself "I'm sorry for.... " Acknowledge any guilt that's appropriate.

IV. Take Up a Moral Challenge So You Can Become More Who You Desire to Be

Take an area in Part III that you acknowledge as a shortcoming or moral failure. Consider what might be done to alter a specific fault or bad habit. Your response might include any number of strategies. Some suggestion are:

- Avoid a certain person or situation.

- Engage a specific person or situation.

- Take an initiative.

- Lessen some behavior.

- Modify a certain judgment or attitude.

- Do something positive.

- Find some quiet time.

- Alter a schedule.

All too often well-intentioned people attempt too much too soon. Growth in the moral life always comes in small steps. Always remember: Step, don't leap! Focus on specific behaviors, feelings, or attitudes you are able to address *now*. Attention to one focused area of your life will spill over to others and, with time, your accumulation of moral victories will make you more who you desire to be.

We all know that attempts to do good and to be good are not made without setbacks. When our moral resolve falters or we fail to live up to our moral goals, we should develop a frame of mind that views such occurrences as minor and brief setbacks. All too often people scold themselves for not following through on their moral resolve, thereby ending up less motivated than before. Yes, take responsibility for slip-ups and wrong turns, but keep the focus on your resolve. Don't dwell on the failure, but ask what you learned from it. Assess your motivation and then get back to your moral challenge.

Let's review DMI's four essential steps:

1. Acknowledge yourself to be a *good* person who wants to be a better person.

2. Provide for yourself a felt sense of being *grateful* and viewing your life as gifted by focusing on one or two experiences that foster feelings of gratitude.

3. Examine your life and identify those *behaviors* that contradict the moral ideals that you hold.

4. *Identify* one behavior you can address that benefits your moral health.

Don't make the DMI a burden! Perhaps for a while you might do only Parts I and II. Or even restrict your efforts to a few daily moments of feeling grateful. If necessary, alter the DMI in a way that makes it work for you.

Using psychic energy productively provides conscience a healthy foundation. It does not mean, however, that conscience will function well automatically. Psychic energy is necessary, but not sufficient, to insure the functioning of a conscience that sustains moral fitness. In the chapters ahead we examine other dimensions necessary for a healthy conscience.

{ Dimension Two }

DEFENSES

===

According to a *Wall Street Journal* poll "a decline in moral values" is the nation's most serious social problem. When asked about the past forty years (the 1950s through the 1980s), Americans were nostalgic about the fifties, looking upon that decade, when compared to the past century's waning years, as a time of higher morals and values.[1] "Many Americans wish they could turn their clocks back to those days. More than 80 percent of those surveyed said the nation's morals and values were much or somewhat higher in the 1950s than now."

Not surprisingly, the concern about our nation's moral decline echoes the results of other findings in our discussion of the moral climate today (see p. 38). What caught my eye about these polling results, however, was another reported statistic. The survey included the following statement: "Rate your own morals and values on a scale from one to 100 (100 being perfect)." Despite the worry those polled expressed about a country in moral crisis, their responses to how they evaluated themselves were the exact opposite:

96 to 100	21 percent
90 to 95	29 percent
80 to 89	26 percent
75 to 79	11 percent
0 to 74	11 percent

As the *Wall Street Journal* points out, "If you can believe them, most Americans are closer to canonization than damnation, even though they say that in general, Americans' morals are poor and getting worse." In fact, half the respondents rate their own morals at 90 or better on the scale. If the morals of that many people were so high, wouldn't America be more like "heaven on earth" than a nation combating moral erosion?

How do we account for this contradiction between serious concern for declining national morals and high ratings of personal moral behavior? For one thing, we expect most people to rate themselves favorably when evaluating their own moral behavior. But the striking finding in the survey is not that people rated themselves positively, but the degree to which they did so — half at or above 90. The article notes that possibly the question required people to make quick evaluations so that they naturally called to mind their positive features and failed to consider moral lapses or weaknesses. Thus if the task had been to write an essay rather than responding to a simple statement, more balanced findings would appear. Perhaps. But having 50 percent of the population rate themselves in the top echelons of moral behavior is too staggering a finding to explain away by the polling method!

In my view, something else played a crucial role in the respondents' answers. My interpretation is a simple one. The individuals polled were *defensive* when offering their responses. When responding to a statement that might lead to a negative evaluation of themselves, particularly around subjects as sensitive as personal morals and values, people are inclined to offer "self-presentations" that portray themselves in positive ways. A score of 90 might well have been the separating line between what people viewed as acceptable and as intolerable. In other words, to rate their own morals and values at below a score of 90 triggers a level of distress that people deem personally objectionable. Moreover, while it remains "safe" to criticize the morals of the nation or consider previous decades as offering a more appealing moral climate, when survey questions hit closer to home and probe directly our personal behavior, the self-honesty required to acknowledge moral frailty proves, simply, too threatening.[2] It has already been pointed out that people will almost always find a means to maintain an adequate level of moral worth, even if this belief rests on self-deception. Conscience makes possible the decisions that provide an authentic basis for our moral goodness, yet the use of unhealthy defenses provides conscience an enormously powerful way to blind us — creating the self-deceptions that lead to the construction of a false measure of goodness.

Behind the Survey

The survey's message is straightforward. In the American population or in any population for that matter, the use of psychological defenses is alive and well. Defenses are interwoven into the fabric of our psychological lives.[3] We all use them. In starker terms, without defenses our psychological nakedness is exposed. Whether alone or with another, no one tolerates such total exposure.

Though humans naturally seek self-knowledge, acquiring such information through fruitful reflection or valued relationships involves risks, and either path eventually invites feelings, insights, or self-evaluations that prove threatening. Defenses become for us, therefore, a protective shield. They silence or at least help us avoid negative feelings (particularly guilt, shame, anger, jealousy, and envy) that trigger emotional upset and distress.

As I write this chapter, several crime stories have made headlines. Just several miles from my home in the town of Boulder, Colorado, residents have lived with the shocking murder of Jon Benet Ramsey, a beautiful six-year-old beauty pageant queen. In the state just north of my own, Wyoming, citizens are trying to make sense of the brutal death of a young adult man, pistol-whipped into unconsciousness and left to die. Matthew Shepard's death triggered a national soul-searching regarding the ways we treat people who are different from ourselves. The media also has publicized numerous cases of parents abandoning their newborn infants. What I wish to point out, however, is that for any of these events to have taken place, healthy defenses either failed or were nonexistent, and unhealthy defenses were activated. In short, whatever the crime or moral wrongdoing, specific defenses contributed to these immoral acts.

Defenses are psychological processes that individuals employ, usually at a nonconscious level, that serve to shield them from awareness distressing feelings and negative self-evaluations. Defenses enable us to adapt to the demands, challenges, and disappointments of life. If the defenses we utilize are predominantly healthy ones (see below) then we nourish our own health and maturity. On the other hand, if we find ourselves frequently responding to life's events with unhealthy defenses, then we sabotage opportunities for happiness and moral growth. Unhealthy defenses serve either to distract us from taking responsibility for our actions or deflect responsibility for our behavior onto another person, situation, or event. By avoiding responsibility for our mistakes, shortcomings, and failures, we erroneously conclude that we function at a higher level of moral fitness than is actually the case. Given human beings' need to maintain feelings of moral worth, defenses are the sturdy allies that insure such moral worth remains both intact and secure.

Defenses originate in our earliest years. To various degrees, depending on life circumstances, every child must cope with feelings of frustration and anger. All children at one time or another feel misjudged and cheated out of the love and care they believe are rightfully theirs. To counter the feelings associated with such perceived disappointments, children utilize an array of defenses to bolster and protect their still developing yet fragile sense of self-worth. As children grow, they begin to rely on some defenses more than others. In the teen years, adolescents, even though frequently unaware of what they are doing, employ battle-tested defenses that serve as a sturdy buffer to shield them from hurt, disappointment, and negative self-evaluation. By adulthood, we forge within our personality a favorite "set" of defenses to employ in specific situations when our moral worth is threatened or at risk.

In daily life we resort to defenses for a number of reasons. For one, significant people we value disappoint or hurt us. Because we share a common humanity and its imperfections, we are bound to be disgruntled at one time or another, even by our deepest loves. Friends and family, for example, do not always live up to our desires and expectations. The fallout from such disillusioned feelings is bound to be hurtful at times. Such feelings can generate in us self-justifying responses that shield us from self-evaluation. For example, Sandy justifies her uncharitable remarks by saying to herself, "He had it coming after what he said about me."

Other sources of defenses are the daily stressors of life that accumulate over time and take their toll on our health — physical, psychological, and moral. Arriving home after enduring ninety minutes of rush hour traffic, Sam justifies his impatience with his children by saying to himself, "I've had a long day and I deserve some peace and quiet."

The rules and norms of society require that we accept behaviors that we find difficult to live up to or even obey. After deciding not to report several thousand dollars on her tax return, Mary justifies her action by saying to herself, "The government just wastes money anyway, so why report it?"

Finally, it can be difficult to hold our own impulses in check. For example, even after numerous requests from his wife that he not criticize other family members, Jose, at a family birthday gathering, makes a cynical remark about his sister-in-law. Driving home from the party with his wife, he responds to her criticism of his behavior with, "It's a free country. I have a right to voice my opinion."[4]

What do Sandy, Sam, Mary, and Jose have in common? They have all conveniently eliminated responsibility for their actions and subsequently their guilt by utilizing a defense mechanism (in this case, the preferred defense mechanism is rationalization, which we will discuss in more detail below).

Healthy Defenses

For most of us, our "set" of defenses consists of a variable mixture of healthy and unhealthy ones. Healthy defenses foster ethical conduct and a mature conscience, whereas unhealthy ones create the illusion of moral health. Moreover, healthy defenses are adaptive. In other words, they allow us to weather the ups and down of life. They encourage us to solve problems in a constructive fashion and seek creative solutions to life dilemmas. Finally, they permit us to enjoy life by finding a meaningful level of contentment. They

promote the joyful aspects of life by helping us to channel constructively our psychic energy, specifically, as pointed out in the
previous chapter through nurturing friendships, regulating emotions, and sustaining a life project. Healthy defenses include the
following:

Sublimation: This defense enables us to channel negative feelings and unacceptable urges into creative pursuits. For example,
a hobby we take up engages our creativity while it transforms
negative feelings into constructive outlets.

Sense of Humor: It is a universal truism that we enjoy people
who make us laugh and feel good about ourselves. Adolescents,
for example, diffuse the pressures of sexual and aggressive urges
through jokes and foolish pranks. When something painful happens to us, a sense of humor helps us put things into a proper
perspective. Can you recall an instance when a friend encouraged
you to "lighten up" or was able to help you see the humor or irony
of a situation you initially evaluated as disturbing? Frequently,
when we can make something humorous, our load is lightened and
our psychic energy is preserved for more meaningful tasks. Finally,
"when we say that someone has a good personality, we are usually
not talking about 'good' in the moral sense. We usually mean that
this person is likeable, is fun to be around, and has a good sense of
humor. Conscience does not function well without humor."[5] Most
well-integrated adults have a side to them that is playful. Fooling,
sporting, and tinkering "humanizes" us. The playful sense makes
us more bearable and humane. Such playfulness contributes to a
"good" personality just as it fosters the moral good. "People who
are 'good' in both senses of the word have achieved a healthy
balance between moral and mischievous impulses in their personalities. The morally minded mischief-maker is careful to separate
the prankster in him- or herself from thoughtlessness or the desire
to be intentionally evil."[6]

Suppression: We have all lost our temper at one time or another or acted in some way that later proved embarrassing. Simply
stated, suppression is the ability to inhibit such impulses. Everyone
has, periodically, the desire to "tell someone off." There are instances when this response is appropriate. If we have been treated

unjustly we have every right to express our wounded feelings. Yet even strong reactions come in degrees, and we have all had the experience of saying something we later regretted. Children learn to incorporate this defense as a key ingredient for building positive social relationships. As a case in point, if we follow a group of children from ages two to twenty-two, there is, on average, a decrease in both physical fighting and verbally abusive behavior.

Altruism: Acting in a caring manner is essential for promoting the common good of society as well as for nurturing personal moral health. I have always thought Mother Teresa to be a noble example of this defense. Possessing a strong personality, she chose to direct her forceful tendencies into selfless acts focused on the care of others.

Anticipation: This defense involves our ability to perceive challenges, struggles, and problems in our lives and to seek realistic solutions to them. When we are hurt unintentionally by the comments of a friend, for example, we take the time to figure out how best to approach him. A conference report requested by our supervisor is given proper attention and preparation. When we anticipate we view life in a realistic and conscientious manner and draw upon the necessary psychic energy to complete tasks and accomplish our goals.

Self-observation: A friend tells Doug, "You know, you really came across as arrogant the other day." Doug could respond in a number of ways to this comment. But assuming that his friend's remark was well-intended and Doug respects his friend, one response would be for Doug to take the time to review the situation that led his friend to make the comment. A means for assessing the truth of his friend's remark is for Doug to "step outside himself," to try to be an objective observer who views the situation realistically. This "objective observer" enables Doug to assess what actually occurred and to acknowledge honestly any mistakes he made. When we take the time to view our own actions and monitor our feelings and our reactions toward others, we are said to self-observe. Many of the questions, exercises, and statements in this book seek to activate this defense. Without ongoing self-observation, moral health is placed at serious risk.

Take a moment to combine the qualities that flow from the healthy defenses discussed above. In other words, imagine someone who is creative and makes you laugh. This person acts appropriately, is caring, displays competence, and possesses a healthy dose of self-reflection. Wouldn't you want someone like this as a friend? As the above characteristics demonstrate, healthy defenses encourage and sustain our moral growth. They are the qualities we wish for in ourselves and our friends, and they promote healthy friendship. Those who utilize them are more apt to profit from their experiences; they learn from their shortcomings and mistakes, and are more likely to take responsibility for their actions. They seek appropriate ways to address their wrongdoings, and in the process they accrue moral wisdom.

The ultimate benefit of healthy defenses lies in their capacity to generate within us a stance toward life that is best characterized as *open-minded*. Ironically, even though we label them "defenses," the most significant advantage they hold is their power to encourage us to approach life nondefensively. When healthy defenses are deployed, we live more authentically the lives we desire. We more fully and openly engage loved ones and colleagues. We partake in and learn more from life's events, challenges, opportunities, and misfortunes. Philosopher Jonathan Lear is correct to assert that "one of the most important truths about us is that we have the capacity to be *open-minded*: the capacity to live nondefensively with the question of how to live."[7] No internal psychological process is more likely to contribute to an open-minded life than a set of healthy defenses.

On the other hand, Lear rightly notes that "human life in general is a study of why this capacity is not exercised: why open-mindedness is, for the most part, evaded, diminished, and attacked."[8] A malfunctioning conscience is a major culprit that subverts our striving to be open-minded, and unhealthy defenses contribute significantly to this malfunction.

Unhealthy Defenses

Human beings have the unenviable talent of being able to activate more than twenty unhealthy defenses that have the potential to

Frank and Ernest

Unhealthy defenses are the favorite "tricks" of the unhealthy conscience.

undermine emotional health. It is a small "set" of defenses, however, that appears to exercise the major role in undercutting the working of conscience. In other words, most of us in our everyday lives use a small, select group of unhealthy defenses that undo the hard-earned moral growth we achieve. Let's examine each of these defenses and the toll each takes on our moral fitness.

Minimization: When we minimize our actions, we downplay their moral significance. The benefit of this defense is that if we believe that an action is not very bad, then we eliminate feelings of guilt and the need to make amends for our wrongdoing. Take the example of Chris, who always manages to overstate his expenditures on business trips. This practice has become so habitual that he no longer even considers it an issue when he submits reimbursement requests. When Chris first started altering his expense account, he found himself saying "Oh, it's only a few dollars and won't make that much of a difference." With time, this internal debate fell silent. Chris's case points out a very troubling aspect of minimizing. Over time, we truly do seem to convince ourselves that our actions are minor foibles rather than serious moral misdeeds. It might be that Chris has now compartmentalized any thought of his wrongful action. When we are blind to our misdeeds, they soon become more frequent and, over time, more serious. Just recall an instance in your life when a so-called "fib" became a lie, which in turn led to lying about something else of a more serious nature.

Rationalization: Whereas minimizing an action downplays its moral significance, rationalizing provides our misdeed the excuse it needs. Usually these two defenses are linked. That is, one who minimizes has little difficulty finding ways to rationalize. We have had a hard day at work, and these toils are used as an excuse for not responding appropriately to a loved one. We neglect an obligation to help a friend and justify our failure by saying we were preoccupied with an important matter. In reality we might have had a "hard day," or we were truly "preoccupied." But the point is that if we employ an unhealthy defense, then we fail to take responsibility for or examine seriously our actions and their harmful effects.

When we find ourselves in situations that are ambiguous or "fuzzy" in regard to the right thing to do, we are especially prone to rationalize. Take the example of a supervisor requesting the completion of a report "as soon as possible" (but not specifying a certain date). The less clear the instruction, the more likely we are to rationalize our actions for our own advantage. Thus the employee may complete the report, but if there is a time crunch, it becomes much easier to rationalize "I need a few more days" than if a specific date had been set. Another way that rationalization seeps into our everyday thinking is the all too familiar "yes but" argument. In other words, we agree about the rightness of an action (the "yes" portion); however, in this specific situation we can make an exception (the "but" aspect). Thus we agree with the moral principle that people are entitled to their good name, but since Al's comments to us were particularly hurtful, we rationalize that in this specific instance (a "yes but" situation) gossiping about him is acceptable.[9]

In America, victimhood has become a favorite form of rationalization. It is true that millions of individuals have undergone enormous physical and psychological hurts as a consequence of trauma, rejection, and violence. Moreover, many people struggle with overwhelming feelings of anger, hurt, and sadness that result from horrific acts such as rape, physical or sexual abuse, or abandonment. I do not wish to downplay or dismiss these events and their painful consequences. Nonetheless, as a society we have become what some call an "excuse factory." For the fast driver there is "road rage." A troubled adult views her problems as stemming

© 1999, The Washington Post Writers Group. Reprinted with permission.

from "toxic parents." Misdeeds arising from Internet usage might be classified as some form of "Internet addiction." People living in urban areas speak of some type of "urban syndrome" as a way to explain away biased attitudes or questionable behaviors. More and more frequently, these explanations are being used as legal defenses in the courts. And, along with the legal community and the popular trend to litigate any grievance, the psychological community must also bear its share of responsibility. Over the past few decades mental health professionals have designated ever increasing numbers of behaviors as mental disorders.[10] In our psychologically minded society, the temptation exists for moral responsibility to be set aside (or at least significantly decreased) in favor of expert witnesses who testify to extenuating circumstances.[11] By raising this issue I am not dismissing an individual's environment or family background as unimportant when we weigh personal responsibility. The concern I have is that as excuse-making grows more prevalent, it becomes an increasingly acceptable way to "explain" misdeeds and clearly wrong actions. As a consequence, both personal and national moral health erodes.

In a similar vein, one of the most subtle but harmful uses of rationalization occurs when the underlying assumptions of how people should treat one another are pared down to the most feeble expectations (or what might be labeled "least demanding morality syndrome"). In the face of blaring headlines and graphic news stories depicting horrific accounts of people's behavior toward others, some individuals try to make sense of such horrors by lowering their expectations of how they and others should behave. Despite

Pepper . . . and Salt

THE WALL STREET JOURNAL

Baloo

"So you see, your honor, when my client looted
the savings and loan, it was really a desperate
cry for help."

Used by permission of Cartoon Features Syndicate.

recently reported declines in crime rates, the growing tolerance
of behaviors once considered inappropriate becomes a convenient
rationalization to then explain more serious wrongdoing. In other
words, we develop a mind-set that makes sense of serious wrongdoing by rationalizing that questionable behaviors are bound to
occur because they are part of everyday life. Such a viewpoint si-
lences guilt and personal accountability.[12] This all too frequently
employed use of rationalization poses a considerable threat to
America's moral fiber.

Displacement: To illustrate displacement's meaning in a classroom setting I always share with my students the following
example. A supervisor is unfairly critical of an employee. This employee proceeds to go home and yell at his or her spouse. The
spouse, wishing not to aggravate an already difficult situation,
snaps angrily at the oldest child, who responds by provoking her

younger brother. The brother yells at the dog who in turn barks at the cat. The cat stares menacingly at the goldfish (please don't ask me what the goldfish does!).

All of us have faced a situation where someone in a position of power has treated us unfairly. In some instances, either because of the supervisor's personality, the situation itself, or the interaction between the two, we are unable to respond appropriately. Prudence dictates we must at times be less than forthcoming about our feelings because if our visible reaction mirrored our true emotions toward someone with power or influence in our lives (for example, a supervisor, a spouse, or a friend), we might be threatened with further punishment (e.g., job loss, demotion, or a strong emotional reaction that we find personally threatening or uncomfortable). But when we decide not to respond directly, we are left with unresolved negative feelings. As a consequence, a natural inclination is to find someone else upon whom to ventilate (displace) our feelings.

By their very makeup, power relationships offer numerous opportunities to displace feelings onto others, but personal relationships are equally prone to be the target of a displacement defense. From a moral perspective, displacement poses two problems. First, it harms others. Innocent people are subjected unfairly to tirades, accusations, and responses that can be hurtful; displacement threatens a basic principle of charity and care that we are called to uphold. Second, displacement postpones or allows us to avoid finding constructive ways to deal with our negative feelings and hurts. Recall from our previous discussion how psychic energy is wasted and the moral life undermined when anger gets the best of us. If we can always "take things out on others," then we never really address adequately our negative feelings.

Like many other unhealthy defenses, displacement is learned early in life. The eight-year-old Little Leaguer called out on a third strike isn't going to attack the umpire, but he might well kick the team's water cooler. All of us have found ourselves in situations where directing our negative feelings at someone or something else (e.g., a friend or an object) "feels" like the safest course of action.

Compartmentalization: Over the past several years most people have heard a story of a single teenage woman who went to extraordinary lengths to conceal her pregnancy. At times, the young mother's response to giving birth to her child was so chaotic that abandonment and/or the subsequent death of the newborn became the tragic solution.[13] These extreme cases graphically illustrate the defense of compartmentalization. Sadly, these women were unable to seek the help they needed and coped with their dilemmas by eliminating from consciousness any acknowledgment of their condition. As a consequence, the baby's birth was an event for which they were totally unprepared. In essence, these young women compartmentalized the fact that they were soon to be parents. For most of us this mental manipulation, or at least one this extreme, is hard to comprehend, but for some of these young mothers there seemed to be a capacity to psychically block even the fact that they were pregnant.

In specific situations, compartmentalizing can be associated with a survival mode. In other words, it serves as a coping mechanism for resisting stress that then affords a sense of control over a difficult situation. For example, Sarah, a parent herself, is worried about her infirm mother. In the next few months a decision must be made about moving her mother to a nursing home. But at the moment, she is preoccupied with her son's school performance and even more upset with his group of friends, whom she perceives to be exerting more and more influence over him. Understandably, a useful strategy is simply to block from consciousness the upcoming discussion she needs to have with her mother about moving to a nursing home. Once this blockage occurs, she is able to concentrate her efforts on her own parental worries. In this situation we could say that Sarah has compartmentalized her role as an adult child to her mother. Of course, the decision about her mother's living arrangement cannot be put off indefinitely, and at some point a painful and stressful discussion with her mother must take place. But for now Sarah makes a prudent decision. First things first. Thus the advantage of compartmentalization is that it enables us to accomplish pressing tasks and deal adequately with troubling issues that potentially could overwhelm us. The downside is that failure to look seriously at our compartmentalizing tendencies can lead us to avoid facing decisions that are integral to living healthy human and moral lives.

Over the years I have noticed an increase in the number of clients whose statements and actions could be interpreted as attempts to compartmentalize. I suspect that the defense of compartmentalization is employed with greater frequency than ever before. Indeed, I would go so far as to argue that use of compartmentalization has made it, unfortunately, *the* defense of the early twenty-first century. Why might this be? Several trends have surfaced that can help us understand the newfound popularity of this defense.

First of all, modern society emphasizes self-improvement and successful performance. Achieving high grades, a certain income, a recognized social status, or superior job performance places the "self" under tremendous pressure. In addition, there are psychological pressures to "have it together" and live up to the media's message that flaunts idealized relationships and physiques that few people can hope to achieve. Tied to these pressures is the growing isolation of people from bonds that have been traditional sources of support such as family, neighborhood, and church. As a consequence, more than ever before in human history, individuals find themselves feeling inadequate and lacking the support they need to withstand this "burden of selfhood." The pressure and isolation of modern life leave many people feeling vulnerable and exposed. If I believe that I must achieve a certain level of success in most areas of my life and if the pressure for such achievement is part of my self's consciousness, then a satisfactory way to negotiate this burden is to compartmentalize specific failings, deficits, or shortcomings in order that the burden of being *this* self does not overwhelm me. In such a pressurized world, compartmentalizing surfaces is an all too convenient escape from the anticipated perils that go with acknowledging personal inadequacies.[14]

Second, technology's information glut eases the transition from a sense of self as unified to selves that are now many, which, in effect, encourages compartmentalization. Television, e-mail, voice mail, fax machines, and car phones expose us to enormous amounts of information, which reinforce the consciousness we assign to the self *at this moment*. Furthermore, this information flood is intrusive, often appearing when we are unprepared to respond adequately. Too many voice mails or an unexpected phone call burden a self already deluged by information. Obviously one way to control the influx of information flow is to carve up consciousness. Thus we are workers at work, spouses at home, teammates while with the team, daughters when at home with parents, and parents when in the company of our children. Of course, this segmenting of the role-at-the-moment is rarely total. For most parents being a parent is a role likely to seep periodically into awareness no matter what other role occupies consciousness at the moment.

Finally, the Internet has spawned a new way of envisioning and thinking about our lives. This new technology and its enthusiastic acceptance by the American public has made e-mail, web sites, chat rooms, and even virtual reality more and more a part of everyday reality. Such enhanced technology provides increased opportunities for personal communication and the dissemination of information. Yet the allure of online communication poses several dangers. Communicating online "feels" anonymous and venturesome. The temptation might exist to experiment with or "try on" a new and daring "self." Lacking face-to-face encounters that convey disapproving facial gestures or voice tone, the interaction that takes place online "feels" safe, secure, and secret and, as a consequence, might stimulate fantasy reflected through increasingly provocative statements and questions to someone "out there." It stands to reason that such behaviors and mind-set would encourage the compartmentalizing of morally questionable actions, feelings, and thoughts in a mental file labeled "my computer self."[15]

The more threatening a role is to our self-esteem or the more ill-prepared we are to handle its demands, the more likely we are to carve out psychically the role's specifically troubling aspects. This psychic division gives us some sense of control over who we are at any one moment. Just think of the working parent who while dropping children off at school gets a call on her car phone from her mother about her father's illness. With this family concern on her mind, she arrives at her office to hear an unexpected voice mail from her boss and to receive an unwanted fax from a disgruntled client![16] Even common sense would dictate that some type of division of the self (into selves), or compartmentalizing, would need to be done for her to cope successfully (and bear in mind that her day is just beginning!).[17]

With some caution I am inclined to conclude that thinking of one's self as truly multiple can lead to a certain flexibility of thought and provide a fresh perspective on various challenges and problems. However, from the viewpoint of moral health, we must preserve the unity of the self in order to sustain a *unified moral being*. This unity is vital for our moral health because only when we view ourselves as wholly moral persons in the midst of our numerous role commitments are we able to apply moral principles with consistency. Without this unity of self, the moral meaning we strive for and the moral message we wish to convey become clouded and ultimately incoherent. Inevitably, the unceasing bombardment of information and the psychic division that produces multiple selves encourage us to ignore or dismiss one or more selves' misdeeds or wrongdoings. In effect we compartmentalize a specific self or some actions connected with our current role as "off limits" to conscience.

Take the working mother described above. Obviously she is flooded with information, and the temptation to compartmentalize is very real. Under stress, she in all likelihood will fail at some point to act as morally as she would like in *all* the various situations that confront her. Compartmentalizing selective responses in some of her roles could easily surface as a solution for any moral failings that occur, thereby insuring her feelings of moral worthiness while at the same time insulating her from any guilt. She might begin to treat a client, her child, her parent, or her boss inappropriately and fail to consider her actions. Since her consciousness has already been grooved to define herself in terms of multiple selves, the slicing off of specific attitudes and actions might be a natural response to times when she feels overly burdened or stressed. After all, both multiple selves and compartmentalization have a similar dynamic. In both instances the psyche in one way or another fragments and separates. If "multiple selves" are the prevailing self-definitions for our lives in the twenty-first century, then I suspect that compartmentalizing our lives is the favored defense we employ to deal with our moral shortcomings and failures. Perhaps one commentator said it best when he noted that "the problem with compartmentalizing in real life is that we are really the same person and we take ourselves with us from compartment to compartment."[18] It is the *same* person who grapples with the consequences of compartmentalizing, many of which are unforeseen, yet harmful to others. Frequently, actions must be explained and relationships repaired, all of which requires time and psychic energy.

Confronting Our Unhealthy Defenses

If the set of defenses we have developed over the years consists of too many unhealthy ones, then we endanger moral health. None of us is without unhealthy defenses. Can you honestly say that over this past week you have not at least at one time or another rationalized a behavior or minimized something of importance? We are all prone to use unhealthy defenses on a daily basis. This issue becomes a problem when we employ these defenses too frequently or over too many issues that directly influence our lives as caring, loving, and just human beings. It is one thing to rationalize not rising early enough to exercise, but it is a far different matter to compartmentalize a marital affair or to rationalize the way we cheat a client.

At the same time, we must be realistic about the defenses we have. Recall their purpose. They serve as a protective shield that deflects feelings and evaluations that undercut our sense of moral worth. At times these feelings and evaluations can be extraordinarily painful. Defenses are often nonconscious. Most of the time we are unaware we are activating them. Still, we *desire* to achieve moral health, and this desire requires a functioning conscience that uses healthy rather than unhealthy defenses. If we are to live nondefensively and approach life with an open mind, then we must do all we can to limit our reliance on unhealthy defenses.

The following guidelines can be helpful for gaining insight into our use of unhealthy defenses. Keep in mind, however, that we have defenses (whether they are healthy or unhealthy) for a purpose. If you are using an unhealthy defense to cope with intense negative feelings or some traumatic episode in your life, then simply putting into practice the suggestions below will not eliminate the defense. In such instances, counseling or therapy might prove helpful.

1. The primary way to avoid unhealthy defenses is to have *good friends*. As we have already noted, healthy friendships serve as guides for self-honesty. The challenge, inquiry, or concern of a friend serves to break the stranglehold of unhealthy defenses. True friends help us to discern when we rationalize and minimize. At the same time, they encourage the laughter and care that help promote healthy defenses.

Try this exercise. Imagine a close friend. Now quickly go through the healthy defenses described in this chapter. Think of ways this friend helps you sustain and promote these defenses. Now go over the unhealthy defenses. Can you think of instances when this friend has helped you gain insight into your behavior? If you have not benefited in this way from the relationship, consider what you might say to your friend that allows him to support your healthy defenses. Are you able, for example, to accept a timely challenge from your friend? If not, what might be the issues that prevent you from responding nondefensively to him? Recall that in the previous chapter we stated that conscience requires that we channel psychic energy into productive pursuits. There are few more productive uses of psychic energy than developing friendships in which friends help one another to gain self-insight.

2. Because defenses are routinely used in a nonconscious fashion and become part of our daily routine, it is critical that we focus our consciousness in ways to enhance self-insight. The Daily Moral Inventory (DMI) discussed above (see p. 95) serves as an excellent resource to probe ourselves gently but honestly with regard to how we truly behave and act.

3. I have often encouraged people to focus on a personal issue. It might be a relationship or some feeling about yourself. Ask yourself what you find troubling, upsetting, or distressful. Ex-

plore this relationship or feeling from as many perspectives as possible. Examples of perspectives include: your personal needs, your situation, your life history, your expectations about yourself or someone else, and any emotional sore points that leave you vulnerable. Now take a specific event or circumstance associated with this relationship or feeling and reflect on the words "rationalize" and "minimize." Consider whether one of these defenses is operating as you look at the relationship or feeling from these multiple perspectives.

4. The defense of displacement can be addressed in the following manner. Think of individuals that trigger within you feelings of both powerlessness and anger. These could include authority figures, loved ones, or colleagues. Now ask yourself how you respond to them. The key element here is whether you have been able to be honest with this person about how you perceive yourself being treated (e.g., unfairly? poorly? with disrespect?). If you have been unable to communicate to this individual in a forthright fashion, then ask whether you take the negative feelings that are the fallout from this troubled relationship and direct them toward someone else. This wronged person could be a spouse, a colleague, a child, a friend, or someone over whom you have authority. At the heart of displacement is the fact that you feel safe directing negative feelings toward certain people rather than others. Quite frequently, this person is at a power disadvantage relative to you, or a person you feel safe using as a target.

5. An excellent technique to counter the temptation to compartmentalize is to make a list of your various roles, for example, friend, spouse, parent, child, sibling, work colleague, supervisor, club member, teammate. Now take each of these roles and rate yourself on a scale from one to ten with the criterion being your level of moral fitness in each role. Compare various roles and ask yourself why some roles scored higher than others. Make a list of issues you associate with each role that contributes to or decreases your moral fitness. Self-honesty is vital in this examination. As you explore each role, do any of them trigger feelings with which you are uncomfortable? What insights does this self-examination generate?

A variation on the above is to inventory the moral principles that guide your life. Then take each of these principles and go over the list of roles you hold dear. Do you notice that with some roles your attempts to be loving, caring, just, honest, and respectful fail to achieve the level you set for yourself? What reasons do you give for these discrepancies?

Human defenses are truly a double-edged sword. When our lives are lived nondefensively, the predominant defenses in our arsenal are healthy ones. We find ourselves drawn to being open-minded toward life and all that it holds. Healthy defenses allow us to assume responsibility for our actions, and they thereby help to insure that we gain insight into our moral frailties. Though we can never live a life without some self-deception and though all of us manage to find some things about ourselves that trigger defensiveness, the healthy functioning of conscience obligates us to do all that we can to examine carefully the defenses we employ. Giving diligent scrutiny to our defenses provides our decision making a direction and quality that are the distinguishing marks of a well-functioning conscience.

{ Dimension Three }

EMPATHY

===

One of the most vivid memories of my childhood occurred when I was nine. It was a fall day, and I was riding a school bus sitting next to a window on the driver's side. The bus stopped at the edge of a subdivision, and the bus driver opened the door. Suddenly I heard the screech of tires and the bus driver scream, "Oh, my God" as he bolted for the door. I have a faint memory of him grabbing the little red emergency kit as he exited. But before leaving the bus he turned to all of us and in a stern but anxious tone announced, "Everyone stay in your seats and don't move."

Apparently, the first child in line to exit had quickly hopped off the bus and bolted across the street before the bus driver had fully extended the stop sign. My eyes were transfixed on the unconscious student lying on the street. Blood was slowly dripping down his face. Even though I did not know him (he was in another grade), I remember feeling upset and worried about him. Several students who had gotten off the bus ran down the street to the injured child's house and got his mother. I will never forget the anguish I saw in her face. Her look frightened me. I wanted to do something to help, but I felt powerless. I started feeling uncomfortable. I sympathized with her and her injured son. My memory then blurs, but I remember an ambulance and police cars and a crowd gathering around the scene of the accident.

Fortunately, the boy suffered only a few scratches and mild concussion and returned to school several days later. As the bus pulled away after what must have been close to an hour I started thinking of my own mom and the hurt she would feel if I had been the injured student. When the school bus came to my stop, I got off, carefully scanned the street for oncoming traffic, and then darted home to tell my mom what I had witnessed. I perceived the concern and what I interpreted as fear in her face as I recounted the story. I realized that she was thinking of me as any parent would, something like "What if this was Charlie who had the accident?" As I finished my story I blurted out something to the effect that I would always look both ways and assured her that such an accident would never happen to me. I found myself reassuring my mother, in my own childlike way, comforting her in the face of the fear I perceived she was feeling.

I share this incident because it highlights starkly the power of empathy. It makes real everything I have read as an academic about this vital human experience. As I reflect back on that event, now many decades old, I realize the empathy I had for the injured student and his mother. I recall that I was distressed, felt powerless, and tried to care for my mom. All these feelings and actions are at least in part due to empathy's power to evoke strong reactions. Over the years I have asked numerous people a simple question: "Could you conceive of yourself as a moral person if you lacked the capacity for empathy?" Some offered an immediate response to my inquiry, whereas others pondered the question for a few moments. However, the answer from every person to whom I have posed this question has been the same: a definite "no." It is inconceivable to think of ourselves as morally healthy while simultaneously lacking empathy. Without the proper dose of empathy, our conscience becomes cold and callous. With little or no empathy, a brittle quality corrodes conscience, leading to moral decisions that are insensitive or heartless. As an example of how empathy's void corrupts the workings of conscience, take the case of the psychopath. One of the consistent findings in psychological literature is the striking way in which psychopaths describe their actions. They recount their crimes in a matter-of-fact style, with little if any feeling for their victims. In essence, "psychopaths view people as little more than objects to be used for their own gratification."[1] The chilling remarks of a psychopath serving time in jail for kidnapping, rape, and extortion demonstrate in dramatic fashion how the lack of empathy corrupts the functioning of conscience.

You've got to look out for yourself, park your feelings. Say you need something, or someone messes with you . . . maybe tries to rip you off . . . you take care of it . . . do whatever needs to be done. . . . Do I feel bad if I have to hurt someone? Yeah, sometimes. But mostly it's like . . . uh . . . [laughs] . . . how did you feel the last time you squashed a bug?[2]

Empathy's significance has both personal and far-reaching effects. At the personal level, we see its influence when we show sensitivity to a friend, help a person in need, or listen carefully to the disappointments someone shares. Empathy, however, also has general effects whose significance for our own moral lives receives far less attention. Empathy allows groups to bond together in order to promote their unity and accomplish their goals. National celebrations such as the Fourth of July are, from a psychological perspective, successful largely because Americans empathize with their country's history, flag, common heritage, and traditions. Empathy might be described as the "psychological glue" that enables groups or nations to endure and persevere. But just as this generalized effect can produce bonding in families, neighborhoods, and even nations, its downside is just as apparent.

Empathy's power can undercut an individual's or a nation's conscience. The bloodletting that has gone on among ethnic groups that at one time formed the nation of Yugoslavia shows, tragically, how empathy contributes to the undermining of both an individual's and a group's conscience. Croats, Serbs, Muslims, and now Albanians display empathy toward their own, but their twisted and tortured histories together and the hostile memories they generate undercut expressions of empathy toward another group's plight. Ironically, the very empathy that, on the one hand, bonds and unites a people's ethnic identity, on the other hand, creates barriers and hardens attitudes toward groups with differing ethnic heritages.

I have often thought about how many wars were started or prolonged or to what degree human suffering needlessly existed because of the failure to respond empathically to others who are different. Because of empathy's power to forge blinding loyalty to one's own group, to what degree have feelings for and understandings of the other side been dismissed or never even considered? How many negotiations among nations might have turned out more positively if negotiators had demonstrated some empathic understanding of the needs and concerns of adversaries or vanquished foes? One particularly tragic example from the last century is the attitude of the Allies as they negotiated (or, perhaps more accurately, dictated) the terms of the treaty ending World War I. The punitive and harsh measures forced on a humiliated Germany returned vengefully to haunt the entire world. Though the depth of the Allies' animosity was understandable, given the enormous human suffering and loss of life of the war, we know now that the conditions imposed on Germany fomented discontent, creating a social, economic, and political instability that contributed to Hitler's rise to power.

Fortunately, empathy and politics are not always doomed to failure. We see examples in our own Congress where empathy influenced how lawmakers shaped public policy. When as senator's daughter was killed by a drunk driver, the senator gave new life to a legislative bill requiring advertisers to add safety warnings to commercials advertising alcohol consumption. Senator Bob Dole's support was critical in enabling the Americans with Disabilities Act to pass the Senate and eventually become law. One senator was able to influence colleagues to vote for more funding to fight mental illness after experiencing its effects in his own family. Other politicians focused their energies on issues such as cancer after witnessing their own or other family members' suffering.[3]

Empathy's Meaning

Empathy is the experience of feeling the pains, hurts, sorrows, joy, hopes, and triumphs of another person (or group of people) as if they were one's own.[4] In other words, the capacity for empathy allows us really to know and be known. It creates the ability to share and attach ourselves to others in relationships that provide intimacy and profound meaning. Lacking adequate empathy, a human being experiences a deadening void that proves emotionally fatal to any desire to become a loving and caring person. Psychiatrist Robert Jay Lifton captures well this dynamic union of empathy and love:

> The quality of that access to another's experience, physical and mental, is also specifically human. It is what makes possible the intense level of caring that can develop with love. That is why human beings can express and experience love in letters, on long-distance telephones, during and after prolonged physical separations, while being mostly indifferent to others immediately around them. So fundamental is this transformation that, in its absence, attachment or proximity becomes the enemy of vitality, and is deadening.[5]

When a child is given adequate care and nurture, there develops a sensitivity toward others that allows empathy to flourish. Though children differ in how much empathy they express, nearly all children show some degree of empathic expression. Even very young children are capable of empathy, though not to the degree of sophistication that adults show. To illustrate, over the years I have gone to several college reunions in order to "catch up" with former students. Typically there is a family picnic for alumni to bring their spouses and children. With so many young children gathered in one place, in addition to all the youthful enthusiasm and joy, there are the usual crying spells and temper tantrums too. What I find fascinating at these gatherings is the reaction of other children to a child who is visibly upset (with crying the most obvious indicator). In some instances a younger brother or sister or even a child from another family will take his or her toy and spontaneously give it to the child who is upset. It is as if the child is saying, "This toy makes me feel good, and I give it to you so you can feel good."[6] Though other interpretations can be given to explain these children's caring behaviors, I have observed this behavior so frequently and arising so spontaneously that it is compelling evidence, I think, of some simplified level of empathic capacity among even very young children.

On the other hand, as every parent can attest, children are not always empathic and caring. All children throw periodic tantrums

DENNIS THE MENACE

"MOM, CAN WE HAVE HAMBURGERS FOR THANKSGIVING THIS YEAR?"

Used by permission of Hank Ketcham and North American Syndicate.

and display considerable doses of selfish behavior. But a consensus now exists among child psychologists that even young children display caring behaviors. Moreover, as children grow older, their caring behavior grows more consistent and frequent. Paralleling this advance in caring behavior is the child's growing capacity for empathy and the corresponding skills to respond appropriately to the needs of others.

Problems with Empathy

Empathy provides conscience its essential *quality* — best described as making choices and judgments that express sensitivity, care, and love. Empathy disposes conscience to be other-centered while it helps to combat natural self-serving tendencies that are a continual source of struggle for us all. In a sense, empathy fuels our con-science, energizing it to make loving and compassionate responses to the needs and concerns of other people.

At the same time, we must resist the notion that everything about empathy enables conscience to make better moral decisions. We have explored how empathy impairs conscience by fostering a bias that favors the needs and concerns of people similar to ourselves (e.g., family, ethnic group, or nation), thus potentially eclipsing adequate consideration of justice and fairness toward those who are different.

Empathy alone does not give us a total picture of a moral per-son (which is why it is only *one* of conscience's dimensions). To illustrate this point, a city official's position allows him consider-able latitude to direct the city's tax dollars among various social service projects. This same official has a niece whose chronically severe mental illness has left her homeless. Empathy with this rel-ative might lead him to allocate a disproportionate share of city funds to projects that serve mental health and homeless causes. But the demands on any city's social service budget are immense, and the official must seriously scrutinize his goals, biases, and inten-tions in order that other legitimate social service needs also receive adequate funding. Let's assume that this city official is described by co-workers as sensitive and compassionate. This personal charac-teristic is admirable and should be encouraged. Nonetheless, this civic administrator must strive to balance his empathic inclina-tions with conscience's other dimensions in order to insure that he fulfills his duties with integrity.

Empathy must be "informed" by the many morally worthy (and at times competing) commitments and obligations we have be-fore us. Having friends is wonderful, but we cannot empathize so totally with one friend that we exclude all other friendships.

A final problem with empathy is that the empathic inclinations of some individuals are so highly sensitized that they are prone to lose boundaries with others. Recall that empathy's definition means we experience what another goes through "as if" we felt what they feel. But for some people the "as if" becomes "one with." Some individuals are so drawn into another person's situation (whether this situation is positive or negative) that they literally lose perspective and end up living out the actual joy, hurt, or distress the other feels. Some fans at football games, for example, are so overcome by their team's victory that they work themselves into a frenzy. In large audiences the ecstasy of victory or the pain of defeat can erupt into foolish or even violent behavior. Witnessing a car accident and viewing a bleeding victim might create so much empathic distress that we are rendered helpless to be of assistance. More typical examples are individuals who have a hard time keeping their own sense of self-identity (boundaries) when listening to another's misfortune. They become highly emotional or so overwhelmed by their feelings that they act as if the misfortune had happened to them. Because people at times are prone to overempathize and in the process lose boundaries, those working in caregiving positions such as ministry, health care, education, or social service where human suffering is all too apparent must be especially vigilant in keeping appropriate boundaries so that the best interests of vulnerable parishioners, patients, students, and clients are adequately served.

But the need to maintain an adequate boundary is not only for the good of the person needing help. When we empathize with someone, we involve ourselves on many levels. On a cognitive level we perceive the problem another person is facing and in the process form an interpretation. Does the person have a problem? Does she need help? How serious is the situation? What are the consequences for her if I do help? Unless we have some sense of these questions, we would have a difficult time even being empathic.

On an emotional level our empathy, once aroused by another's situation, might generate any one of several feelings. Our emotions might be negative (e.g., fear, distress, anger) or positive (e.g., joy, gratitude, hope). If the situation leads to the interpretation that someone is in need and we empathize with this person's plight, then our response might lead us to offer help or aid to the person.[7] But note that such personal involvement usually comes at a cost. The distress empathy triggers stems in part from our physiology, which reacts with a heightened state of arousal. Thus if we encounter too many empathy-producing situations, then a likely consequence is burnout. Consider the case of a caring teacher attempting to respond adequately on a daily basis to the needs of a hundred students, each of whom has his or her unique needs, problems, and home situations. Perhaps this is why teachers are often encouraged to implement any creative ideas early in the semester because by the end of the term instructors are simply trying to get through the day! Indeed, the teachers I have known in my academic career and whom I rate as the most empathic in responding to student concerns are most frequently the ones who feel burnout at the end of a semester.

Symptoms of burnout are more likely to surface whenever we empathize with a person for a prolonged period of time. Think of a friend who has experienced a number of personal setbacks. We care deeply for this person. Naturally our conscience prods us to take initiatives in order to be present, supportive, and helpful to him. But sometimes if this friend's problems become chronic or never seem to end (and particularly if our friend's personality is contributing to his problems), our empathic responses become taxed. We might begin to notice ourselves becoming annoyed, which might trigger from us a remark that is biting or cynical (about which we frequently feel guilty afterward!). Even though we might be strongly attached to this person, we find ourselves having mixed feelings toward him. At times, we might even find ourselves withdrawing or avoiding our friend.

Can Empathy Undermine Our Moral Health?

My suspicion is that most readers of this book are sensitive people genuinely interested in improving their moral lives. The characteristics that make up our lives are double-edged swords, and the trait of caring is no exception to this rule. People who are described as compassionate and sensitive sometimes overly involve themselves in the lives of others. In other words, they lose boundaries with those they care about. They worry excessively, or try to do too much, or become dissatisfied with how they are responding to the person in need. All of these behaviors can be warning signs of future burnout.

The other part of the equation is the person who is the object of our concern. When we stop and consider the people we love and reflect on each one of these individuals, we soon discover the enormous *complexity* of every loved one's life. There exist so many factors that influence any person's life history. If we stop to reflect on the life of just one person we know well, we are sometimes struck by the amount of hurt, pain, sorrow, and hardship that person's life contains, for example, the illness of an aging parent, concern over a child, a breakup of a relationship, unemployment, inadequate financial resources, family disagreements, an unexpected loss, a difficult upbringing. Now go beyond the people who are close to you and consider the numerous people who are only acquaintances and the issues with which they struggle. Branch out even further to stories you have heard from friends, families, or colleagues about people you don't even know but who have suffered because of some misfortune. Finally, just think for a moment about what you read in the newspaper, view on television, or hear on the radio about catastrophes, tragedies, and individual suffering. As we stop to ponder all of this information, it becomes apparent that most people at any given moment are aware of numerous hardships, heartaches, and hurts in other people's lives.

Now connect people's tendencies to be sensitive and caring with their awareness of so many misfortunes. This two-part equation causes many caring individuals to become overly stressed and show symptoms of burnout. Stated another way, people of good conscience, particularly those with a strongly developed empathy, will often lose boundaries and become stressed themselves. To some degree, such responses are unavoidable. Our family ties and commitments to others will pull us into a level of involvement that causes us serious worry and concern. Nonetheless, for moral health to flourish in our lives and for our consciences to be functioning well, we must monitor carefully empathy's role.

If we find ourselves getting too involved or exhibiting a level of care that seems never to let up, we need to make a concerted effort to assess our situation and alter at least some behaviors. Obviously, we won't change overnight. Nonetheless, recognizing empathy as a "potential" burden is a first step (consciousness-raising). Practicing some of the suggestions below can allow our empathy to operate at an optimal level.

1. *Repeat often a reality-based statement that fits the situation of someone for whom you have concern.* Examples of reality-based statements include: "I can't solve all of his problems," "I care about him, but I can't change his behavior," "I can't take responsibility for his situation or his behavior," "I'll do what I can, even go the extra mile, but I can only do so much," "I can be here for him, but he has to make his own decisions," "I can't change everything," "Being burned out myself won't help him; I need to take care of myself, too." Develop other reality-based self-statements or modify some of the these so that they fit your situation. Repeat them often to yourself, especially when you begin to worry about someone you care about. At first, such self-talk might seem "odd" or make you feel guilty (see the discussion of unhealthy guilt in the next chapter). If this happens to you, try to keep in mind that the self-talk we are proposing does not deny the compassion you have or the love you feel. What it does is help your compassionate and loving responses remain appropriate.

2. *Make an assessment of your personal needs.* What are your needs at this point in your life? Examine each of the needs you mention and ask yourself: "Is this need of mine a healthy one?" Reflect on what actions you take that help you fulfill your needs. Would you evaluate the means you use to meet your needs as healthy? If unsure of your answers to one or more of these questions, check them out with a trusted friend and take seriously her comments. Because of perceived selfish overtones, focusing on meeting your own needs seems an odd subject to include in a chapter devoted to empathy, but it is of vital importance. You might describe yourself as having a "need" to help others. But if other legitimate needs in your life are not being satisfied, then the need to care for others has the potential to become so consuming that it fills up the void left by other legitimate but unmet needs. People with unmet needs always get their needs met; the *problem* comes from the unhealthy means they use. For a caring person with too many unsatisfied needs, the temptation is to become pre-

occupied and overly worried about others. Becoming too absorbed with others' concerns can become a convenient distraction from acknowledging our emotional deficits. This lack of awareness in turn can form the basis for compulsive caregiving. Such tendencies sabotage a healthy conscience by undermining other dimensions such as psychic energy and self-esteem. Compulsive caregivers unwisely invest too much psychic energy in others and structure their self-esteem around being perceived by others as caring and helpful.

3. *Allow for time alone.* People who show highly developed empathy need solitude. Our mental health in part rests on the capacity to use productively time spent alone. When the arousal of our empathy is unrelenting, we sometimes feel depleted and discover, over time, that we are drained by the continual effort to comfort and support others. Solitude offers a necessary antidote allowing us to reinvigorate our empathic responses. Taking a walk alone, writing in a journal, enjoying a hobby, meditating, reading, and reflecting on our lives are all useful ways to replenish ourselves. Being gentle to ourselves and using time alone productively nurtures our capacity for empathy, thereby enabling our empathic response to feel natural and truly genuine.

4. *Reflect on your recent empathic responses to others.* Have you felt that you respond out of duty? Obligation? Necessity? Or has your empathy been spontaneous, feeling both free and natural? If your answer leans more toward the former, reflect on which people and situations have the tendency to elicit this "dutiful" sense of empathy. In some situations or with some people do you display characteristics of a compulsive caregiver? Are there some situations where you find yourself losing boundaries and becoming too involved in another's misfortune? Is burnout an issue that concerns you? Ideally, when you respond to someone empathically, you do so in a natural and spontaneous way. When we respond naturally to someone in need, empathy produces a sense of self-pride and wholeness. By contrast, the more we feel duty-bound, the greater the danger that burnout, compulsive caregiving, and personal frustration take root. Some situations, however, leave us little recourse. Caring for a chronically ill loved one or worrying about a family member or a dear friend is taxing and at times over-

whelming. In such situations finding balance in our lives is difficult, especially if the loved one's situation lacks any ready resolution. A parent who empathizes with her adult child whose marriage is in turmoil or with a son who has recurring alcoholic binges faces ongoing anguish. In such cases, the worried parent must rely on the social support from healthy family members and friends. Developing such a network of support can itself be a form of boundary setting, provided limits are set on topics for discussion. Finally, those deeply concerned over a loved one's plight should make efforts to attend to the other six dimensions of conscience, with special attention to the ways they invest psychic energy. As we saw above, such profitable investment of psychic energy holds out the best hope for a sense of personal peace and contentment.

Fostering Empathy

When we respond in an empathic manner to others, we not only connect to them but also, in a sense, place ourselves in their shoes. As adults, the single most productive strategy to make sure our moral decision making includes empathy is to do exactly that: place ourselves in the other person's shoes. Depending upon the situation we are facing, one or more of the following might prove helpful.

1. Take a moment to identify who will be affected by an action you are about the take. Make sure you consider the "ripple effect." Your action might affect another person directly, but there could well be others who face unintended consequences. For example, Megan, after thoughtful consideration, feels the need to disclose a painful event from her past life to her close friend Hillary. In coming to her decision to disclose this information, she needs at least to consider its impact on Hillary. But she might also think about Barb, who is a mutual friend, and consider whether what she shares with Hillary might have consequences for Barb. Of course, what Megan communicates and the reasons she discloses information to Hillary are determined by many factors, such as

the nature of what is shared, personal motives, the situation, past experiences of shared histories, her friend's expectations, and her potential reaction. All of these factors and more help to determine what Megan divulges to Hillary. The point is that when conscience calls us to respond, an integral aspect of our response is the empathy that identifies those who are affected by the judgments we make. In other words, part of any moral decision making is simply recognizing how our decisions affect other people's lives.

2. When you make a moral decision that directly influences others, try using a third-person perspective. Imagine yourself as an observer or bystander viewing the conversation you are having with the other person. As you view this imagined situation, what do you notice about yourself? About the other person? Focus specifically on the other person's reactions as you imagine them. How do these reactions make you feel? How does this experience help you gain insight into yourself and your relationship? Does it help bring clarity regarding your motivations for helping someone?

3. Place yourself "in the shoes" of this other person. Do you understand what she is actually going through? Can you understand her perspective? Always show respect to the other person by trying to understand her situation and what she is experiencing.

4. Finally, reflect on the importance of boundary setting. Resist involving yourself excessively in another's problems or misfortunes. If you become too involved, you might not be showing empathy as much as creating some type of psychic merger or dependency that will undercut any sense of objectivity. Helping others effectively always includes *not* becoming them. It does mean that you have compassion for them, understand their situation, and take whatever action you can that provides appropriate benefit and support. Quite naturally, relaxation of boundaries and intense empathic responses occur when the distressed persons are close friends

or family members. Yet when you feel profoundly their distress and experience the forceful tug to become excessively
involved with them, in reality, truly helping them requires
that you regain your perspective and relate to them as persons for whom you have deep love and care. Moreover, you
need to remind yourself periodically that you are in any love
relationship precisely because you are *someone else.*

Empathy and Conscience: Some Final Thoughts

"Empathy" is one of those words nearly everyone endorses with
high enthusiasm. Empathy is aptly viewed as the "heart" of morality. It is truly morality's core. Empathy contributes significantly to
nearly everything we view as vital to being the human beings we
are. It underlies the attachment we have with special people in
our lives. It creates opportunities for profound moments of intimacy that endure and deepen with time. It promotes the care that
leads us to be men and women of compassion. Love, intimacy,
compassion — what could be more significant to us?

Yet, viewing empathy critically is of vital importance to our lives
as moral beings. In a sense, empathy's pull can be seductive. The
positive evaluation we assign it can lead us to ignore its potential
pitfalls. For people of good conscience, failing to think critically
about how empathy functions poses a danger to moral health.
Like all other dimensions of conscience, empathy has its downside.
When it is triggered too strongly, we can lose our boundaries, mis-
judge situations, or act unfairly. The intensity of empathy can lead
us to be biased toward some individuals or groups (based on our
loyalty to those who are similar to us) or become so emotionally
upset that we are incapable of taking appropriate action.

Intense emotions can surface when we empathize with others.
Emotions can energize our moral actions, but persons of good conscience cannot let emotions blind them to other considerations.
Emotions might ready us for action, but they don't necessarily
tell us the right thing to do, and sometimes they can undermine the right course of action. For example, suppose we have
good intentions and sincerely desire to aid a colleague at work.

Our colleague's situation provokes our empathy. But suppose this colleague is playing on our sympathies or manipulating us. Or perhaps our immediate inclination to help simply encourages her to avoid taking responsibility for her own behavior. Or perhaps our actions in the short term could cause more difficult problems in the future. Having good intentions and a strong empathic response is necessary if we are to be people of good conscience. But they are *not* sufficient in themselves. Sometimes "tough love" is necessary.

Nonetheless, we do not want to downplay empathy's significance. It provides a *quality* to our responses that sustains a caring and compassionate stance. We never want to lose this quality in our moral decision making. Without it we would soon see a growing insensitivity or even callousness in the moral decisions we make. In summary, the conscience that functions well does so precisely because empathy, though at the core of conscience, remains only one of seven vital dimensions.

{ Dimension Four }

GUILT

For many people, guilt equals conscience. Feeling guilty is all the evidence most people need to respond positively to the question: "How do I know that I have a conscience?" Popular phrases like "Do you have a guilty conscience?" or "Is your conscience bothering you?" exemplify this view. Do you recall a discussion about conscience that was not linked to guilt or wrongdoing? A primary goal of this book is to challenge this shortsighted understanding of conscience and explore more fully its complexity as well as its relevance for everyday living. Nonetheless, guilt is a fundamental dimension of any well-functioning conscience. We do not want to dismiss guilt but to view its role as one of the seven dimensions that make up a healthy conscience.

On a public level, it is safe to say that guilt has made a big comeback! Anyone reading magazines or newspapers is aware how courts, neighborhoods, and local community organizations are attempting to instill a sense of guilt in individuals convicted of crimes. Typically, their illegal deeds are highlighted through a public display that invites ridicule. Supporters of this method of punishment believe exposure to public scorn creates such humiliation and embarrassment that offenders will abandon their errant ways. In one city, people arrested for prostitution are brought to the precinct, where they must stand before a "shaming detail" of local citizens who taunt them with verbal ridicule and scorn. A judge in another state orders a man to place a sign at the end of his driveway informing people that he is a convicted felon. Such public punishments are sometimes combined with community service in hopes of creating behavioral change.

All across the country similar examples are carried out with increasing frequency. Shaming those who in the eyes of the community have behaved illegally has a long tradition in American history, dating back to the seventeenth century Puritans. Since the mid-1980s, however, legal and civic efforts to embarrass offenders have taken on new life as local communities, elected officials, and judges seek innovative ways to discourage and prevent crime. Are such methods effective? No one really knows. On the one hand, they galvanize members of the community, foster awareness of civic obligations and wrongdoings, and, ideally, sensitize offenders to the seriousness of their misdeeds. On the other hand, such public contrition can stir resentment, anger, and ill-will in those who are convicted, and in their families and friends. Such measures can also raise public outcry among citizens who view such sentences as overly harsh or vengeful. Answering the question "Is public shaming effective?" depends upon many factors, including the offender, the type of offense, the locale where the public shaming takes place, and a host of other influences.[1]

Society's Moral Authority

An interesting question emerges from this social trend. From the standpoint of society, what is the motive behind public scorn toward those who break the law? More than anything, I suspect society is attempting to reclaim its moral authority. Public humiliation is an attempt by society to instill *guilt* in offenders. The offender who experiences guilt is viewed as acknowledging society's moral authority to establish specific codes of conduct that deserve respect and obedience.

But the public's increasing intolerance of crime (note the huge increase in public expenditures for building prisons), its escalating disgust with "victim excuses," and the movement toward harsher sentences also suggest a shift in people's personal attitudes toward guilt. For example, in giving workshops across the country over the last fifteen years I have often made the statement that "guilt is good." When I first made this statement in the early eighties, I noticed members in the audience wincing or shaking their heads. Over the past few years, however, I have had more and more workshop participants nodding affirmatively and some participants taking the initiative to thank me for stating such a view. Why was it so difficult to endorse guilt in the seventies and early eighties (and even today it meets with firm opposition from many)? Let's briefly explore the reasons.

Hierarchical Model

First, many baby boomers were raised in a period of relative economic, political, and social harmony. Even if for some this was not the case, a commonly held belief in the late forties through the early sixties (and still today to some extent) was that success is possible for any who take personal initiative. Reinforcing this belief were the assumptions that respect for authority figures and working through the "system" were the ways to happiness and personal fulfillment. It was faith in this *hierarchical model* that reinforced perceptions that government officials could be trusted, school teachers were right and should not be challenged, and "Leave it to Beaver" parenthood was a reality in place. Of course, this was not an idyllic period (particularly for the poor and minorities), and during this era there were criminals, gangs, and numerous individuals who never quite fit in ("beatniks" or "hobos" come to mind). Even so, the ruling ethos was the "expectation" that people obey the law and not question authority. One of the most compelling pieces of evidence of the hierarchical model's grip on Americans is the fact that into the sixties, many medical, legal, and psychological authorities viewed the sexual abuse of children as a rare occurrence. Given the assumptions of the hierarchical model, to which so many Americans subscribed, how could we conceive of a parent doing such a ghastly thing to a child? In hindsight, and with the publicity of the last thirty years, such a viewpoint seems today ridiculously naive. But during the fifties, such a view of family life and parenthood held powerful sway on the American psyche.

Relational Model

A number of factors in the sixties led many to reconsider their allegiance to the hierarchical model of authority: the civil rights movement, the Vietnam War, the Watergate scandal, and the movement for women's rights, among others. These factors led many to doubt the merits of accepting so uncritically the hierarchical model of authority.

As a consequence, many sought more freedom and new methods for self-expression. An ethos developed to compete with the hierarchical model, best described as the *relational model*. A linchpin for this model was the growing acceptance of popular psychology. Self-knowledge, personal experience, inner subjectivity, interpersonal communication, mutually satisfying relationships, personal fulfillment — these became the lens many people used to understand and evaluate their lives. Proof of the relational model's influence can be found by looking at families today. Hierarchy might still be important as parents must set limits, enforce rules, and discipline their children. Even so, today's parents are encouraged to communicate with their children, to share their feelings, to be more open and honest, and to negotiate privileges as the children grow older. For most young people today, doing something simply because a parent "said so" is much less acceptable than it once was.[2]

Nor is this shift to the relational model limited to family functioning and communication. Corporations have adapted many of the basic beliefs of the relational model to their own structures in hopes of improving corporate morale and efficiency. Whereas three decades ago the typical (and ideal) "company man" would make a geographic move whenever requested, no matter what the hardship caused to himself or his family, today many employees show increasing resistance to relocation without discussion and negotiation with corporate supervisors. Today's workers (popularly referred to as Generation X) seek to balance quality of life issues (e.g., spending time with family, participating in leisure activities, living in a favored geographic locale) with work commitments.[3] In a similar vein, leadership in corporate America increasingly recognizes the role of supporting positive relationships and team building. In the public mind, today's successful corporate leader possesses a vision of the future and good interpersonal skills.[4]

Striking a Balance

What does all this have to do with guilt? The hierarchical model, with its message of respecting authority and complying with authority's wishes, has the potential for creating greater guilt. In the hierarchical model, disobeying one's parents or one's boss often resulted in self-blame. The hierarchical model originated within a cultural climate that encouraged acceptance of authority and minimal dissent. If you defied authority, guilt would be a natural response. Here I am not attempting a sociological analysis of American society. Rather, I am merely pointing out that with the rise of the relational model we are increasingly becoming a psychologically minded society in which psychological analysis is prized, psychological experts are consulted, and relationships are considered a primary means for personal happiness. On high school and college campuses, for example, in just a few decades going to counseling has gone from being a stigma to finding acceptance among youth.

Just as an unchallenged hierarchical model has shortcomings (unfair laws, social injustices, denial of rights, or misdeeds carried out by unscrupulous authority figures, whether abusing parents or publicly elected officials), the relational model is not without its own defects. When the relational model goes without challenge, it can produce a cultural climate that creates erroneous assumptions regarding how relationships should function. Individuals uncritically accepting this model's premises are prone to excesses across a broad spectrum of behaviors, including: rampant individualism, narcissism, unchecked self-indulgence, victimhood, and the denial of personal responsibility — the consequences of authenticity gone astray. Such expressions reveal a warped sense of what it means to enjoy personal fulfillment. The excesses of the relational model subvert conscience by stigmatizing guilt. The question is not "moral versus unhealthy" guilt but whether we should feel guilt at all.

A telling sign of the relational model's power is the popular movie genre that displays rugged heroes who have been betrayed by all the traditional establishments (formerly the legitimate sources of hierarchy). The local police, the FBI, the newspapers, elected officials, the legal system — not infrequently even friends and families — fail as trusted confidants so the solitary hero must take matters into his own hands. This rugged individualist, usually male, is immune from laws others must obey. To catch the "bad guys" virtually any means is acceptable. Lawbreaking for these heroes is condoned and rarely meets with adverse consequences. The actor highlights his own importance and superiority through incredible physical feats, uncanny insights, superior knowledge, and firm resolve to bring about "justice" at all costs.

Others have written eloquently on the narcissistic tendencies of our culture and its focus on self-indulgence and excessive individualism.[5] On a daily basis we experience the fallout of such excesses, including rudeness and selfishness. One mundane but very telling sign of this self-indulgence is the increasing friction between restaurants and their customers. Rudeness and conflict are increasingly the norm. Hefty tip charges, deposited credit cards, and prompt departures are demanded by restaurants, while customers fume over poor service and the business-like atmosphere. Arguments and shouting matches are more and more common even in top dining establishments.[6] In a similar vein, many airline flight crews now receive advanced training in how to mediate conflicts and, if necessary, subdue unruly passengers. On flights today people are more likely to see arguments between ill-mannered passengers that at times lead to verbal abuse or even physical assault of other passengers or crew members. This "air rage" has risen dramatically in recent years.[7]

Guilt and the Therapeutic Culture

The relational model, with its focus on self and personal fulfillment, though having merits, can weaken or undermine an individual's capacity for guilt. Comparing models, we can say that the hierarchical model's excessive focus on authority too often enhances unhealthy responses of guilt, while the relational model's shortsighted emphasis on the self is prone to downplay or ignore the vital influence guilt has in shaping us as moral beings.

The decline of guilt is aided by a particular aspect of the relational model: the therapeutic culture. Far too many therapists view guilt as an obstacle to living a happy, normal life. Typically, a Freudian or psychodynamically trained therapist views guilt as a primitive, punishing part of the superego that wreaks havoc on the ego's attempt to maintain self-esteem. A behaviorally trained counselor understands guilt as a learned response needing correction so one can enjoy personal fulfillment. A cognitive-oriented clinician is apt to see a client's expression of guilt as arising from some type of dysfunctional or irrational belief system that needs alteration. A therapist with a humanistic viewpoint is likely to see guilt as an obstacle to the client's reaching full potential. Of course, not every therapist, counselor, or clinician subscribes to one of these points of view, but my own dealings with mental health colleagues over the years lead me to conclude that such thinking is the prevailing view: guilt is an experience needing correction and often elimination from the client's life.

As I reflect back over the years of my clinical study and training, and the numerous conversations I have had with fellow students, clinical instructors, and professional colleagues, I realize that the word "guilt" was almost always cast in a negative light. It invariably elicited impressions of people crippled by low self-esteem, depression, or some debilitating anxiety. The only exception was when we were discussing or interviewing a person fitting the diagnosis of Antisocial Personality Disorder (APD) — which includes the "psychopath." As the previous chapter indicated, psychopaths often show no empathy toward their victims and fail to experience remorse for their misdeeds.

An essential issue here, of course, is the "biased" population therapists encounter in clinical settings. Quite frequently, individuals entering therapy struggle with painful feelings. Their sufferings frequently flow out of a poor self-image, a feeling of incompetence arising from their inability to master some skill or task, or an interpersonal conflict. Their difficult situations are revealed through a wide variety of negative and often painful emotions (e.g., anger, shame, guilt, and sadness). In most instances, when the therapy focuses on issues surrounding guilt, what is being addressed is "unhealthy guilt." Such guilt is emotionally crippling and impedes the development of a healthy conscience. But therapists make a grave mistake if they leave clients with the impression that most guilt is unhealthy or they generalize from their biased client base and conclude that everyday guilt reactions nearly always need "correction." It is my impression that far too many therapists view guilt with such bias and distortion.

Another reason for the therapeutic culture's problems with guilt has to do with the very nature of counseling. A proper and central goal of counseling is to eliminate personal distress and to help the client develop coping skills that maximize a sense of contentment and personal enjoyment. With this goal in mind, therapists are often prone to categorize feelings of guilt as a distressed state that impedes the client's attempt to achieve personally fulfilling goals.

Additionally, there is a belief among some therapists that they should not impose their own values on clients. In other words, a mental health expert should strive to be value neutral and not interfere with the client's worldview or belief system. But there is no such thing as value-free therapy. Every counselor, therapist, and clinician has a certain therapy orientation, brings up or encourages the discussion of certain topics and not others, and believes some outcomes for the client are preferable to others. The therapist is always in one way or another endorsing some value or belief system. If we can accept the assumption that counseling has as a basic, general goal the well-being of the client and maximizing this well-being, then guilt (or what I term "moral guilt," discussed below) is a natural human experience that the therapist helps the client acknowledge as appropriate. My impression is that psychologists whose specialty is mental health work (e.g., clinical or counseling psychologists or other clinically focused specialists such as social workers, mental health counselors) appear less inclined to see guilt as a positive human experience, whereas psychologists in other specialties (e.g., developmental psychologists) have a more enlightened approach to guilt.[8]

Guilt and Family Life.

Parents loom as powerful figures in the lives of their children. Being so vulnerable, the children are exposed to and absorb much of the fear, anxiety, and guilt that each spouse brings to the marriage. Sometimes even adult children will act out these feelings and respond to an event or person with feelings of guilt or attempt to create guilty feelings in another. By doing so, such children perpetuate through others what they themselves experienced while growing up. The very fact that families develop emotionally deep bonds serves to promote guilt. When adequately fulfilled, the emotional needs and desires that arise from these deep bonds are sources of joy and contentment. But because each family member is also a human being existing in a family of human beings, inevitably regrets, hurts, disappointments, and remorse are triggered. In other words, the experience of guilt is an unavoidable aspect of human and family life.

As Jerome Kagan suggests, a sense of guilt might serve as an adaptive response in family upbringing. Human beings, whose maturity and independence require a more prolonged period of family bonding and rearing than other species, experience guilt as a protective buffer among siblings. A child's capacity to become resentful or angry toward a sibling or the impulse to hurt a brother or sister can be short-circuited by developing an appropriate guilt response.[9] Kagan's observation makes sense. Even though siblings squabble, quarrel, and grow jealous and engage in occasional fights, rarely does conflict reach the point of violence. Indeed, "the frequency of such seriously violent acts is so tiny, each occurrence is a screaming headline in the local newspaper."[10] Guilt exercises a prominent role in helping children to contain their aggressive impulses.

Early Childhood Development

As children develop into their adolescent years, they acquire an increasing capacity to empathize not only with individuals, but also with more extensive groups of people and larger social entities. Such empathic understanding can lead them to feel distress (guilt) in the face of others' misfortunes because of their own fortunate state. Examples include showing sensitivity to victims of a natural disaster, attempting to help the underprivileged, or aiding members of a minority group.

As children develop they also come to understand that they have the capability to harm others. If a child begins to believe that his behavior is the source of another child's feeling bad, then he might empathize with the other child's distress and feel guilt about the misdeed that caused it. As they grow older, children also develop the realization that they can wish harm or imagine something bad happening to someone. Realizing they have this desire can itself become a source for guilt. Children also develop awareness that they have choices. They can choose to engage in a harmful act or make the choice not to respond positively to another's need. In each case, the resulting feeling might be one of guilt.

It has been demonstrated by carefully monitored observations that even very young children provide comfort to one another. As children continue to develop, the increasing interconnection of guilt, empathy, and cognitive growth form the basis for caring behaviors.[11] In their review of a wide range of published data, two prominent researchers noted that "studies support the notion that children in the first years of life are endowed with the cognitive, behavioral, and social-emotional competencies necessary to experience/express empathy and guilt."[12]

This brief review points to one inevitable conclusion: from both a biological and psychological perspective, guilt is part and parcel of the fabric of human life. A sense of guilt and being human go hand in hand. Moreover, having a capacity for guilt is beneficial to the human species. Ideally guilt helps both families and other significant relationships through reparative actions (e.g., saying "I'm sorry," making amends, asking forgiveness).

Parenting

Unfortunately, because guilt's influence on those we love can be so powerful, family members are prone to use it as a source of control. Recall that one definition of a family (albeit a cynical one) is a group of people who know how to push one another's buttons! Family members know all too well the vulnerabilities of other family members. Typically, using guilt as a way to control behavior originates with the parent as a method for controlling a child. Unfortunately, the effects of guilt used as control endure far beyond childhood. A certain statement, a tone of voice, a specific topic can send even an adult child into a tail-spin. A parent, for example, can make statements that give the message of "poor me," which in turn creates in an adult child a variety of feelings including guilt, anger, and frustration.

At the same time, older children and teens know that responsible, sensitive parents can be manipulated too. A teen might "hint" how other parents are allowing her friends to do something her own parents have refused to give permission for in hopes of stirring just enough guilt to make one or both parents yield to her wishes. In any case, it comes as no surprise that being raised in a family where guilt was utilized as a primary means of control easily triggers resentments and hurts that resist any age boundaries. For some adults, a natural reaction to such an upbringing is trying not to dwell on the feelings such guilt generates. Because experiences of guilt come to us so naturally, using them at times (or often) as a means of controlling others we love is alive and well today in many families and interpersonal relationships.

It stands to reason that misuse of guilt was more prevalent among baby boomers' families with their hierarchical model of authority. As a consequence of this upbringing many baby boomer parents today face a quandary. In discussion with parents of the baby boomer generation (my own peers) I sense at times the desire, on the one hand, not to rely on guilt. As one parent recently told me, "My children will not be manipulated by guilt as I was." On the other hand, in today's climate where children face so many temptations, so many choices, and so many opportunities to be led astray, there exists a vital need for rule setting. But if rules are to be effective, children need to develop a healthy capacity for guilt. As a way to resolve such confusion, I discuss with parents the difference between guilt used as control (an example of unhealthy guilt) and the natural sense of guilt that parents can rightfully desire for their children. This healthy sense of guilt I designate as *moral guilt*.

A final reason that guilt has been in disfavor is, simply, that it is an unpleasant experience. As in the case with conscience itself (to which it has been equated), most people believe that little can be gained by talking about guilt or discussing its positive features. Hence, an avoidance cycle develops. We fail to discuss guilt because it proves distressing, often reminding us of uncomfortable feelings from our past history, but in the process this avoidance leads us never to consider its positive features and vital role in leading a healthy moral life. In specific instances, such as a gruesome crime, we may wonder how such criminal acts could be carried out and ask "How can he not feel guilt?" Ordinarily, however, guilt is not a topic that most people are inclined to discuss among themselves or, for that matter, to reflect upon personally. When it is a topic of conversation or personal reflection, unhealthy rather than moral guilt all too frequently becomes the focus of discussion.

Distinguishing between Moral and Unhealthy Guilt

If you did not have the capacity for guilt, what type of person would you be? I would be a moral monster. I have no doubt that failure to experience guilt would incline me to offensive, unacceptable, and wrongful actions. Over the years these actions would degenerate into habits that increasingly would bring suffering and hurt to others. Feeling no remorse for hitting siblings would have made striking peers all the easier. Deceit, thoughts of revenge, and snap judgments would be my ordinary response to other people. Would I have ever even uttered an apology or developed the capacity to say, "I'm sorry." After all, doesn't such a statement, when genuine, stem from a personal sense of guilt?

It is important that we not allow healthy guilt to deteriorate into chronic feelings of remorse or ongoing worry over imagined wrongs. The guilt I am speaking of is a judgment we make about ourselves as a consequence of actually having done something wrong or having failed to act when we believed it right and necessary. In other words, guilt, when it is healthy, is a judgment we make about ourselves that is the consequence of having violated some moral rule or principle. The emotional, social, and personal states associated with such judgments of guilt include embarrassment, disappointment, distress, humiliation, intense self-focus, a feeling of isolation, a sense of failure, self-directed anger, and self-criticism.

Moral guilt is absolutely essential for the development of a healthy conscience and, consequently, personal moral health. Experiencing such guilt is an internal signal that because of my actions "I am guilty." At times this can be acutely and painfully felt, particularly if the misdeed causes serious harm to others. Nonetheless, moral guilt places the emphasis on the personal responsibility that we acknowledge our wrongdoing and accept the consequences. With moral guilt the emphasis is on this personal responsibility for wrongdoing as well as on the amends we make and our future actions. On the other hand, when we experience "unhealthy guilt" we are aptly described as prisoners held hostage by negative feelings and shame. Some people's self-criticism can be so resistant to rational reflection and common sense that they become emotionally crippled by their negative self-evaluations.

Here we will describe in more detail the essential features of each type of guilt. To better appreciate the distinctions between moral and unhealthy guilt first reflect on an instance when *you felt guilt* over something you did or didn't do (something you should have done). Then go through each list and determine which set of features best captures the state of guilt you felt.

Moral Guilt

1. With moral guilt I take *personal responsibility* for my misdeeds. There is a realism to the responsibility I assume for my action. As I reflect on my misdeed I realize I actually could have acted differently or refrained from doing something. Personal responsibility assumes a realistic appraisal of possibilities. For example, if Brenda upsets her teacher with behavior in clear violation of school or classroom policy, then her feelings of guilt are appropriate. On the other hand, if Susan's boss at work is

angry over worker performance and Susan is a good employee and not even on the shift of workers whose poor performance caused her boss's reaction, then any feelings of guilt would be unhealthy.

2. One of the results of moral guilt is a healthy sense of *humility*. Moral guilt fosters a personal humility that jolts the self-complacency that builds over time in work and relationships. A specific feature of healthy humility is ongoing awareness of my need to expand my moral horizon through the insights of those I respect and acknowledging my dependence on them. In other words, the humility that flows from moral guilt acknowledges my reliance on others.

3. Moral guilt frequently serves as a force freely motivating me to *repair* the wrong that I have done. Examples of reparative actions include making some type of restitution or asking forgiveness.[13]

4. Moral guilt can help *alter* wrongful behaviors. Understandably, the influence guilt has to change my misconduct depends upon the significance a relationship has in my life and the history I share with the offended person. If years of hurt have built up in a marriage, family, or friendship, I might find myself continuing to be hurtful to a loved one by what I say or do. Even here, however, moral guilt can serve as a protective buffer that diminishes or limits my hurtful responses.

5. Moral guilt is *other-directed*. It motivates me to build meaningful connections and resolve or minimize conflicts in a realistic fashion.

6. Moral guilt is a natural ally of *empathy*. The more I am aware of another person's feelings or feel distress over his situation, the more I might be motivated to respond positively toward him. Here we see moral guilt's power to promote caring and altruistic acts. Moral guilt serves to promote the personal responsibility I take for being a member of the human community. Even if I did not specifically cause hurt to someone, perceiving his distress and feeling his hurt (empathy) might lead me to offer a helping hand. As we have already pointed out, however, there is need for clear boundary setting; otherwise my empathy and guilt could make such unrealistic

demands that I am unable to devote time and psychic energy to other legitimate obligations.

7. Another valued feature of moral guilt is its ability to prompt *self-insight*. Moral guilt leads me to acknowledge my error, but it also triggers a new perspective. Moral guilt evokes questions such as "What have I learned from this misdeed?" or "Can I learn from this mistake how to be a better person?"

8. Finally, moral guilt encourages a *future perspective*. It links me to my moral vision. If Ben has hurt his friend and experiences moral guilt, he is likely to apologize to his friend and do what he can to repair the relationship and make amends for his wrongdoing. In addition, however, moral guilt nudges Ben to reflect on what kind of friend he desires to be. In other words, moral guilt encourages Ben to take seriously his aspirations, his dreams, and his hopes for the friendship. Moral guilt aids Ben in confronting his mistake but does not seek to extract an unreasonable psychic price by triggering in him excessive worry over his misdeed. On the contrary, moral guilt serves to refocus his contrite evaluation of himself into something beneficial. His moral failure slowly transforms itself into a focal point that stimulates his deeper desire: to be the "good" friend to the person he injured. As he reflects on his wrongful act, the focus slowly shifts to what "can be" rather than what happened. This orientation to look ahead to future possibilities is taken up later in our chapter on idealization.

Unhealthy Guilt

Because guilt is so pervasive in family life and significant relationships and because our emotional lives are not perfect, everyone experiences instances of moral failures that lend themselves to the chronic worry, the recurring self-devaluation, and the hurtful shame we associate with unhealthy guilt. In essence, unhealthy guilt sabotages moral health.

1. With unhealthy guilt I live in the *past*. The importance I give to specific misdeeds or moral failures is never relinquished. My moral failings intrude periodically or even frequently into consciousness. As a result, psychic energy is drained, and I am

distracted from initiating the positive steps that help insure moral growth. Obviously, certain misdeeds in my life might never be forgotten, particularly if they involved serious harm to a loved one or caused significant personal disappointment, failure, or embarrassment. In such instances periodic recall of my misdeeds reminds me of my frailty and the need to take appropriate steps to insure moral fitness. But when such recollections are accompanied by intense emotional pain and turmoil, then I need to consider if these memories and the feelings they generate are more appropriately labeled as the aftermath of unhealthy guilt.

2. Unhealthy guilt *stymies my emotional and moral growth.* It highlights my moral failures and discourages me from considering what insight I have gained as a result of my wrongful action. It is content to wallow in the negative feelings it generates.

3. Unhealthy guilt *prolongs personal suffering.* As I give undue attention to my shortcomings and failures, I soon find a list that "feels" never ending. I am caught in an endless loop in which I recall a misdeed that triggers negative feelings, which in turn fuels my memory of the misdeed even more, and so on and on.

4. Frequently, unhealthy guilt's greatest ally is my *imagination.* I find myself feeling responsible for situations or actions that are beyond my control, or replaying in my mind instances in which I could not possibly have made a difference no matter what I did (but still feel the responsibility). I might misinterpret my actions in a way that creates worry or makes me beat myself up psychically. An extreme example of unhealthy guilt is what mental health experts label "survivor guilt." A family on vacation is involved in a serious auto accident, and one parent survives while her spouse and two children die. Such traumatic episodes become breeding ground for survivor guilt. When someone to whom I am significantly attached dies as a result of some strange or freak accident while I manage to survive, a common response is to feel guilt simply because I survived. I grope to understand such senseless loss of life and wonder "Why me? Why did I survive?" As I struggle with such questions, my imagination breeds endless and emotionally draining responses.

5. Unhealthy guilt never moves beyond feeling misery and up-

set. All in all, its only purpose is the assurance of *continuing distress.*

6. Unhealthy guilt frequently triggers *unhealthy defenses.* As a way to deal with the unhealthy guilt I might fixate on it, incurring in the process chronic worry and upset. On the other hand, I might find myself minimizing wrongdoings or rationalizing my actions.

7. With unhealthy guilt, *I* always prove to be the victim. Frequently I feel a *sense of personal shame.* We must be careful to distinguish between guilt and shame. A sign of a maturing conscience and increasing moral fitness is appropriate guilt, which allows me to assume responsibility for my actions and the harm I cause another. Shame, on the other hand, is a self-evaluation that "I am bad." Shame degrades the self, viewing "me" as contemptible and unworthy of nurture, love, and respect. Chronic anxiety and self-punishing thoughts are allies of the shamed self. Such a negative personal evaluation cripples emotional growth, creates enormous personal pain, and drains psychic energy. As a result, there is diminished psychic energy for building healthy relationships, planning realistic goals, and making everyday moral decisions. The shortage of psychic energy required for healthy and adaptive living inevitably disrupts the functioning of conscience and leads to declining moral health. After all, if my own evaluation of self consists to a significant degree of the experience of *being bad,* then how can I allow myself permission to feel the contentment of friendship, feeling the pride of accomplishing appropriate goals, or knowing the satisfaction of making good moral decisions?

The subjective experience of guilt is so uniquely personal and so intricately interwoven with how we interpret our life histories that the criteria listed above are meant to serve as guidelines rather than a neat package that distills in crystal clear fashion the differences between the two types of guilt. Over any person's life span, there exist so many self-evaluations that must be made and so many negative feelings to sort out that it is inevitable that these two types of guilt overlap. We can frequently experience both moral and unhealthy guilt. Guilt, all in all, is "messy."

Coping with Guilt

We all have experienced moral failures. Generally speaking, the "key" to moral growth is not the misdeed but learning from such failure. The points below explore how this growth can be accomplished.

1. Admit your shortcoming, misdeed, or moral failure. Utilize the DMI discussed above (see p. 95). Strive for self-awareness and self-honesty.

2. When you realize your moral failing, try to unravel the pieces. For example, ask yourself:

   a. What moral principle did my moral failing violate? Call to mind the moral principle and repeat it to yourself.

   b. What made this action wrong?

   c. What were the effects of this choice on myself and others?

   d. Does the guilt I feel fit the criteria associated with moral guilt or unhealthy guilt?

   e. What were my intentions?

3. If you determine that your guilt fits the criteria for healthy guilt, then *congratulate* yourself for feeling this guilt! This statement may sound strange, but remember, moral guilt is essential for a healthy conscience.

4. Building on number three above, pose to yourself these questions: "Now that I take responsibility for my action and experience this guilt, how am I a different person?" "What have I learned about myself?" "How can I learn from this moral failing?" "What might I do differently next time?" Ultimately, the fruit of moral guilt is wisdom in making future moral choices.

5. Recall that essential features of healthy guilt include (a) acknowledging your wrongdoing, (b) making whatever amends that are necessary while accepting appropriate consequences,

(c) realizing what you have learned, and (d) focusing on the future. The guilt you experience, though distressing, can prove in the long run to be a positive experience for personal moral growth.

6. As you reflect on your past behavior you will recognize reactions to your moral failures that contain elements of both moral and unhealthy guilt. When you reflect on these misdeeds you need to be realistic. The unhealthy guilt that contaminates your moral guilt-response does not cease to exist just because you understand it better. You most likely have already tried reasoning with yourself and chances are this too has failed. Recall that guilt reactions are complicated and messy affairs that are difficult to unravel. The best strategy is to concentrate on your moral guilt. In other words, identify those aspects of your reaction that are healthy and focus your attention on them. Go over the list of characteristics of moral guilt and pay particular attention to those that are not part of your guilt response. This strategy broadens the moral guilt aspect of your reaction, while shrinking the unhealthy guilt portion. Instead of refuting and trying to change unhealthy aspects of your reaction simply *make the choice* to concentrate on moral guilt and build up these healthy aspects. If you concentrate on the healthy guilt, you might find over time that you are able to contain or at least limit the attention you give to unhealthy guilt and the upset it causes. The benefits of *choosing* to focus on moral guilt are reinforced by gradual improvement in moral fitness. This approach calls for *patience*. Since unhealthy guilt exerts a powerful grip on our emotional lives, focus on small improvements, and consider each small step a victory!

Sadly, many people are so victimized by unhealthy guilt that the most apt description for them is "hostages." This creates not only emotional turmoil and upset, but undermines the healthy functioning of conscience. Unhealthy guilt holds conscience hostage. The acute pain of unhealthy guilt obstructs moral awareness and blinds us from making realistic moral evaluations. A conscience plagued by unhealthy guilt is absorbed in the distress of the moment and ill-equipped to discern accurately or wisely a future moral course. Individuals experiencing serious unhealthy guilt frequently can benefit from professional counseling to achieve greater understanding of the toll such guilt takes as well as to find coping strategies for dealing with its harmful effects.

Moral guilt is vital for a healthy conscience. Guilt fosters self-honesty and humility, which enable me to discredit or at least limit the inevitable self-delusions and self-serving biases that falsely inflate my sense of moral goodness. When I deceive myself into thinking my moral health is better than it truly is, I am traveling down the slippery slope of self-deception — slowly eroding any moral gains I have made, thus impairing conscience still further. More than any other dimension of conscience, a healthy sense of moral guilt underlies the self-honesty needed for a realistic appraisal of my intentions and behaviors.

{ Dimension Five }

IDEALIZATION

═══════════════

Living ethically is much more than not living unethically. It is much harder to live out exemplary standards of professional conduct than it is to avoid wrongdoing.

— MARTIN SELIGMAN, former president,
American Psychological Association

Psychologist Martin Seligman made this comment in his monthly column addressed to members of the American Psychological Association. In it he urged members of the profession not only to work toward healing and correcting "the worst things in life" but also to strive toward fulfilling "the mission of building the best things in life."[1] He believes psychologists are expected to be ethical professionals, but in the fullest sense being an ethical psychologist requires more than avoiding "wrongdoing." Extending his idea, we can view not doing wrong as the bare essentials of an ethical life, but it falls far short of a full and rich ethical life. To live an "ethical," "moral," or "good" life to the fullest extent possible requires something more.

Seligman's statement applies to all of us. We can be a good friend or the best friend possible. We can be a good work colleague or the best work colleague possible. In the introduction we noted that conscience is a uniquely human attribute that sets us apart from all other species. We adhere to moral principles to guide our behavior as we determine right from wrong.[2] But we not only want to avoid wrongdoing; we want to be "exemplary." We discover something within ourselves, an ideal of being the *best* friend, parent, or colleague imaginable. These are the ideals we cherish, relish, and even, at times, die for.

The process whereby we attempt to live up to our potential is what I label "idealization" — the fifth dimension necessary for conscience's healthy functioning. This dimension of conscience all too frequently fails to receive the focus it deserves. Regrettably, this absence deprives conscience of its most *positive* quality. Idealization is conscience's invitation to the self to seek the greater good. It articulates a positive morality whose goal is striving for what is better rather than merely avoiding any wrongdoing. It creates possibilities for goodness instead of simply forbidding what is unacceptable. It weds conscience to a moral horizon that inspires hope while shaping a moral vision we are invited to embrace.

Where Are the Role Models?

Several years ago I gave a workshop to teachers, and during the morning break one of the participants asked me a question that I think about periodically to this day. Her question was direct and to the point: "Can you think of one hero who is looked up to today by young people who is portrayed by the media as having the qualities of intelligence, compassion, and moral character?" Taken aback for a moment I started thinking. After a few moments I looked at her and said, "I'm sorry but no one comes to mind who possesses all three of those qualities." She responded, "I can't either, and that's one reason why being a parent today is so tough."

As the week went on, I grew more disturbed by this encounter. From the perspective of moral health, role models or heroes hold great significance for a culture. On an interpersonal level we usually know several people whose qualities we admire and respect. Historically, and etched into national consciousness, are individuals we as a nation admire: Presidents Washington and Lincoln come immediately to mind. Such public figures embody the ideals for which we strive. They enflesh the good we hope to attain. More than anything, moral heroes communicate to us that living a moral life *is possible*. Their lives tell us that human beings can achieve the ideals they cherish. Role models who command national attention embody a nation's values. Their lives bridge the natural differences dividing us, forging a consensus of common interest upon which different groups converge. Their lives and actions reflect core character traits the culture deems significant. When we acknowledge their successes and admire their achievements, society itself is the beneficiary. The residual effects of heroes' feats encourage people to "try harder" or put forth their "best effort."

One baseball season highlights this dynamic of the hero's effects on the rest of us. A home run race between Mark McGwire and Sammy Sosa captured many people's attention. Individuals who never cared for the sport began to take an active interest in baseball. Over the summer months I heard conversations at movie theaters, in restaurants, or while browsing through a store. A frequent question was, "Did he hit one today?" The spillover effect of this interest had benefits far beyond baseball. People discovered a common interest they never before had shared. Most importantly, both players are nice men. Even though they were competing against one another and even though their respective teams (the St. Louis Cardinals and the Chicago Cubs) had a long and hotly contested rivalry, they wished each other well. Their reputations as good people were well deserved. Big Mac gave a substantial part of his salary to help abused children, and even though he could have gotten more money with another team, he chose to stay in St. Louis, a city he enjoyed. Who can forget the endearing picture of him hugging his son after breaking the home run record?

Sammy's vault to the national spotlight caught sports fans by surprise. But there he was, bursting into the national spotlight with smiles and kind words for all. Born in the Dominican Republic, he was raised in an impoverished background and overcame numerous obstacles to achieve his goal of becoming a major league ball player. He is described by those who know him as likeable, unassuming, and a good teammate.

But perhaps the most striking feature of these two men is how they treated one another. They complimented each other's feats and rooted each other on, refusing the media bait to speak ill of one another. *Sports Illustrated* hailed their achievements by naming them "Sportsmen of the Year," and it went on to say of them:

> It wasn't just the lengths they went to with bats in their hands. It was also that they went to such lengths to conduct the great home run race with dignity and sportsmanship, with a sense of joy and openness. Never had two men chased legends and each other that hard and that long or invited so much of America onto their backs for the ride. Rarely has grace so swiftly begotten grace, $2 million pouring into Sosa's foundation for hurricane victims in his native Dominican Republic and a flurry of checks for $62 and $70 into McGwire's Los Angeles–based charity for abused children.[3]

No one has any way of measuring the influence of these two sports figures, but I have no doubt their influence was overwhelmingly positive. I can't help but think that during and after the summer of '98 some children tried harder on the field, some teammates were better teammates, some fathers became better fathers, and some competitors did not let their rivalry degenerate into personal grudges — at least in part because of the influence of these two men.

Unfortunately, surveys point to a scarcity of national heroes. Some writers label this period in American history as "a post-heroic age." Two-thirds of Americans believe that the culture has shifted so dramatically that individuals who carry out noble deeds find it "much harder" to acquire recognition. More than 70 percent of those polled believe Americans have taken a more cynical view toward heroes. While more than half of older Americans said they had heroes and thought national role models were important for the country, 60 percent of baby boomers reported having no heroes. Raised in the climate of Watergate and the Vietnam War, this post–World War II generation is apt to be cynical about the very notion of a hero, and this group makes up a majority of Americans who raise children today. What baby boomer parents communicate to future generations about heroes remains to be seen. Finally, more than 80 percent of those surveyed, in trying to account for the lack of national heroes, saw the media as part of the problem. In the view of survey respondents, the media always look for negative things to say about public figures, therefore making it easier to tarnish a well-known person's name or destroy his or her reputation.[4]

Increasingly, Americans, especially young Americans, do not look to political leaders for heroes. Over the past few decades government officials have come to be viewed more realistically and more cynically.[5] In a recent survey, American teens were asked what qualities they desired in a national leader. These adolescents reported that in order of preference they wanted a national leader to have the following qualities (a) cared about average people; (b) held consistent beliefs; (c) possessed personal leadership skills; (d) had strong ethical values; and (e) communicated well. "But a majority of students could not name a single public figure — in government or outside of it — with such qualities."[6] Some major sports figures have tremendous recognition (e.g., Michael Jordan or Tiger Woods), but many athletes take their knocks from the media (some deservedly so) even as the media highlight their on-the-field feats.

What are the consequences of a heroless culture? No one knows. On a practical level, true role models are individuals whom young people (or any of us for that matter) "can see, feel, and interact with"[7] in everyday life. Dave Sanders, the Columbine coach killed in the Littleton Massacre, fits such a description. His efforts on that fateful April day saved the lives of over two hundred students and cost him his own. He was always there for students, even on his last day on earth. Every school has such role models. His dying words, uttered to frantic students doing everything they possibly could to save his life, were "tell my girls I love them."[8]

Perhaps the baby boomer generation will grow increasingly concerned about the dearth of national heroes as they grapple with building the character of their own children. Reflecting this view, moral educator Thomas Lickona senses that "people are eager for their kids to identify with figures of moral excellence — with heroes."[9] The public outpouring of sympathy at the death of the great Chicago Bear running back Walter Payton (whose nickname was "Sweetness") might be evidence of the hunger for heroes in this increasingly heroless age. Most tellingly, in an interview shortly before his death, Payton told writer Don Yaeger, "Those athletes who say they're not role models and that they don't care never want to have that discussion with me."[10] Only time will tell what form moral heroes and role models will take in the years ahead.

Do You Have Moral Heroes?

1. Can you list five people (living or deceased) you personally admire and look up to?

2. What three characteristics do you associate with each of these individuals (be as specific as possible)?

3. If you had to explain to someone why these characteristics are significant *for you,* what response would you offer?

4. If you had to rank all these characteristics, which would be your top three? Why these three and not other characteristics you mentioned?

5. What do the individuals you listed convey to you about the meaning of a *good* life?

6. Define the *good* life.

7. How would you evaluate your own behavior in living up to the good life you just defined?

Two Forms of Idealization: "Bad to Good" and "Good Becoming Better"

We spoke earlier about idealization. As I use the term here, to idealize requires that we aspire to something, we strive to become better than what we are. In this process we do not become different from who we currently are, but we do become better.

Bad to Good

Idealization promotes moral health in two ways. Let's call the first one the "bad to good" approach. For example, if we lie or steal, the capacity to idealize might have enough sway to motivate a change in our behavior. In such instances, when ideals influence us to alter our behavior, the actual workings of conscience typically are the following. We grow uncomfortable with our behavior; we realize we are not living up to some ideal, what it means to be the "good" person we desire to be. This personal discomfort finds support in a moral belief such as "stealing is wrong." Moral guilt also plays a role. These three dimensions all contribute to our change of behavior. Naturally, other factors also might alter our wrongful behavior. For example, we might feel guilt, but we might also fear getting arrested. Suppose that two individuals, Cassidy and Mary Beth, periodically steal from stores. Cassidy, on the one hand, ceases stealing because her conscience — especially idealization, moral beliefs, and guilt — leads her to feel troubled and embarrassed over what she has done. Let's also say that Cassidy's grandmother recently died. Cassidy loved her grandmother, and her death made Cassidy think about what her grandmother meant to her. She recalled that her grandmother was a "good" person (idealization). Further, she knows her grandmother's goodness would endorse the moral belief that "stealing is wrong." The more Cassidy reflects the more remorse she feels (guilt). Here we see the workings of conscience. Cassidy doesn't really think about getting caught, and being a juvenile, in her view, reduces the consequences of arrest to a minor inconvenience. But the result is that on her own she has ceased stealing.

Mary Beth, on the other hand, stops her stealing at around the same time, but for different reasons. Recently, while in a store where she periodically snatched merchandise, a store clerk's gaze proved sufficiently unsettling to cause her to rethink her thievery. She also has a classmate who got a suspended sentence with fifty hours of community service for shoplifting. Mary Beth walks out of the store and says to herself, "That's it. I don't want to get caught." She too quits stealing. For both adolescents there has been a positive change of behavior. But if you were asked which of the two has the most "potential" for improving her moral health, you most likely would respond, "Cassidy." Cassidy's behavior change, though triggered in part by an external event (the death of her grandmother), is mostly prompted by a healthy conscience. The three dimensions of conscience noted above work together to alter her behavior. Her moral growth, in other words, is fueled by her own inner dynamics rather than fear of external sanctions, which is the motivation for Mary Beth. Given Cassidy's attachment to her grandmother, idealization's role is likely to be crucial.

Good to Better

Cassidy falls in the *bad to good* approach. But often we are already attempting to be good human beings, and idealization's role is to inspire us to be better ones. I'll label this the *good to better* category. This form of idealization occurs with great regularity in our lives. The problem is that we don't take the time either to recognize or to savor its benefits to our moral health.

Frequently, the joys, satisfactions, and happiness in our lives as well as the disappointments and disillusionments we struggle with are at least in part the consequences of these meaning-making, good-becoming-better moments. Most of the time such moments are not about major triumphs or catastrophes but have more to do with ordinary daily events. Indeed, they are so commonplace that most of the time we are oblivious to them. Also, when we do attend to such moments, we are likely to frame them in factual and psychological ways and *ignore* their moral significance.

At times, all of us find ourselves in our worlds of work and relationship struggling with competing claims, interests, and conflicts or caught in situations that are complex and perplexing. Melissa is told on short notice by her boss that she "must" represent him at a human resources meeting late tomorrow afternoon. She feels trapped by this request because she promised her sister and brother-in-law, who are out of town, that she would pick up her ten-year-old niece the next day after she finishes soccer practice, which happens to end one-half hour after her meeting begins. As a regional sales supervisor, Steve has authority over how a recently received bulk shipment of electrical cables is to be allotted to the five salespeople in his region. His company's production of cable lags behind demand, and each of the sales employees could easily sell close to half the cable in stock. Steve prides himself on the relationships he has with each of his salespeople.

Both Melissa and Steve could approach the very human events and the dilemmas they find themselves in on a strictly *factual* level. For example, Steve could simply allocate 20 percent of the electrical cable stock to each salesperson or utilize an already established seniority system to resolve the competing interests among his salespeople. Sometimes life requires that we operate in such factual modes to conserve energy, to resolve pressures, and to obtain goals. Our lives would be chaotic if we didn't have some order, regularity, or direction about how we allot time or make commitments. Besides the factual, we also could engage these dilemmas on a *psychological* level. Melissa feels the need to take into consideration her relationship with her sister before deciding how to handle the next day's scheduling conflict. Several months before, she and her sister had a major argument that caused hurtful feelings among a number of family members. Now she feels that her relationship with her sister has improved significantly, and she wants to insure that no obstacles or misunderstandings interfere with the healing taking place between them. Obviously, both of these individuals would be wise to take into account their relationships with the various parties involved as well as any specific personal issues that could lead to misinterpretations of motives or unfair judgments. Not to consider psychological factors and what is prudently possible can lead to alienation, misunderstanding, and hurtful feelings.

Notwithstanding the importance of these two levels, I would propose that each of these individuals add another level to the analysis — *the unspoken desire for goodness.* This is not to say that moral considerations are not present in the previous two levels. At both the factual and the psychological levels moral issues surface. Obviously, Melissa can't just forget about her niece, and Steve has to consider "what is fair" when allocating electrical cable. A sense of what they believe is morally right or wrong is a central element in each of their deliberations as they try to resolve their dilemmas. My point is, however, that to *savor* the conscious experience of being moral beings they might engage this third level by introducing the question of goodness. In this way, they allow themselves to articulate what might well be the most troubling aspect of their dilemmas — the clash of various ideals they hold dear.

Melissa and Steve are dealing with idealization — being a good employee versus being a good sister and aunt; being a good manager versus being a good colleague. Both Melissa and Steve struggle with *competing* goods and wish to be the best they can be in each commitment. "What is the good thing to do in this situation?" or "What does it mean to be a good employee?" or "What does it mean to be a good sister and aunt?" Such questions will surface several important issues. First, they are likely to increase their self-awareness as moral beings. Second, they are given the opportunity for a fresh perspective. Just reflecting on the notion of goodness and how it applies to life's roles might broaden our understanding. From this reflection new insights can emerge. They might approach their dilemmas in a new way or with renewed zeal.

Reflecting on the good does not guarantee clarity about what course of action to take. Both Melissa and Steve might still experience confusion and distress even after reflecting on their ideals — articulating the good, searching for the greater good. They might still lack sufficient clarity. Even so, they engage their situations with a qualitative difference. They more *authentically* engage their dilemmas. Whatever decisions they make represent more fully what they know to be the most fundamental truth about themselves. It is within this framework of articulating the good that any of us can say, "My life is lived with integrity."

When idealization is operative, there is a shift in the reality at hand. In its first form (bad to good) it joins with other dimensions of conscience to change behaviors and attitudes. When idealization functions in its second form (good to better) the shift is more subtle, but just as critical. When conscience functions well, both forms of idealization are likely to operate simultaneously. Nonetheless, whether it is changing (bad to good) or improving (good to better), there remains a common endpoint. Both forms of idealization lead the self to live more authentically its moral vision.

Idealization and the Moral Imagination

Knowing how to act requires more than idealization. Other dimensions of conscience most surely come into play. Melissa and Steve each has a unique life history. Each has invested psychic energy in differing pursuits; each has a unique set of defenses. For each the trigger threshold for empathy and the intensity and type of guilt experienced is unique. The moral principles each holds as guidelines for behavior differs as the result of age, upbringing, and reasoning. External pressure, the situation itself, and individual personality styles (e.g., the ability to handle stress) play a part in how they resolve their dilemmas.

Melissa and Steve are struggling with *how* to be good people. Inherent in any idealizing is the presence of what some call the "moral imagination." Any time we seek a solution, look for an alternative, come up with another option, apply a creative idea, offer a novel response, explore more deeply a situation, or discover new insights grounded in the desire for goodness, we employ moral imagination. Moral imagination fuels our idealizations.[11] Recall that within the framework of moral health, to idealize is to aspire to a fuller realization of the good. It points to conscience's moral horizon. Inherent in this process of idealizing, then, is a future, something becoming, a product yet to take shape.

But to aspire to be better or to peer into the future that we desire requires creativity. It means perceiving experiences or events in new ways that allow for goodness to flourish. But such an endeavor can never be pursued alone. It requires that we elicit others' perspectives and in the process engage in conversations that generate fresh insights. "It is only imagination that allows us to speak to other members about the chasm that exists between the hopes and fair expectations of the community and the failures of our lived lives."[12] This is the role moral imagination takes on when we engage the idealizing dimension of conscience. It provides our idealizations a vitality and freshness that otherwise would be lacking and nurtures hope in a future that is workable and sustainable.[13] And when we think of the innumerable dilemmas and challenges we face as we struggle to be the people we desire to be, and then consider the serious national challenges we face as a pluralistic nation if we are to live in harmony in the midst of shrill and acrimonious debates, the need for imagination proves vital. Those who are immoral "need not worry about moral dilemmas. Those of us who aspire to something better will have to make some hard choices."[14] The idealization that is part of a healthy conscience ensures that such choices are firmly rooted in the good. These decisions guide us toward the moral horizon we desire. The educator Thomas Green offers a most compelling argument of imagination's power:

> It is an important paradox that if human beings had the power to know the future, such knowledge could only help them in rendering the forecasts false. It would aid us to avoid the malignant future and thus negate its coming or to hasten the happy future and thereby also render its forecast false. Thus, though the work of prophets, seers, and utopians is framed in the future tense, it is not knowledge of the future that we either seek or find in it. It is its transformation — the urging, the invitation to enter now into the realm of possibilities that so far exist only in the imagination and that being acted on will change the future.[15]

Return to the situations of Melissa and Steve. How might the moral imagination enhance each of their idealizations?

We Are Not What We Desire

If we randomly took twenty adults from any city in the United States, I bet you I could make statements to each of them that would be among the most hurtful things they have ever heard. Of course, a context would have to be provided, so let's create one. Let's suppose these twenty adults volunteer for a psychological experiment. To begin, each one completes a short questionnaire that requests some very basic information, for instance, marital status, family background, and work history.

After filling out the questionnaires they are led to a large room and asked to be seated. An associate of mine comes into the room shortly thereafter and announces, "Dr. Shelton, a licensed psychologist, will go over your questionnaires and speak privately with each of you. Please remain seated until your name is called. He will make some comments to each of you that are based on observations and facts he has gathered. Please listen carefully to what he has to say." My associate then leaves and after a wait of several minutes returns and calls out the name of the first person on the list. He leads the participant down the hall to a small room with two chairs. After the person sits down, the associate leaves, and a few moments later I enter. I close the door and sit directly across from the participant. In my possession I have only a clipboard containing the participant's completed questionnaire. Though I closed the door there is another door to the room that is left open with an exit sign above it. I introduce myself and, with as much seriousness as I can muster, proceed to say to Mike (as we'll call him):

"Mike, I have just a few things I need to say. First of all, based on my analysis it is my opinion that you are a lousy parent. I want to say further that you were a terrible son to your parents. You are for the most part an unreliable person, not to mention an awful friend. Quite frankly, as a spouse you pretty much have failed. At work, you are the weak link, and I seriously doubt most of your co-workers trust you as a colleague." I abruptly stop and simply stare at Mike.

Now suppose for a moment that you volunteered for the experiment and, having gone over your questionnaire, I make comments similar to these but appropriate for your particular situation. What would you feel? What would you think? How would you respond?

Before we go further, I can offer some consolation by saying that the experiment described above would never be carried out for a number of reasons. For one, it violates in numerous ways the discipline of psychology's ethical standards. My behavior would be considered so inappropriate that I could lose my license. Second, there might be legal repercussions. I as the experimenter could be sued for defamation of character or perhaps brought up on other legal charges. Finally, I had better have my insurance card handy because if Mike is a strong man, outraged (as he most certainly has the right to be) and impulsive, it is possible that he could physically assault me.

But let's say none of the above applies. Let's suppose the above really happened. I wagered that I could make statements to total strangers, people I had never met before, and the statements I made would hurt them about as deeply as anything ever said to them. Of course, the fact that I am a psychologist might give me some credibility as an expert, thus compounding my stinging comments. But even if we could somehow eliminate any influence that goes with being a psychologist, my sense is that these twenty people would be highly distressed. They might shout, cry, run away, withdraw, attack, or be in such shock that they are left emotionless and speechless. But I submit that with few or no exceptions, what underlies all these varied and highly personal responses is emotional hurt. If you interviewed them later and probed their reactions, what would emerge would probably be significant anger (recall that anger is frequently a symptom of some emotional hurt). Most, if not all, would say they were *hurt* by my statements.

Now suppose that I was not making these statements to them, but their own son or daughter, spouse, parent, sibling, colleague, or teammates were. How do you think each would then feel? Most likely, hearing these statements from someone to whom they were emotionally attached would increase their distress level enormously.

The Pain of Coming Up Short

What is most intriguing is not only the hurt but the degree of hurt that most individuals would feel. As the experimenter, I could trigger some level of hurt by my remarks, but this distress would be compounded and result in far greater harm if it were spoken by a family member, friend, or colleague.

Recall an event in your life when a family member, friend, or colleague made an accusation or comment that deeply hurt you. Concentrate on the incident: pay close attention to the location, what was said, and the tone of voice used. Now take a moment and explore your reaction. What did you feel? How did you respond? Now, let's go back to the question of why we feel deep hurt when important people in our lives make derogatory statements about us.

From a psychological perspective the answer is simple. We are emotionally attached to this parent, friend, spouse, son, daughter, brother, sister, colleague, or teammate. Or in place of or along with this emotional connection this person has some type of power over us (frequently this occurs with an authority figure such as a parent, older sibling, or boss). Regardless, there exists some type of relationship. Recall that emotions provide a portrait of our concerns. They point to what we find most meaningful. Emotions are powerful conveyers of information (through a tone of voice, a facial look) that significantly reinforce or undermine the words we vocalize.

However, from the perspective of moral health, what response can we give to the question: "Why do we feel such hurt?" The answer involves who we are as human beings. Let's start with the most basic question: "Who am I?" This question goes to the heart of our identity, our self-definition. But I can never respond adequately to such a question unless I discover what motivates me. What do I want? What do I hope for? What are my deepest desires? Unless I can respond honestly to these questions, my self-definition remains incomplete, my self-understanding remains a hollow outline containing little substance. When we add to our self-definition our wants, hopes, and desires, we lock into the power that idealization offers. In the moral context, to idealize is to experience the movement of our desires toward something — the longing for something better. Thus, we endorse the good, but we desire the greater good. "In order to have an identity, we need an orientation to the good, which means some sense of qualitative discrimination, of the incomparably higher."[16] Human beings, in other words, possess a sense of *quality* about their lives that reveals itself through the desire for something beyond what they are at any concrete moment in time.

The Longing for the Greater Good

Recall that we are addressing the original question "Why do we hurt?" within the context of our moral health. When we idealize we aspire to the greater good. And we must view "all these diverse aspirations as forms of craving, which is ineradicable from human life."[17]

Who we are is inseparable from what we desire — which is something *more* — what I term the *greater good*. From a moral perspective, it is inconceivable to define the meaning of what a person is without reference to this longing, which in its most acute moments, is an aching to achieve the "greater good." An example might be helpful. Most of us don't devote much time of thinking about how we are "good" friends. We just naturally interact with our friends and do things with and for them. Yet when we go out of our way or make a sacrifice for a friend, we exhibit idealization in action. When we help a friend (particularly when it calls for sacrifice), the good friend that we are is transformed into the better friend to which we aspire. Our lives are spent in routine and reaction, and we must develop ways to nourish the questioning, the reflecting, the probing of our experience to make us consciously aware of how we have grown. As we have said before, just as physical fitness requires exercise, a balanced diet, and adequate rest, in a similar vein, we must identify opportunities, consider their significance, and become *aware* of the shifts from being good to becoming better. When such moral growth occurs in our lives, we must savor and relish it!

Idealization and the Ordinary Life

One of the most significant shifts in the modern era is to the belief in the value of ordinary life. Over the past few centuries, great numbers of human beings have rid themselves of social castes and stereotypes that reflected specific ways to work and relate. Such a breakthrough does not mean, of course, that inequality in regards to income, prestige, or influence has disappeared. People's earning power, status, and authority vary considerably. But the attitude about what constitutes ordinary, everyday life has changed. Today, caring for family and providing for them and other loved ones through some type of socially productive labor constitutes the meaning of ordinary life.[18] Here we might revive Freud's thought that the healthy life consists of loving and working. In addition, the ordinary life, for many, expands beyond ties to family and work to incorporate the enjoyment of friends, leisurely pursuits (e.g., sports), and public commitments (volunteer work, political activity, civic duties).

The roles we take on in the everyday living of ordinary life are far more than mere social habits or perfunctory duties. The roles we live out and value are the means through which we actualize the ideals we cherish. They encapsulate the good and portray to others what is meaningful to us. These valued roles are our reference points that demonstrate how the good life is truly lived. The way we live these roles is utterly crucial to our moral health. Think of a time when you were very upset with yourself. Now if I ask you why you were upset, you might respond by describing an event and what you said, did, or did not do in the situation you describe. On the factual level you have recollected accurately. But you probably have not tapped into a deeper reason for your disgruntled state. You were probably upset because in the situation you remembered you failed to "live up to" being the "good" parent, spouse, friend, worker, brother, sister, teammate, colleague, teacher, team captain, supervisor, attorney, nurse, physician that you desired to be. Your actions did not measure up to the good you desired. *In other words, you viewed yourself as retreating from the moral horizon that provides meaning to your life.* You let slip away the opportunity for the good to become better, for the greater good to be realized. The guilt, dissatisfaction, or discontent we so often feel arises because we judge ourselves as having failed to live up to the good we desire.

From the perspective of moral health we can perceive "why" we hurt when someone's accusation or disparaging comment is directed at us. We *hurt* because to say, "you are a lousy parent," or "you are a terrible friend," or "you are a failure as the team captain" strikes directly at our meaning-making capacity. When such an accusation is leveled at us, the very core sense of who we are becomes, at least momentarily, unraveled. The moral horizon recedes. We are vulnerable not only because the statement is made by someone we are emotionally attached to or by someone who has authority over us. More significantly we are wounded because our moral center, specifically its idealizing dimension, has lost its way.

Our Life Project

In American culture most adults have a set of meaning-making roles that express their desire for goodness. The various roles, our investment in them, and the priority each is given constitute for every adult a uniquely fashioned framework that embodies his or her life project. Or, to say this another way, our life project is the investment of our lives in a set of cherished roles that constitute for each of us a uniquely ordinary life. The notion of a life project expands consciousness by requiring each person to consider not only "Who am I?" but also "What provides my life with meaning and purpose?" The prioritizing of, investing in, and assigning significance to each role identify the project's uniqueness because it is one only "I" could author. Each treasured role in our life project contains its own idealization and so provides us with an opportunity to make the transformation from being good to being better.

The life project we each author through our various life roles sustains our sense of moral worth. For example, a friend recently called me to cancel a dinner invitation. Not having seen each other in over two months, we were planning to go out and get a pizza and "catch up" on what was going on in our lives. The day we were scheduled to go out Bill called and with regrets said he had to postpone the engagement because he needed to be available for his daughter, who was having "some problems." We rescheduled for the next weekend. In this instance, Bill was pursuing his life project and nourishing his moral goodness. His statement to me indicated how fundamental being a parent was to who he was as a moral person. The way Bill responded to his child promoted a good that was absolutely central for his life as a moral being.

In modern American society our life projects, though unique to each of us, are grounded in and selected from a large but common grouping. That is, the roles of being a friend, spouse, parent, son or daughter, co-worker, or colleague are brought together to make up the central elements of our life project. But along with this basic core, numerous other roles emerge that, for some, are the focal points for intense idealizations. A parent, for example, who devotes time to organizing neighborhood projects or to planning a summer little league schedule also taps into idealization. A research scientist who limits his friendships or forgoes marriage in order to devote his life to discovery and truth-finding comes immediately to mind. A public servant who sacrifices a hobby and leisure time to serve the common good offers still another example. As our society becomes more diverse and opportunities to find personal fulfillment expand, the number of roles available for finding meaning increases.

The Problem of Distorted Ideals

Inherent in the life project we create is the tremendous idealizing power it offers. Yet, all life projects are not equal, nor should society endorse all of them with the same enthusiasm. Furthermore, some life projects must not be permitted. What I am speaking about is what I term the "distorted ideal."

The ideals that we treasure and that are lived out in the roles we value do not necessarily promote the good. Culture influences the roles and life projects we embrace, and the cultures in which some roles are rooted actively oppose the good. The most glaring example of this distortion is Nazi culture.[19] We could maintain that a member of the Nazi party was engaged in a life project that provided purpose and meaning. Moreover, his idealization was intense and deeply rooted. Though his conscience was erroneous, he followed it and believed himself to be a "good" citizen. Yet no reasonable person, and most certainly no person of good conscience, would accede to the idea that inciting hatred or participating in genocide was a "good" form of idealization. Idealizations themselves can be distorted and at times grossly so. Like every other dimension of conscience, idealization too can go awry. Just as defenses can be either healthy or unhealthy, so too can idealizations either embrace the good or succumb irrevocably to corruption.

Because idealizations are so tied to culture, their distorting power is vast. A gang member kills to fulfill the "ideal" of be-

Reprinted by permission of Newspaper Enterprise Association, Inc.

The distorted ideal comes in many forms!

ing a good gang member. A corporate executive subtly uses his power to curtail the hiring and promotion of minorities. A perfectionist forms idealizations that wreak havoc on her marriage and co-workers. Yet in all the instances just cited, none of these individuals experience conscience as a burden. The perfectionist comes closest to having what we might term a troubled conscience, but in all likelihood she attributes her shortcomings to personal flaws rather than viewing critically her irritating behaviors.

The corrupting power of distorted ideals goes a long way in explaining why we can have a "racist" or "sexist" conscience. Idealizations can evoke such blinding and intense allegiances that they warp conscience and thereby make it impervious to reason or the emotional pleas of those in need. From idealizations can originate the holiest saint or the worst criminal. When distorted idealizations corrupt the life project of someone wielding great power or influence, then the possibility for evil grows immensely. Adolf Hitler, Pol Pot, Mao Tse-tung, and Joseph Stalin are some of the more horrid figures who aptly fit this description. But gang leaders, corporate executives, elected officials, sports figures, or well-known Hollywood personalities, as a result of their well-publicized behavior, can also weaken the moral climate of society. Frequently, this moral diminishment takes the form of a subtle corrupting influence on people's overall attitudes and behavior. Tragically, these individuals all have their life projects. All of them might view themselves as "good." They might sincerely believe they are striving for the greater good, and they might enjoy some significant degree of personal fulfillment or conclude that they live lives of authenticity. But for any person of good conscience the only possible conclusion to be reached is that something is horribly wrong.

Conscience and Our Ideals

The problem centers on the standards used to measure our life projects and the idealizations that fuel them. Typically, understandings of conscience have focused on the sanctity of individualized forms of expression regarding what is right. Conscience is so precious to us and so genuinely portrays who we are, that we do not compel people to violate their conscience if they sincerely believe it demands a certain course of action (society, of course, can limit people's actions for the sake of the common good).

I have no difficulty with upholding the sanctity of conscience. What I do take issue with is the highly individualized perspective we give it. Such thinking is unidimensional. This viewpoint too often depicts a person of conscience as standing alone against a group. When we think of conscience, typically what comes to mind is this isolated individual. There is truth to this perspective, and over the centuries individuals and even groups of people (martyrs, for example) have given their lives for the sake of the good. The life projects they lived out and the idealizations they aspired to demanded they offer this ultimate witness.

However, an unintended consequence of this understanding is that it creates an individualized sense of conscience. It gives the message of "me versus them." If the person's intentions are noble, we might have a saint, but if the person's idealization is deeply distorted, then a fanatic, a narcissist, or a person of a true ill-will might surface — all in the name of following one's conscience.

Only when we conceive of conscience as possessing numerous dimensions can we hope to prevent its becoming overly individualized or distorted. Conscience is the guide for our life projects. It directs our idealizations to aspire to what is noble and good. *Only a multidimensional focus for conscience can insure such direction.* Recall that the dimensions interact among themselves. In terms of idealization, healthy defenses foster an open-minded perspective that directs our idealizations toward noble aspirations. In a similar vein, empathy steers our idealizations toward a compassionate rendering of our desires and sensitizes our life projects in ways that foster care. Moral guilt, realistic self-esteem, and the proper investment of psychic energy each contributes to idealizations that continuously strive for the greater good. In other words, only a multidimensional approach to the functioning of conscience allows our idealizations to thrive and our life project to flourish. At the same time, this approach to conscience helps to limit any distorting tendencies that might arise. When conscience functions as depicted above, the necessary safeguards are usually in place.

A CHECKLIST FOR YOUR IDEALS

1. List the cherished roles in your life. Which ones receive the highest priorities? What do these priorities say about you as a person of good conscience?

2. How would you describe your life project? What dreams, desires, and hopes does your life project convey? What significant relationships in your life help you to sustain this project?

3. What kind of person do you hope to be in ten years?

4. What other dimensions of conscience most contribute to keeping your life project on course?

5. Make a list of your desires. Now make a list of your *deepest* desires. Finally, what few desires lie closest to your heart? In light of these aspirations, how do you define the good and how does your life project foster this good?

{ Dimension Six }

SELF-ESTEEM

As we have already seen, throughout the seventies and early eighties, guilt was generally viewed as an unhealthy emotion. An interesting question emerges: If guilt was the villain, who was the hero? It seems that role fell to self-esteem. Few words captured the fancy and received such uncritical approval both in academic circles and the popular press as "self-esteem." Educators, counselors, administrators, and parents began to view low self-esteem as one of the root causes of numerous misdeeds and social problems. When we read the popular press during this period, we can't help but be fascinated with how willingly the educational and mental health fields, not to mention the media and the general public, jumped on this bandwagon. At the time (the late seventies) I was a high school teacher, and when an adolescent's rule-breaking or problem behavior prompted discussion among the faculty, it was only a matter of time before the buzz phrase "low self-esteem" surfaced. In the popular press of those years, "low self-esteem" at one time or another was associated with school discipline problems, academic failure, depression, juvenile delinquency, violence, anxiety, drug abuse, child abuse, spouse abuse, teenage pregnancy, welfare, discrimination, and poverty.

But these issues are complex. Does low self-esteem cause these problems? Do the problems cause low self-esteem? Is there some other factor that causes them both? Frequently low self-esteem is only one of several factors that shed light on a social or behavioral problem, but the exact influence it exerts on behavior or a social problem remains in many cases an open question. Yet even though there were many questions regarding the role of self-esteem, the seventies and eighties saw widespread support develop for this concept.

Why was self-esteem viewed so positively and accepted so uncritically during that period? For one reason, positive self-esteem had a certain appeal if not charm. Who doesn't want high self-esteem? Who can be against having it? Second everyone has problems with self-esteem at one time or another; thus advocating self-esteem touched a sensitivity in each of us. Promoting self-esteem soothed any inadequacy we found troubling. If we can help build someone else's self-esteem for the moment, then it might take the sting out of some personal deficiency we ourselves are trying to cope with or work through. Third, as we noted above, low self-esteem is associated with many personal and social issues. Some depressed people suffer from low self-esteem. Many people living in poverty, likewise, feel a lack of personal worth. Thus there is some merit in the position that many individuals' problems are related in some way to poor self-esteem. But as we have seen, that relationship is often difficult to untangle. Fourth, in popular consciousness self-esteem was associated with positive feelings and personal fulfillment. Since finding authenticity through personal self-fulfillment is a goal most people find desirable, self-esteem becomes a natural ally in the quest to achieve an authentic self. Finally, given the lingering shame-based feelings many baby boomer parents grappled with as a result of their own childhood during the late forties to mid-sixties, promoting self-esteem served as an ideal method for correcting in part a parenting style many found hurtful.

Self-esteem's universal appeal has provided it remarkable staying power in the public mind. Nowhere is this more evident than in education. "By the mid-1990s, thirty states had enacted more than 170 statutes promoting self-esteem."[1] Enhancing children's self-esteem has become the goal of numerous curriculum programs and teacher workshops. The state of California even set up a task-force on self-esteem, which in turn recommended that every school district in the state have the goal of promoting self-esteem among students.[2] Teachers are encouraged from kindergarten onward to create a learning environment that builds self-esteem in their students. This is usually accomplished by praising the children or complimenting them on almost every behavior that appears positive, even the most ordinary. Some critics of the self-esteem movement correctly observe that excessive praise of student behavior eventually makes all forms of praise trivial.

A second approach taken by the self-esteem movement is to refrain from criticizing the child. Or if it must be done, to do so minimally. Within this mind-set, self-esteem is associated with compliments, commendations, and praise. This positive thrust deemphasizes criticism and correction with the hope of preventing student discouragement. Critics contend that the push for self-esteem inevitably leads to watered-down versions of subject content and grade inflation.[3] I encountered a stark example of such thinking several years ago. A friend shared with me his frustration over the fact that his nephew's spelling was not corrected by his teacher. When my friend's brother inquired about his son's writing skills, he was told by the teacher that correcting the spelling might hurt his self-esteem!

In an American Psychological Association publication an article appeared entitled: "Is Self-Esteem Really All That Important?"[4] Given the mind-set of the preceding few decades, I doubt that such an article could have been written prior to the mid-nineties. I note this article because it not only provides a short summary of the disputes among psychologists surrounding the issue of self-esteem, but it also shows a rethinking among some researchers about the wisdom of viewing self-esteem as "the" cause of behavioral and social problems. It appears that as guilt has emerged in public and scholarly consciousness as a vital attribute for human living, self-esteem — in the thought of some scholars and clinicians — has begun to recede from its vaunted position. Many psychologists now view self-esteem more critically and acknowledge how complex its relationship is with the numerous problems to which it was previously linked.

A Realistic Sense of Self-Esteem

Research indicates that differences exist between individuals with high and low self-esteem.[5] However, one finding stands out among all others. Increasingly, the evidence seems to suggest that individuals who possess high self-esteem, defined as "a favorable global evaluation of oneself") are more prone to be violent and aggressive and to commit crimes than people with low self-esteem. Of course, this does not mean that all people with high self-esteem are prone to violence. But when we look at specific categories such as rape, domestic abuse, juvenile delinquency, murder, assault, and homicide and examine the culprits, the evidence is clear. From the schoolyard bully to the terrorist, there exists little evidence they suffer from low self-esteem. Most likely, these aggressors have a distorted view of themselves, that is, they have high self-esteem but their self-appraisal is an unrealistic one. They inflate their sense of self and maintain an overly favorable self-impression rather than accurately evaluating themselves and the true facts about their situation. When events, situations, or individuals are perceived as threatening their false sense of superiority, they are prone to respond angrily, and at times violently.[6] If low self-esteem were the cause of violence, then those who abuse, rape, murder, and torture others could work with their therapists to increase self-esteem. Would any therapist endorse such a therapy for these individuals? If anything, violent-prone individuals need to alter their self-evaluations so that they can experience humility, modesty, empathy, and guilt. For those struggling with low self-esteem, such outcomes are rarely the focus of therapy.[7]

A key element in this discussion is realism or, more accurately, the lack of realism among those who commit violence. These individuals have inflated self-evaluations and falsely view themselves as superior to others. From a more clinical perspective, these people are frequently observed to have narcissistic traits — a sense of entitlement, indifference toward others, and preoccupation with their personal well-being.

Like many other critics, I view a lack of realism as a major difficulty in the self-esteem movement's thinking.[8] Endless praising and flattery of children or adults make no sense. Such compliments trivialize the true purpose for commending others. We offer praise or acclaim typically when an individual accomplishes something worthwhile. In other words, it is effort, achievement, and accomplishment that merit others' acknowledgment and kudos. Indiscriminately applauding someone's actions might actually encourage an unrealistic view of life. It sends the message that effort and achievement are secondary "to feeling good." For some people, this message can develop into a sense of being entitled to rewards and acknowledgment without exerting the necessary labor and effort. Most of us have had the unfortunate experience of knowing someone whose sense of self includes a feeling of being "privileged." Such individuals expect to be rewarded even though the effort they put forth is minimal at best.

Coping with Failures

Self-esteem must be associated with more than positive feelings. To overemphasize the positive and ignore the failures, disappointments, heartaches, and disillusionments that are part of everyday life promotes a lack of realism that over the long run undercuts maturity and emotional health. Children, of course, need encouragement and praise. They need to feel positive about themselves and encouraged in their efforts to achieve. But children must also learn to *master* negative feelings that arise from disappointment and failure. A sure way to foster low self-esteem in children is to allow them to enter young adulthood without the necessary coping skills for successfully negotiating situations of failure and disappointment.

As a college professor I work with students entering their young adult years. I am always struck by the various ways these young people cope with personal failures and disappointments. For example, somewhere along the line during their undergraduate years, most students receive an unfavorable mark on a test, paper, lab project, or final exam that they find disappointing. The common and reasonable response is to make an appointment with the instructor to talk about the grade. Students' reactions are wide-ranging. Some are calm, open-minded, reasonable, curious, and pleasant. More often than not these students genuinely want to learn, to find out where they made mistakes, and to use their disappointment as a motivating force for future improvement. I also have had students who are argumentative, hysterical, cynical, or irresponsible. These students frequently exhibited one or more of the following: (1) they refused to believe they could do so poorly; (2) they thought it was my fault that they received their low mark; (3) they were outraged and perceived me as not liking them; and/or (4) they didn't understand the need to put significant effort into their work.

By no means am I suggesting that most college undergraduates fit this negative description. But some do. And from talking with faculty colleagues from other universities I have the impression that this group's number is increasing. I frequently wonder about this group of students and why they respond so negatively. It appears they cannot accept responsibility for their poor performance. These students are, I believe, the product of a an educational system that fostered in them a distorted sense of self-esteem. Their view of life and themselves is simply unrealistic. I sense most of these students have never been taught adequate ways to cope with the pains, hurts, and letdowns that are part of everyday life.

Respecting the Person

In addition to a realistic sense of oneself, self-esteem involves an appraisal of a *person*. Because the person is the focus of inquiry, he or she must be given *respect*. Advances in ethical thought over the past several centuries have increasingly recognized the principle that human beings are worthy of respect. Even with technological advances that threaten humankind's existence (e.g., weapons of unthinkable power and destruction such as nuclear bombs), there has gradually and persistently emerged a growing respect for the human person. Being a person is accorded a dignity and status today that was inconceivable several centuries past.

Showing respect for others does not mean that we must agree

with them or that all opinions are equally valid or that we must go along with whatever they choose to do. Nonetheless, what has grown increasingly apparent in ethical writing from the eighteenth century onward is a growing consensus that each human being deserves respect. Outside of despotic or corrupt regimes, punishment is guided by laws that strive to be fair and that impose limits on government power. The number of governments adhering to the democratic process has advanced remarkably in recent decades, and unjust and cruel punishments so commonly carried out only a century ago have declined. In addition, the subject of human rights enjoys greater emphasis in ethical writing and scholarly debate. "The impact of the idea is undeniable. Human rights ideals have been accepted by people around the globe, whether they are students seeking democratic reform in China or women demanding equal protection under law in Pakistan."[9] Though we do not live in a perfect world by any means, few would deny the advances in respecting people's right to believe and follow their consciences during the last century. Noting the respect our modern era gives to individuals, Charles Taylor writes:

> The moral world of moderns is significantly different from that of previous civilizations. This becomes clear, among other places, when we look at the sense that human beings command our respect. In one form or another, this seems to be a human universal; that is, in every society, there seems to be some such sense. The boundary around those beings worthy of respect may be drawn parochially in earlier cultures, but there always is such a class. And among what we recognize as higher civilizations, this always includes the whole human species.[10]

Building on this insight, Taylor notes that "respect" in the modern era has acquired certain attributes that include prizing freedom, acquiring some sense of control, seeking to curtail suffering, and cherishing one's productivity and family life.[11]

For self-esteem to hold any relevance for moral health, I believe it must be based on both realism and respect. Self-esteem includes the acknowledgment (1) that I am a person, (2) that as a person I realistically and responsibly appraise my unique combination of talents and limitations, and (3) that I possess as a person a basic respect that I in turn offer to others.

Emphasis has been directed more on "how we feel" than on "what we do." From the perspective of moral health, an imbalance arises when we emphasize internal states (feelings) at the expense of observed behaviors (moral actions). If Sarah has "high self-esteem," we presume she feels good about herself. We also assume that Sarah's positive self-image will lead her to be caring and respectful of others. But note the emphasis. The focus is Sarah's internal feelings, which are *prior* to her moral behavior (how she treats others).

There are two false assumptions present in this line of reasoning. First, as we have already noted, it is high-rather than low self-esteem individuals who are likely to act cruelly toward others. But more importantly for this discussion, it is the dominance of a *psychological* viewpoint that creates the second erroneous assumption. An imbalance in the self-esteem debate has occurred that shifts the focus from external behavior to internal feelings. Feeling positively about oneself is a worthy goal, but in issues of morality, our behavior needs equal emphasis. In other words, feelings need to sustain right action. Only when we define self-esteem within the boundaries of respect and realism are we capable of eliminating its faddish excesses.

Self-Esteem and Conscience

When we possess positive self-esteem we approach the world with a hopeful, yet realistic, stance. We believe in our basic worth as human beings, and this allows us to experience self-approval and realistic appreciation for who we are and what we do. Assuming responsibility for our actions allows us to expand our self-knowledge because we admit our mistakes, shortcomings, and failures. Every time we acknowledge a mistake, we realize something about ourselves. Those who fail to take responsibility for their actions avoid this opportunity to learn. Responsibility joins with realistic self-appraisal to create a healthy humility. Positive self-esteem connects us to the wider human family because it reminds us that all men and women possess dignity and deserve respect. Positive self-esteem functions productively with conscience's other dimensions. Optimally, psychic energy is channeled into constructive tasks whose accomplishments provide self-worth. Responsibility encourages the use of healthy defenses just as recognizing the respect we owe others encourages an open, empathic stance. Responsibility and realistic self-appraisal support moral guilt reactions when appropriate. When we live with a sense of dignity, our focus turns to the ideals we cherish. Finally, respect for who we are supports the moral beliefs we uphold.

Feeling Needy

Frequently as I give workshops to educators and professional care-givers, the question of self-esteem arises. In these situations I am usually standing at a podium while participants in the audience are seated. I begin with a question such as: "Will all the people who have low self-esteem please stand up?" As the reader might expect, no one in the audience jumps up, and after asking this question, I rush to the nearest empty seat. With no one now standing the audience breaks into laughter. My point is made.

Generally speaking, we might even have what is considered "high" self-esteem, but when we narrow our focus and examine our lives there are several areas where we feel unsure about ourselves. The inadequacy we feel might come from any of several sources. Perhaps we believe we are unfit to accomplish a task or fulfill a goal. Maybe we draw upon past failures and doubt our ability to perform adequately. Most of us worry about some personal attribute we find distressing. Perhaps it is the way we look or the way we speak or the way we present ourselves to others. Even with a fairly positive level of self-esteem, we might struggle with the fear of rejection or exclusion. Do any of these statements have a ring of truth for you?

At some point everyone has been rejected, disappointed, hurt, disillusioned, or has not measured up to some standard (whether it is set by one's family, in a relationship, in the classroom, or on the job). And no one has always had all of his or her expectations met. When we consider the negative events of our lives and our tendency to remember or dwell on the negative, we can only conclude that it is impossible not to feel inadequate on some occasions about our self-image.[12] When such situations occur, we find ourselves feeling deprived. We feel a deficit within ourselves. Something seems missing from our lives. Given this reality we all experience periodically, along with the intensity with which it may be felt, feeling needy is a crucial fact we need to consider when exploring how conscience functions. Even if we have relatively high self-esteem, we are vulnerable at times to such neediness.

From the standpoint of moral health, we can frame this concern through a question: *What do you do when you are needy?* Frequently, a needy state makes us prone to ignore or overlook the moral beliefs we cherish. We seek ways to alleviate our needy state, such as misbehaving or acting immorally. When we are needy we are *not* the people we desire to be, and all too frequently we compromise the very standards we set for ourselves.

A Checklist for Self-Esteem

1. What situations, thinking, or actions help you to sustain the positive self-esteem this chapter describes?

2. As you examine your life, how do the twin themes of realism and responsibility relate to your viewpoints and behaviors?

3. Being as realistic as possible, make a list of your talents. Make a list of your limitations or shortcomings.

4. What situations, personal thoughts, or relationships are most apt to make you feel "needy?"

5. When you find yourself in a needy state, how do you behave? What thoughts do you dwell on?

6. How does your needy state prevent you from being the person you desire to be?

7. Can you think of times when your needy state overrode your conscience? Which dimensions of conscience were most weakened by your neediness?

{ Dimension Seven }

MORAL BELIEFS

It is hard to find an example that better illustrates the tensions in American society than the recurring debate over what to teach our children. Yet even though intense debates erupt over the content to be taught, the specific programs to be adopted, and methods of instruction to be used, there is an increasing consensus among the American public and educators that some common ground on morality is necessary if American society is to carry on an intelligible and constructive discourse about the quality of life future generations will inherit.

Few events have more galvanized the public's interest in moral education than the recent rash of school murders. During the last decade we saw the painful reality of child killing child and student murdering student. In the 1950s there were no multiple murders of school-age children at schools, yet in the final decade of the twentieth century Americans on several occasions awakened to TV news that grimly announced that yet another young persons's life had been lost at the hands of another student. The offenders were almost always boys or adolescent males. How do we account for such events? Psychologist Martin Seligman writes:

> The outer world of boys has, of course, changed, but their inner world has changed as well — in an astonishing and dismaying way. The outer changes are better known, but they bear repeating: easy access to guns, contagion fostered by the media and the waning of parental supervision.[1]

Seligman devotes his attention to this "inner world" of youth. As already noted, individuals who commit violence often possess high rather than low self-esteem. Some young people mistakenly believe themselves to have more talent and ability than is actually the case. Moreover, says Seligman, American society is awash in victimhood. A young male who believes himself superior but views himself as a victim possesses a highly volatile and potentially explosive inner world. Media portrayals add to this explosiveness. Further, American children view several hours of television every day, exposing themselves to the depiction of thousands of acts of violence each year. According to Seligman, this daily witnessing of violence becomes so ordinary that inhibitions for some youth begin to wane. Feeling aggrieved in their victimhood, these young males start to fantasize about getting even or seeking revenge. This sad and frightening chain of events, when taken together, adds up to "a recipe for violence."

Seligman rightly notes that we must alter the inner world of these impressionable and misguided youth:

> What I believe needs changing is the way kids think about their troubles. Baseless self-esteem is easily shattered by the usual setbacks of growing up; when, in a boy with a mean streak, it combines with blaming parents, peers and the school — blaming anyone but himself — it can become violent. We need to teach our children warranted self-esteem and realistic optimism — based on the skills of doing well in the world, on doing well with others and on personal responsibility.[2]

When we read the above closely, we discern the basis for some distinctive moral beliefs. Among these are (1) belief in a basic respect for self and others, (2) belief in taking responsibility for one's actions, (3) belief in acting honestly and competently in one's personal endeavors.

Moral Beliefs in American Culture

The American political landscape is characterized by an emphasis on rights and personal freedoms. Sad to say, in these early years of the twenty-first century, many Americans interpret this belief to mean the right to pursue not only their own interests, but even their own *selfish* interests. The interests we choose to pursue can be based on any number of perspectives: philosophical or religious grounds, cultural popularity, emotional ties, or simply a highly prized and privatized form of personal preference. The reasons behind our choices cover an almost endless spectrum, but common to them all is the quest for the authentic self. To be authentic requires that we achieve our destiny and follow our personal version of the truth wherever it might lead:

> Being true to myself means being true to my own originality, and that is something only I can articulate and discover. In articulating it, I am also defining myself. I am realizing a potentiality that is properly my own. This is the background understanding to the modern ideal of authenticity, and to the goals of self-fulfilment or self-realization in which it is usually couched. This is the background that gives moral force to the culture of authenticity, including its most degraded, absurd, or trivialized forms. It is what gives sense to the idea of "doing your own thing" or "finding your own fulfilment."[3]

Being truly authentic requires that we embrace what is most unique about our humanity. And what satisfies most clearly that claim is that "I have a conscience."

In the seven-dimensional system I propose, conscience acts as a moral guide for making decisions that attain the good. Decisions of conscience ground us in the good, encourage us to be good, and guide us to embrace the good more fully. When the seven dimensions of conscience work properly in an individual's life, that person's life story has a simple yet eloquent conclusion: *a life became better.* This by no means says that that person led a perfect life or had no moral setbacks. But in the end, that person's conscience was able to sight and strive toward the moral horizon.

To say we are drawn to the good does not mean there is a singular good with which everyone concurs. Nonetheless, in the seven-dimensional framework proposed, there is not an equality of goods. A healthy conscience rules out some behaviors as wrong or immoral. People of good will can reason differently and argue, debate, and disagree over issues and behaviors. Our pluralistic culture insures that such disagreements will continue. The "good," however, is not simply some vague, meaningless word. On the contrary, the very discussion of the seven dimensions of conscience leads to some generally accepted standards. In the case of empathy, for example, compassion is essential, and thus moral beliefs must reflect compassion.

In Western culture, particularly in moral and ethical theory, the power of rationality has a long and enduring tradition. In fact, as we have already seen, conscience was for a long time viewed from a narrow cognitive perspective, and emotion received little consideration. Without the rational life living itself becomes almost unbearable. Through rationality, meaning, significance, and choice can take on a persuasive if not compelling sway. As Sidney Callahan says so well:

> Even if persons claim to dedicate themselves to irrationality and propose to decide issues by spontaneous, random whim, they must, in their rebellion, recognize the ground of order and rational purpose against which they protest. Only the most sophisticated, decadent, or despairing human beings can truly pledge themselves to irrationality — and even they find it almost impossible to be consistent.[4]

Without a rational perspective, the moral life is reduced to sentimental choosing. Indeed, this is a problem for an increasing number of people. These individuals give too little time to reflecting on *why* their choices were made. For some, the moral life becomes simply making a choice of convenience or opting for a personal preference because the opportunity is there. In such situations there seems to be little forethought or critical thinking, and conscience itself is left rudderless. Without well-reasoned moral decisions, there is little hope for psychic energy to be invested wisely or self-esteem to be realistic.

Whose Good? Whose Moral Beliefs?

If moral beliefs are integral to a well-functioning conscience, then we must move from the general discussion of the "idea" of moral beliefs and attempt to specify a set of moral beliefs that guide conscience. But to make this move is to invite intense debate. Reasonable people agree that "we must do good and avoid evil." Fair enough. Clearly, the question begged is "whose good?" for as we all know, one person's good is another person's evil. Abortion rights and homosexuality are just two areas where the moral discussion is shrill and intense.

The pluralistic nature of American society makes forging a moral belief system we can all agree on an imposing, if not impossible, task. Or is it?

If we do not have a common moral grounding, youth today will opt increasingly for a privatized morality that threatens the fabric of community. Without some common moral assumptions accepted by all, debates about proper social behavior will intensify, and conflict over "my rights" will become more heated.

As a result of these concerns, "character education" movements have been launched in numerous school districts throughout the nation to stem this tide of moral confusion and ambiguity. Character education seeks to instill virtues in youth and require responsible behavior by children and adolescents. Virtues are essentially good habits, which means that they are not just taught, but practiced in the classroom, the cafeteria, on the playground, and at home.[5] Leading proponents of this movement include psychologist and educator Thomas Lickona, who has lectured throughout the country on the role of character education. Perhaps the most prominent spokesperson is author William Bennett, whose bestselling book *The Book of Virtues* generated interest in the role of virtues in helping to raise moral children.

The concern about the lack of moral direction among youth was a stimulus for a meeting in Colorado in 1992 that produced what has become known as the "Aspen Declaration." This document argued that character consists of six core virtues that all young people should model in their everyday lives: (1) trustworthiness, (2) respect, (3) responsibility, (4) fairness, (5) caring, and (6) citizenship. As these elements are spelled out, they lead to more specific behaviors such as exercising the right to vote, showing compassion, being honest, acquiring self-discipline, etc.[6]

Moreover, Harvard psychologist Jerome Kagan has spoken of the school's "moral function" to influence youth's behavior and argues that schools should promote "kindness, restraint on aggression, honesty, and a reasonable blend of pride and humility."[7] Sociologist Gerald Grant has framed the question in terms of a school's character. The value neutrality that for so long characterized the American public school system has yielded no common understanding of what it means to be a responsible member of society. He argues that schools must recommit themselves to positive behaviors that enable a democracy to thrive. For Grant, these include: "the minimal order required for dialogue, the willingness to listen to one another, respect for truth, the rejection of racism (or openness to participation in the dialogue), as well as those transcendent values that shore up the whole society — a sense of altruism and service to others and respect for personal effort and hard work."[8]

But education is not the only area where the search for a common morality has surfaced. Indeed, before the character education movement received attention, American companies were busy writing ethical codes. Rushworth Kidder describes a variety of ethical codes that point to a set of "core values." Frequently, corporations' ethical codes emphasize similar values such as fairness and honesty. Kidder cites evidence showing trends such as more and more United States companies are adopting ethical codes, more CEOs are speaking out on issues related to business ethics, and a growing emphasis on training employees in ethical analysis of issues.[9] No doubt ethics training on the job has, if anything, increased as a result of the legal issues surrounding sexual harassment and discrimination and the ambiguities many workers feel about what behavior is appropriate in a work setting. Recent rulings by courts have galvanized companies to be proactive. By issuing guidelines and promoting in-service training to familiarize workers, corporations are increasingly taking the initiative in hopes of heading off misunderstandings, complaints, and lawsuits before they occur.[10]

Social scientist James Q. Wilson argues that there indeed does exist an innate moral sense that is fueled by four sentiments he labels as sympathy, fairness, self-control, and duty.[11] Kidder's study of this issue leads him to conclude that, despite cultural differences, human beings share a common interest in certain core values: love, truth, tolerance, responsibility, fairness.[12] Whereas two decades ago scholars would insist that cultural differences made a common morality impossible, today there are respected writers and academics who are sympathetic to this position. Given the role of conscience and the priority it is assigned, at least in Western culture, and the more universal notion of a moral sense, it could be argued that there is a common morality. But the exact form it takes varies according to cultural influences. Jerome Kagan observes that "although the surface virtues children develop will be relative to the cultural demands they encounter, we can count on the appearance of empathy and an appreciation of right and wrong in all children before the third birthday."[13]

The need to establish some guidelines for behavior and to evaluate their ongoing moral adequacy requires people everywhere to render judgments of right vs. wrong, good vs. bad, and moral vs. immoral. Given the diverse and pluralistic makeup of American culture, the ability of conscience to function smoothly will be enhanced considerably if some consensus could be reached regarding an acceptable set of moral beliefs. Universal agreement will never be totally possible, for some Americans will accept no constraint on their privatized moral worlds. Nonetheless, traditionally understood fundamental moral beliefs such as honesty, fairness, caring of others, and participating in the democratic process are eminently worthwhile moral beliefs upon which most Americans can find common ground. Such a set of moral beliefs provides conscience a basis upon which intelligible and critical analyses of moral dilemmas and conflicts can be carried out.

Maintaining Our Moral Beliefs

During a recent holiday season the movie *A Simple Plan* opened to enthusiastic reviews. Set in the bleak Minnesota winter, it tells the story of three ordinary men who, when walking in the woods on a cold wintery day, stumble upon an abandoned plane and the four million dollars it contains. The find is everyone's dream: instant riches. The old adage that money does not guarantee happiness, however, prevails. The initial joy and anticipation among the three instant millionaires shatter as greed, suspicion, and betrayal take hold. Their moral universe not only collapses but degenerates into violence and mayhem.

On at least two different occasions in the film, a character finds out about the money and the possibility of instant wealth. For both these characters the initial response is that to keep the money is "stealing," but in both instances this moral belief falls quickly by the wayside as the lure of wealth becomes intoxicating and obsessive. Four million dollars, of course, is a huge sum. Furthermore, the money was discovered in a remote area, and there was no person in or around the plane who asserted, "It belongs to me." In these circumstances, the moral belief that "stealing is wrong" evaporated so effortlessly that it raises a critical question: *What enables us to maintain our moral beliefs?* How do we sustain moral beliefs as an integral dimension of conscience in the midst of what are at times tremendous pressures? What keeps us from simply abandoning our moral beliefs at the earliest possible convenience and altering our moral courses?

We have all felt the anguish of not following the choice to which our conscience beckoned us. We have all minimized some moral belief, which then turned feeble or, for that matter, might as well not even have existed at all. How do we preserve our moral principles and keep them as moral reference points and guiding lights for our actions?

Loving Our Moral Ideas

We must make deep commitments of affection to our moral beliefs. With the advent of adolescence, young people for the first time form the capacity to fall in love with their own ideas. During high school or college or at any time in your teens or early twenties did you become absorbed in some cause? Or find some idea or principle so compelling that you lost interest in other pursuits and poured your energies into this idea you treasured so highly? Before the early teen years, young people are unable to make such passionate commitment to their beliefs. This is one reason why abstract ideas, belief systems, and ideologies become persuasive to a person only with the dawn of adolescence.

The ethical codes we have studied, absorbed, tested, and altered serve to guide conscience. If the moral ideas that direct conscience are to be compelling, they must not only be part of conscience; they must be truly cherished, treasured, and relished. We cannot simply *have* moral ideas; we must *love* such ideas. Mother Teresa and Martin Luther King (or any other moral hero) not only had moral beliefs, but were also *in love* with them. Justice and mercy were not intellectual abstractions for them. They were valued friends to be embraced. Likewise, unless our moral beliefs become valued friends who are truly loved, we run the risk of weakening an essential component of conscience.

Psychologists use the term "hot cognition" to describe an idea that is emotionally charged. Such ideas tend to galvanize us. They energize us and prepare us for action. To have a vibrant moral belief system we need to think of the moral beliefs we hold in this light. Unless we passionately embrace such beliefs, they are inclined to remain shallow and passive participants in the functioning of conscience rather than bold leaders that decisively guide our moral commitments.

Why Is It So Hard?

Sometimes individuals discover an ongoing or renewed commitment to their moral beliefs through some form of spirituality or religious belief system. Prayer, meditation, and solitude hold out the possibility of strengthening our moral beliefs. Some trends in spirituality are self-focused and stress self-fulfillment or self-actualization. Other forms of spirituality frequently make reference to the "spirit" or humanitarian themes, all of which might or might not nourish a vibrant moral belief system.[14]

There are many reasons that our moral beliefs remain passive or succumb to pressures or situations. Sometimes we simply take them for granted. We always thought this way and assume we always will. Our parents instructed us in certain ways of behaving, or in church we were exposed to a certain belief system that has stayed with us. We might have strayed here or there, but these beliefs, at least in some vague or general form, are still with us. The Golden Rule, the Ten Commandments, the Boy or Girl Scout honor code, or some other moral story or list provided ethical rules that remained part of us.

Another reason we fail to have a deep, conscious love for our moral beliefs is the stress and pressure of life. Our lives are pulled in so many directions that we simply feel we don't have the time or energy to think and feel deeply about our moral belief systems. If some serious moral decision needed to be made or a crisis developed in our lives, then we would refocus time and energy on our moral beliefs to resolve the situation. Otherwise, however, they are not a conscious part of our lives.

Our own defenses might also play a role. The very purpose of unhealthy defenses is to eliminate any role for moral ideas. We rationalize or minimize the violation of a moral belief in order to short-circuit the reaction of moral guilt. We thus remain unaware of our wrongdoings and deny responsibility for our actions.

There are other reasons, too, why moral beliefs fail to muster the energy and attraction they deserve. We are creatures of habit and go about our days following the twin guides of routine and reaction. Spirited discussions about moral beliefs hold little attraction for many of us. Some people have experienced serious psychological torment from their upbringing ("I was robbed of my childhood" or "I was burned"), which has left lingering, painful memories — seriously impairing or even negating a commitment to a meaningful set of moral beliefs. Such individuals know right from wrong, but their psychic energy is poured into surviving in life rather than reflecting on it. Finally, just as physical exercise poses a challenge for many of us, as we resist even the thought of regular physical exertion (I am struggling to refrain from using the word "lazy"), so, too, with our moral belief systems. We are content with some generalized or vague commitment to certain moral beliefs, but we do not reflect on them with any regularity.

No matter the reasons, unless we feel some fondness for and attraction to our moral beliefs, then the probabilities are high that when the stressors and pressures of life's challenges occur, our moral beliefs will be compromised or even abandoned. Misdeeds and wrongful acts are more likely to take place without even the recognition that they occurred ("It never occurred to me that...!"). Or we are inclined to get lured into unhealthy situations, especially if they evoke in us intense emotional states. Examples include moments in which we experience negative feelings (e.g., anger), sexual desire, or a sense of incompetence or deprivation ("I honestly can't explain it! I just got so caught up in...that I...!").

MY MORAL BELIEFS

1. List three moral beliefs that give your life direction and clarity of purpose.

2. Add to each moral belief the following three-words phrases and then complete the sentence. Run each moral belief through the entire list.

   (a) [Moral Belief] rouses me to...

   (b) [Moral Belief] stirs in me...

   (c) [Moral Belief] provokes in me...

   (d) [Moral Belief] inspires me to...

   (e) [Moral Belief] awakens in me...

   (f) [Moral Belief] stimulates me to...

3. After completing the six sentences for each of your moral beliefs, ask yourself:

   (a) How would I describe the *quality* of my attraction to these moral beliefs?

   (b) What do these moral beliefs evoke in me?

   (c) To which beliefs do I find myself most attracted? What criteria do I use to assess the quality of my attraction?

Moral beliefs are not just guides for action. They point to an *end state*. They lead somewhere. For too long, I believe, psychologists have made a serious error when analyzing human responses. The psychologist observes behavior and compares groups to see if their responses differ. What is crucial, however, is not so much responding "to something" as responding "for the sake of something."[15] There exists within our moral belief system *a deeply intentional aspect*. There is an end point to which our moral beliefs point. Our moral beliefs direct us, ultimately, to a moral vision.

{ Conclusion }

CONSCIENCE IN WORK AND RELATIONSHIP

═══════════

The goals and motives that guide human action must be looked at in the light of all that we know and understand; their roots and growth, their essence, and above all their validity, must be critically examined with every intellectual resource that we have. This urgent need, apart from the intrinsic value of the discovery of truth about human relationship, makes ethics a field of primary importance. Only barbarians are not curious about where they come from, how they came to be where they are, where they appear to be going, whether they wish to go there, and if so, why, and if not, why not.
                                        — ISAIAH BERLIN

Our discussion has ranged far and wide. Ultimately, however, the ordinary life we live must be the testing ground for how our conscience functions. The quality of our relationships and the caliber of our everyday efforts are the most revealing indicators of whether we are truly women and men of conscience. By exploring the intricacy of conscience through the seven dimensional framework set out in the previous chapters, we heed Berlin's call to examine our lives. Indeed, we have done even more. We have investigated the most significant ingredient of the moral life.

Applying Conscience to Everyday Life

One evening after dinner you are sitting down with the newspaper and enjoying a cup of your favorite coffee. Midway through your

206

reading, your daughter, Janet, comes into the living room, where you are sitting and plops on the sofa. She flips on the television, but out of the corner of your eye you can tell that she really isn't interested in watching TV. You think to yourself: "Maybe she's bored." But then you sense she might want to talk, or she has something on her mind that is causing her concern. You play your hunch and ask her how her day was. She responds, "Fine." You try again and ask her about last weekend and how school is going. After a minute or two you find yourself talking with your daughter. Finally, you ask her, "How's work going?" Your daughter has a part-time job, roughly fifteen hours a week, mostly on weekends, at a fast food restaurant. When she hears your question, you sense something troubles her. Janet shifts a little in the sofa and looks away. You probe gently, finally asking, "Is everything okay?" She responds, "Not really." Janet then tells you how several of her friends at work have been taking food and even shortchanging customers in the drive-by and pocketing the change. She goes on to admit that on occasion she has given free food to friends, but she assures you that she has not taken any money. However, she admits she feels pressure to do so by her peers. It is clear she is troubled. She pauses. How do you respond? What do you say?

No doubt we could present more dramatic cases, filled with life-and-death issues, but for Janet and for many other teens (and their parents) situations like this are meaning-making moments where the struggle for moral health is won or lost.[1] Janet in her own roundabout way is seeking guidance, but not saying so explicitly. As Janet's parent, how would you handle this situation?

Janet is an adolescent, and during adolescence friendships and the peer group take on great significance. Janet now feels a dilemma between her moral beliefs and the "pull" to be more like her friends. Janet is wondering: How do I "belong" and still remain a moral person?

I believe the seven-dimensional framework of conscience can help you to help your child grow morally. You wouldn't need to go through every dimension. Two or three would easily suffice. If I were Janet's parent and she came to me, I would engage her through a few questions that reflect some of conscience's dimensions.

First, I would encourage her to talk about her friendships and what they mean to her (psychic energy). I would also invite her into a discussion of what being a "good" friend is (idealization). For example, "good friends" don't encourage their friends to steal. Just sharing reflections together would help ease the burden she feels.

Second, I would reaffirm Janet's moral beliefs (conscience's seventh dimension). I would invite her to talk about right and wrong and underscore that stealing is wrong. Also, I would compliment her on holding this belief and talk about the tension between her moral belief and the peer pressure she is feeling.

Third, if she did not raise the issue, I would comment that I sensed she feels guilt over what she has done. I would affirm that this is an appropriate feeling to have, and it says something positive about her.

Depending on where the conversation leads, I might wonder aloud with her about how she invests her time (psychic energy) in terms of the people she hangs out with and the work schedule she keeps. Hopefully, too, we could employ the moral imagination and think creatively about how to resolve her concerns.

I think if you could talk through several dimensions of conscience, asking a few key questions and providing periodic feedback, then Janet would leave the conversation with greater moral health. Your concern for your daughter will have touched something in her — her conscience (as well as your own, for you will have lived up to the challenge of being a "good" parent). Indeed, as is so often the case when two emotionally connected individuals engage in moral conversation, both profit and leave the discussion with gratitude for one another and for their moral health.

I invite you to return to the introduction (p. 25) and the six examples of daily-life dilemmas that involve work and relationship issues. Place yourself in one of these dilemmas. Now use the seven-dimensional conscience system and reach a conclusion on what to do. Then respond to the following questions.

Testing Yourself

1. What insights about conscience have you gained from working through this example?

2. For the example you chose, which dimensions of conscience proved most helpful in your search for a solution?

3. After working through the example, take a situation from your own life and use the seven-dimensional conscience model to arrive at a decision. It could be an issue about work, your home or family life, an important relationship, or a lingering concern from your life history. Then ask yourself the following: (a) Does what I have learned offer any fresh insights about the choice I face? (b) Which dimensions of conscience prove most helpful in leading me to a moral choice? (c) What is it about these dimensions that make them particularly helpful in this situation?

4. As you think about your life situation and moral choices you will encounter, which dimensions of conscience are likely to prove most helpful for your decision making?

5. On a personal level, which dimension of conscience most attracts you or is of greatest interest to you? Why do you say this? What is it about this dimension of conscience that inclines you to favor it over the others?

6. Take seven file cards and write one of the seven dimensions of conscience on each card. Now go through the cards and assign a number from one to seven to each card, with one as most favorite and seven as least favorite. Now place the cards in ascending order with one on top and seven on the bottom. Go through these cards slowly, and write on each card two or three words, or phrases, that explain why this dimension appeals to you *as a moral person*, not just as a person but as a *moral* person. Now take a few moments and read through the cards. This exercise might offer you insight on how you make moral choices as well as what you overemphasize or underemphasize when you make moral decisions. Make a

special effort to evaluate your comments on dimensions you rated five, six, and seven. Could these be dimensions you need to give more consideration when making moral choices?

The Problem of Evil

It is difficult to discuss the moral life without making reference to the topic of evil.[2] A number of psychological researchers have dealt with this question.[3] Concurring with the common-sense wisdom of everyday thinking, evil actions are viewed as more than bad actions. There is an extreme to these actions that qualifies them as evil. To do something wrong (e.g., to hit someone on impulse) for most of us does not qualify as an "evil" deed. Evil involves an excess of cruelty or harm. To hit a person is wrong (though some situations such as self-defense make it morally defensible), but to hit someone and then to stomp on the injured party and cause serious injury and gleefully laugh in order to show bystanders your enjoyment over your action would in all likelihood be labeled an evil action.[4] Generally speaking, for an action to be labeled "evil" requires serious harm to be inflicted on another person and that the deed be carried out with the intention of inflicting such harm. Furthermore, the action is more extreme than a bad action, misdeed, or wrongful act as commonly understood.[5]

How Does Evil Influence Us?

Many have heard discussions of terms such as the "banality of evil," which refers to how ordinary people can commit heinous, truly evil acts, or to psychological experiments where participants are ordered to increase the intensity of electrical shocks and do so willingly in apparent disregard of any injury caused to the person shocked (who in fact is faking the injury). Some have reached the conclusion that in certain situations most people are capable of serious wrongdoing, cruelty, or evil. This viewpoint is termed the "situationist" position in social psychology and holds that the situation is the primary influence on human behavior. There is merit in this position. In some situations, such as complex organizations like corporations or large bureaucratic or governmental agencies, there exist so many organizational layers that we might not even see the harmful consequences that result from our actions. We might also blame someone in another part of the organization or rationalize that we are just following orders. Then, again, we might simply go along with the climate of the organization and do what everyone else does.[6]

I do not deny the power of situations to influence our moral decision making. Moreover, when the situations fall outside what we consider "ordinary" experience, our behavior is more likely to be unpredictable. Who could predict, for example, what we might do if caught behind enemy lines during combat, or held hostage by a terrorist, or caught in a burning building with co-workers? In the ordinary experiences of our lives, however, I don't agree that situations are the most significant factor in determining our moral decisions.

I base this position on the multidimensional understanding of conscience this book sets forth. If we tend carefully to each of its dimensions, this uniquely human attribute we call conscience settles us within a moral experience offering sturdy resistance (though not immunity) to the lures of specific situations. A high level of moral fitness means that our conscience functions reasonably well across its seven dimensions. If we invest psychic energy in good friendships, find time for solitude, sufficiently monitor our feelings, and draw purpose and strength from our life project, then I believe we have inoculated ourselves to some degree from situations that could trigger actions we deem wrong. The same effect comes about through employing healthy defenses. If we live a life that controls our rationalizing and minimizing tendencies and strive to be open-minded with all that such living entails, situations will not easily lure us into serious wrongdoing. Each of the other dimensions, when operating properly, offers its own inoculating power to the assorted enticements a specific situation might pose.

Stopping the Spread of Evil

We must never lose sight of our moral weaknesses, the moral entropy we always carry within, nor the evil to which it might lead. But there remains another fact that, though given little attention, sows the seeds of hope. Jerome Kagan wisely notes that "the number of acts of rudeness, vandalism, theft, abuses, rape, and murder that occurred yesterday, throughout the world, is infinitesimal when compared with the total number of opportunities each adult had to display any one of these behaviors."[7] What could account for this truth? Simple answers abound. We might conclude that it is the force of law or some other external constraint. Certainly, as we have noted, situational pressures exert influences that encourage or impede our actions. But I would argue that each of us, using some creativity and a little deceit, possesses the potential for committing numerous misdeeds on a daily basis, some quite serious, without being noticed or being caught. Yet the vast majority of us never try or even consider activating such "potential." Why?

The answer to this question, I believe, is not found in external constraints such as laws or the pressure to conform (though both factors play a role). Rather, the answer lies within us. For the true enigma of the human being is not that obnoxious, inappropriate, bad, or evil deeds are committed, but that there are not more such actions. As we ask the question of ourselves, we might respond, "My guilt keeps me honest," or "I have too much empathy to be mean," and like the external pressures we cite above, each has its validity. But if we take seriously the notion that conscience is complex and view it in the framework of the seven dimensional system this book proposes, then solitary answers like "guilt" or "empathy" appear simplistic. The best explanation of the enigma lies in the rich and intricate nature of conscience itself.

In sum, does evil exist? Most certainly. There is simply too much data and evidence in human history and perhaps in our own personal histories to question its existence. Nonetheless, devoting our lives to being and remaining men and women with good and healthy consciences offers the best insurance for containing evil's lurches and limiting its effects.

Helping Others Make Moral Decisions

Conscience does not exist in a vacuum. Its initial boost comes from the affection, support, and challenge of family members who take our initial plunges into the moral life seriously. Assuming there is no serious neurological or developmental impairment, at the earliest stages of our lives, even as toddlers, we are moral beings just waiting for the moment to be switched on. Those flicks of the switch were our initial ventures into becoming moral persons. For the vast majority of us the process took shape more or less as follows. Around the age of two we proudly uttered our first evaluative assertions about the world: "doggy bad" or "me good." Over the years those labels were transformed into increasingly complex and sophisticated moral evaluations of the world and our own role in it. Thus, who I am as a moral person today is a consequence not only of my capacity to have a conscience, but also of those significant people throughout my life who helped make my conscience possible. The questions, encouragement, feedback, discussions, challenges, instructions, and rebukes of family members soon branched out to a wider family and other significant adults (e.g., teachers). As this process of moral growth unfolded in each of our lives, there also developed relationships with friends, pals, and confidants. As we have pointed out, investing psychic energy in these relationships formed an integral ingredient for moral growth. As we took more seriously the wider world, cultural influences such as educational systems as well as our own personal preferences and unique modes of perceiving, feeling, and interpreting interacted to help shape conscience as we walked (some faster than others) down the path to our current level of moral health.

In sum, human beings are embedded in relationships. We are a sociable species. We form networks of relationships that are diverse and of various quality. Family connections, friendships of varying depth and intensity, and colleagues or co-workers make up our ordinary lives of relating and working. Since all of these individuals, like us, have consciences that need support and challenge, it is only natural that some individuals will at one time or another, and sometimes when least expected, be drawn into moral discussion. Just as we desire moral health for ourselves, we wish the same for those with whom we have connections. We are challenged to help others along the road to moral health. We don't have to have a Ph.D. in ethics to do so.

Though every situation, person, moral question, or dilemma has its own distinctive quality, I believe there are some general guidelines for promoting the moral growth of others.

Guidelines for Helping Others Build Their Consciences

1. *Remember this person has a conscience.* We can't make our friend's decision for her. We can, however, promote the growth of her conscience to help her achieve the highest level of moral fitness possible.

2. *Take the time to listen to what the person has to say.* Let others speak about the issue or dilemma before them.

3. *Be sensitive to nonverbal cues.* Voice tones, facial expressions, and body movements all can indicate how important a moral issue is to our friend. We might simply want to give some feedback about how certain feelings such as worry, upset, sadness, or anger might influence the decision our friend makes. We don't need to play therapist and help resolve these feelings for her, but we can alert her to the fact that she might have such feelings and that they might influence how she resolves her moral dilemma.

4. *Appeal to the "good" the person desires.* Moral health requires making the "unspoken desire for goodness" spoken. If Rick is struggling with how to fulfill his role as a husband, father, or employee, encourage him to talk about what it means to be a "good" husband, "good" father, or "good" employee.

5. *Remember a person can only be where she is.* If Nancy confides something to us and what she says disappoints us, stay focused on the truth that this is the reality at hand. From a moral perspective, where we are at any point in our moral lives is the *only place we can be.* This is true for us, and it is true for those who share with us their concerns. In accepting Nancy where she is we might ask the right questions or give the necessary encouragement that helps her shift her focus toward becoming a better person. Though she can only be where she is, she doesn't have to stay there! Loved ones nudge loved ones down the road to moral health.

6. *Encourage a future perspective.* If John is trying to determine how to handle a personnel situation at work, reflect with him on what happens to him when he makes one or another option. Ask

him what he is *becoming as a person* by his choice. Focus on this future perspective and how he is shaping his own moral life by his decision.

7. *Try to provide compassionate care and loving challenge.* The art of encouraging another's moral growth requires displaying appropriately our care for her while at the same time fostering her growth. Frequently we feel a tension between these two approaches — showing care and challenge. Obviously, if a colleague is crying, showing compassion might be the more appropriate response. If a family member is repeatedly getting himself into situations that are hurtful to himself and to others, then perhaps challenge is more fitting. A true friend offers whichever response is most appropriate.

8. *Keep your boundaries.* We should not try to rescue someone from her dilemma or resolve a situation that is beyond our means to control. When someone comes to us seeking moral advice about an ethical dilemma, remember the importance assigned to keeping boundaries. Denise seeks our counsel because we are someone else. Be with her, but don't try to become her is good advice. We need to monitor our empathy. Do we feel the pull of getting overly entangled in Denise's concern?

9. *If guilt is an appropriate response and the person acknowledges his guilt, then be supportive of his admission.* If Al confides that he has done something wrong and it appears he is genuinely contrite, acknowledge this fact. Afterward, help him focus on what he has learned, what insight he has gained from this experience, and what he might do differently next time.

10. *Engage the moral imagination.* Don't rule out the role of novel and creative strategies and solutions. If there is a real dilemma, pose a number of "What if...?" questions. Often some idea surfaces that, when creatively applied, offers an adequate solution.

11. *Help people clarify their moral beliefs.* Dilemmas and conflicts frequently involve the clash of moral beliefs or certain values. Encourage Michelle to express her moral beliefs. Is there concern about a moral belief she is violating? Is one belief in conflict with another? Help her to make such beliefs explicit.

12. *Be willing to say that something is wrong.* If Larry has clearly violated company procedures or treated his family insensitively, then give him this feedback. Of course, the tone and manner in which it is expressed depend on the situation and the history of your relationship. Nonetheless, we do a disservice to those we love and care about if we fail to provide honest feedback. On the other hand, we need to be prudent. We must factor in the nature of the relationship and the consequences for ourselves and others when giving moral advice. In such cases, viewing conscience the way we have might offer insight on how to respond. Our idealizations (what are the competing goods involved?), moral beliefs (which beliefs are most important to me?), and defenses (what does being open-minded in this situation call me to do?) can prove especially helpful in difficult and delicate situations.

13. *Help the person cultivate a sense of gratitude.* We are apt to make the best moral judgments when there is a sense of gratitude in our lives (see p. 96). At some point in the discussion, usually toward its end, help the person be aware of something for which to be grateful. When the person is struggling with a complicated and painful situation, experiencing gratitude might prove difficult. In such circumstances at least convey your own gratitude for the conversation, the time together, and the relationship itself. Frequently just mentioning these facts can spark a sense of hope in the other person.

14. *To help others grow morally, let others help us do the same.* In the long run, we can neither engage others in moral conversations nor offer moral advice if we ourselves do not have people we trust and can confide in about our own moral struggles, dilemmas, and uncertainties. Above all, having such vulnerability prevents an all too typical temptation to be the wise sage rather than the humble friend.

Some Tips about Conscience

Because we have touched on numerous topics and because conscience involves so many factors, I thought it might be helpful to include some friendly "tips" to help keep us mindful of our moral worth. They provide a summation of this book's message.

1. *Conscience is highly personal. Only "I" can make a particular judgment of conscience.* When I make a moral choice, it is "I" who makes it. Decisions that flow from conscience are the most truthful thing I can say about myself. It is for this reason that to act in good conscience is to convey what is most authentic about me.

2. *To make decisions of conscience implies that I have freedom to make such judgments.* It also means that I have responsibility for them. Conscience always implies that I have freedom. In reality, the freely chosen decisions we make are limited. I may lack the necessary funds to take a trip, or laws might limit my options. But when I make a moral choice, I acknowledge my freedom to have chosen otherwise. In the realm of moral decision making, however, being free goes beyond "choosing this" or "not choosing that." For a conscience that functions well, the act of choosing denotes a movement toward something. The moral choice to act well implies moving in the direction of my moral vision, an opportunity to live and realize a "greater good."

When moral choices are made well, freedom reflects a decidedly positive thrust. Such freedom mirrors more wholly who I am. The free moral choice I make conveys my deepest truth, that *I am a moral being.* Thus the moral choice to be good conveys what is most authentic about me. For example, consider for a moment a time when you chose to be good or you did the right thing, especially if the choice was filled with challenges and pressures. Nonetheless, you still chose the right thing. Your decision produced the self-contentment that is freedom's gift. Related to such freedom to choose is the responsibility I assume for my moral choices. Because I made this choice in this situation to be good or to act wrongfully, I take responsibility for this decision.

3. *Even though the judgments of conscience are highly personal, this does not mean that they are entirely subjective.* On the contrary, to invest psychic energy in relationships, to labor in the world, to have empathy for others, to live life in an open-minded manner means that there is an objective world that I must consider and be open to. This world exists independent of my judgments, and my decisions must always take into consideration the evidence this world offers.

For example, empathy, psychic energy, defenses, and self-esteem imply the presence of other people who relate to me and make choices that affect me. None of conscience's dimensions would function adequately if it was not for this active engagement. Recall, for example, that psychic energy poses questions about how I invest my time and what attracts me. The reality of this world with all its perspectives and complexity poses for me wonder and danger. It is where I might triumph or fail, be loved or rejected, and find happiness or misery. But even these polarities and the extent to which I have experienced them lead me to grow and complexify. As such, my stance is one of open-mindedness or, more accurately, the struggle to maintain an open-mind. The moral choices I make in good conscience are carried out with conviction and a commitment to the moral beliefs that guide them. But to live in this world is also to be surprised by it. I know that being human means that I rationalize, minimize, and compartmentalize to some degree. Thus, with conviction do I make a moral decision, but I am open to broadening this conviction and understanding it more fully. Only engaging this world allows such growth.

4. *Conscience cannot exist without ties to communities.* The decisions I make are inseparable from my heritage, family, background, culture, and locale. I have been influenced by communities as small as the family unit and as large as the nation state. I have the obligation to consider seriously their traditions, rules, and accrued wisdom as it has been passed down over time.

The definition of myself as a moral being arises both from the capacity within me to evaluate (recall that it starts as early as two and is spurred on by empathy) and from the encouragement, feedback, and challenge of the numerous social groups that have helped shape the conscience I now have. Each community has its perspective on the world that provides me a coherent frame of reference for interpreting my actions. Family rituals, stories of grandparents, histories of neighborhoods in which I lived, and ethnic ties have shown me ways to do or think about things. Organizations (e.g., work settings, clubs, faith community) to which I belong and faith communities in which I am a member likewise have an accrued wisdom. Some are more significant for me than others, but each has influenced me, and many are still teaching me. I must take them seriously and listen to what they say. Frequently, too, each group has an authority structure that conveys its group's message. Am I able to hear the message, whether it be the repeated warning of an aging parent, an appeal by a civic organization, a public pronouncement by a city official, or a position taken by a faith community?

5. *At the same time, I have the obligation to contribute to my communities.* Being a responsible member of various communities requires that I contribute actively to them. This contribution might mean challenging certain customs or patterns of behavior the community utilizes.

I participate in these communities that are part of my life because I am a person of conscience. What I do or say, how I relate or act, to whom I provide help or resources, the feedback and challenge I offer all engage these communities, not only because of my affection for them but also because such behavior conveys my most authentic self. The cherished roles that link me to these groups require that I take seriously being the good son, the good brother, the good team captain, the good worker.

However, though I belong to these various communities, I am not them. I am foremost a moral being, a person of conscience seeking the greater good. Like an individual, a group can live with a closed mind or be entrenched in its ways. For example, an alcoholic family might be in denial of a family member's alcoholism and the chaos it causes. A family, a neighborhood, a work environment, a city, or a nation likewise possesses its own blind spots that can prove hurtful. As a person of conscience I might at some point have to take a stand on an issue or challenge personally someone I care about deeply. I do not take such action lightly. It is done with respect, and any challenge I issue, intervention I make, assertion I state, or stand I take is *never* done with the intention to humiliate in any way other persons or the group. Of course, I cannot control the response or interpretation of a group or its members to the stand I take, but if it is done with respect for them, no matter what their reaction, I have preserved my integrity as a person of good conscience.

Moreover, because authority figures can't help but be influential in my life and are integral to groups, I need especially to examine my defenses to insure that I utilize healthy ones and that I, too, am open-minded. In other words, I might rationalize my challenge under the guise of some moral principle or take a specific stand as a way to displace my anger from an authority figure onto another person or group. Thus there is always a need to be open-minded, and even if my stand is a strong one, I carry it out with interior humility.

6. *I owe respect to other people, who, like me, are individuals who make judgments of conscience.* This respect does not mean I must agree with their position, for even people of good conscience can reason to opposing viewpoints and legitimately disagree. Nor must I necessarily give in to their demands or go along with their actions. At times, I might oppose their statements or actions, but my opposition is appropriate and done in a manner that does not humiliate them but is respectful of them. In addition, I listen to those whose positions conflict with my own judgments to under-stand them better and perhaps learn from them, even in the midst of my disagreement with them.

My opposition to others is presented in a manner that respects others as men and women of conscience. However, there is a mis-taken assumption in our society that respect equals tolerance of everything another does. On the contrary, respect is the acknowl-edgment of the other person as an individual with dignity, a moral being whose ideas I take seriously. Yet as a person of conscience I have the right to oppose the other person in debate, at the voting booth, or, depending on my inclinations, in some type of overt or symbolic protest. Nonetheless, my conscience also tries to em-pathize with him — to understand his position and why he believes as he does. This point is critical because when I stop trying to understand, my open-mindedness slowly yet inevitably erodes. I become fortified in an "I versus you" mode of thinking, where the links for discourse grow increasingly weak.

7. *The moral decisions I make are inseparable from who I am.* And who I am as a person includes my life history. Therefore, I am committed to acquiring self-knowledge about my life and how life events have influenced, whether positively or negatively, the moral decisions I make.

Socrates' maxim to "know thyself" bears directly on my moral decision making. I must attend to my past, be aware of my present, and have goals for my future. As such, I welcome self-knowledge whether the source is reflection, inquiry, solitude, study, or conversation. To invite self-knowledge and where it might lead is to live an open-minded life. On the other hand, along my life journey I must make decisions with the data at hand. A decision-less life, at least with regard to significant issues and life events, leads to a drifting, diffuse state that loses coherence and purpose. I look back over my life with regrets over some decisions, but the question must be whether *at the moment* in which my decision was made I used all available self-knowledge to arrive at my decision. For example, I fall in love with someone, and we make the decision to marry. I love this person and believe that she completes me and helps me to become a better person, so I propose to her. I have thought about this decision carefully and sought the counsel of people I respect. However, after several decades, I realize that I was not as open-minded as I had thought. Though the good intention was there, I have come to realize that I married this person to provide myself with a certain emotional security, although I was unable to acknowledge this at that time. We might stay married, separate, or divorce. The point is that throughout my life I continue to acquire self-knowledge.

8. *My conscience seeks always to do good and avoid evil.* I take seriously the task of understanding and articulating the good for which I strive.

As discussed in the chapter on idealization, the road to becoming an authentic person is the seeking of the good and the use of conscience to guide this search. I must strive, on a daily basis, to make spoken the unspoken desire for goodness. I must continually reflect on the *meaning of being good* in the cherished roles that define me. In a sense, to be a person of good conscience is to fall in love with the desire for the greater good. To live authentically, I do all that is reasonable or even heroic, if the situation calls for it, to bring this good about.

9. *There exists within my conscience a humility that I must always seek to maintain.* Although I have the courage of my con-

victions, my conscience must be informed and supported, and I actively seek ways for it to be kept informed and supported. I am open to the possibility that a decision I now make or have previously made might be in error. When such realizations occur, I have the humility to alter my judgment.

To be humble is to view my life as an invitation. Humility conveys a hospitality. In this process I literally do "entertain." I think about and take seriously ideas and perspectives differing from my own. They are welcome. They are like guests at a party. When they visit my home, we might have an enjoyable time and discover a wonderful compatibility that leads to more visits and great familiarity. On the other hand, they might leave, or I might ask them to leave, but they have at least the opportunity to visit my home. In sum, to say that I am humble is always to acknowledge that there is "more than me."

As we have already discussed, moral ideas potentially evoke strong feelings within us. These ideas can affirm the good but in the process can wreak havoc and alienation on others or be the source of deep hurt. For example, I might agree with a friend's moral beliefs and respect her highly. I know her to be a genuinely sincere and good person. But some positions she takes (which again I agree with) are argued so strongly, even vehemently at times, that she alienates others. We truly can and should love the moral ideas we cherish. But true love is not infatuation. From a moral perspective, to lack humility is to be infatuated with my moral beliefs rather than to love them truly. Just as with a person, infatuation with ideas breeds, a turning inward that loses awareness of any need to attend to others. True fanatics are infatuaters, not lovers. Humility and fanaticism are mutually exclusive.

10. *There is a frailty to my conscience.* Conscience arises out of a life history that consists in joys, hopes, fears, successes, triumphs, failures, and disappointments. My judgments of conscience, though sincere, are not immune from the influences of the many experiences my life history holds. The emotional impact of some life experiences might linger, and I must take seriously the possibility that some effects might adversely influence my judgments of conscience.

I need to be aware of those events in my life that caused me pain and disappointment, especially if the event was traumatic. A person sexually abused, for example, might form harsh and punitive attitudes on issues of sexuality and make them part of her moral belief system. On the other hand, various types of abuse might so overwhelm and tax one's psychic energy that unhealthy defenses develop that sabotage conscience. In such cases, the self is truly damaged, and conscience lacks the fertile soil necessary for suitable growth. For some individuals, there is a striking failure even to recognize the moral significance of their actions. It is as if moral awareness itself fails to register. A typical response to an inquiry is: "I never thought about it" or "It never even crossed my mind." When people hurt deeply, moral health is frequently an early casualty.

11. *Conscience cannot function adequately without healthy friendship. Therefore, I commit myself to developing good friendships.* My true friends help me direct my goals and actions to a "greater good." Through conversation with good friends, I am able to maintain open-mindedness. Like moral beliefs, friends are moral reference points. This is why sometimes when struggling over a moral dilemma I am apt to reach out to my friends and seek their advice. Perhaps the greatest compliment I can offer my friends is one that they might never know about: In the midst of making a moral choice, when they are not around, I ponder what they might do if faced with a similar situation. Good friends sustain and nurture for each other a life project oriented to the good. And only seeking the good prevents any friendship from sliding into a subtle but alluring narcissism.

12. *My conscience acknowledges that justice and compassion are vital moral beliefs. I am always willing to inquire how my judgments reflect justice and compassion for others.* There is no end to the debate on what moral beliefs individuals should adopt as guides for their behavior. In the previous chapter I maintained that there are some moral beliefs that appear to have near universal appeal, such as fairness to others. One of the first and most serious moral assertions a child vocalizes is the rebuke that "you're not fair." Because of its central place in helping maintain our emo-

tional and moral lives, a compelling case can be made that my moral belief system requires room for some moral assertion that advocates fairness (or its philosophical cousin, justice). Likewise, the psychological glue that binds individuals and communities together is the capacity for empathy, which first surfaces in rudimentary form at around two years of age. Empathy is morality's core, without which I am left heartless and indifferent to the sorrows and needs of others. Thus, I maintain that any person's moral belief system must contain a belief in the requirement to live a compassionate life. As we have seen, two moral positions — justice and care — are at times in conflict or tension. Should I comfort my friend over his misdeed or challenge him? Should I contest a colleague's statement or let it pass because of her difficult life history? Should this student receive a final grade based solely on class performance or should I take into consideration his effort and the personal problems he is trying to overcome? Such questions can be answered only with an understanding of the context of a specific situation and a consideration of all of conscience's dimensions. Nonetheless, I believe that fairness and compassion hold a privileged status so unassailable that the requirement they be part of every conscience's moral belief system is a nonnegotiable point.

13. *Conscience functions best when we have a grateful heart. I am committed to making gratitude a central experience in my life.* Chapter 3 concluded with a Daily Moral Inventory that included a section on gratitude (p. 96). Living gratefully energizes conscience. As I approach the world gratefully, my conscience is imbued with optimism that moral decisions can be made and consequences accepted.

A Final Word of Hope

My daughter wonders whether she should report a teacher who drinks with students. A corporate executive hints that an accountant should provide exaggerated sales projections at the end of the month to make his division appear more profitable than it really is. A company memo instructs all salespeople to emphasize in their sales pitches a soon to be discontinued project in order to deplete inventory; this will require customers to purchase spare parts, at higher cost, from a new product line. A person wonders whether he should spend a weekend with a friend from out of town who recently lost his mother even though it will put a strain on his spouse to manage schedules for their children's sports events and complete household chores. A friend of your child asks him for his homework, and your child comes to you for advice. A scientist ponders whether to write an endorsement for a chemical product manufactured by a company that is funding her research. A neighborhood friend spreads what you know to be false rumors about another neighbor; you suspect a reason for his gossip is that the neighbor being talked about belongs to a minority. These and countless other examples are the terrain that our consciences must navigate in order to insure our moral health. Sometimes the decisions are clouded ones, sometimes they are clear, but in either case it is in the joys, tensions, successes, and disappointments of being human that our consciences must navigate in order to adopt the right choice. It is in this decision making, ultimately, that our moral health either increases or declines.

James Q. Wilson reminds us that humanity's

> moral sense is not a strong beacon of light, radiating outward to illuminate in sharp outline all that it touches. It is, rather, a small candle flame, casting vague and multiple shadows, flickering and sputtering in the strong winds of power and passion, greed and ideology. But brought close to the heart and cupped in one's hands, it dispels the darkness and warms the soul.[8]

Wilson's words inspire hope and highlight what must be cherished, nurtured, and protected at all costs: our conscience.

NOTES

Introduction: Humanity's Unique Attribute

1. Jerome Kagan, *Three Seductive Ideas* (Cambridge, Mass.: Harvard University Press, 1998), 151–200. See also Jerome Kagan, *The Nature of the Child* (New York: Basic Books, 1984), 112–53.

2. Kagan, *Three Seductive Ideas,* 157.

3. For excellent discussions of "self-awareness" and "free will," which are vital to any understanding of ourselves as moral beings, see Michel Ferrari and Robert J. Sternberg, eds., *Self-Awareness: Its Nature and Development* (New York: Guilford Press, 1998), and Benjamin Libet, Anthony Freeman, and Keith Sutherland, eds., *The Volitional Brain: Towards a Neuroscience of Free Will* (Thorverton, U.K.: Imprint Academic, 1999).

4. Roy F. Baumeister, "Identity, Self-Concept, and Self-Esteem: The Self Lost and Found," in *Handbook of Personality Psychology,* ed. Robert Hogan, John Johnson, and Stephen Briggs (New York: Academic Press, 1997), 687.

5. James Q. Wilson, *The Moral Sense* (New York: Free Press, 1993), 130 and 121–63. See also Kagan, *The Nature of the Child.*

6. Barbara M. Stilwell, Matthew R. Galvin, and Stephen M. Kopta, *Right vs. Wrong: Raising a Child with a Conscience* (Bloomington: Indiana University Press, 2000), 15.

7. Obviously such a unique capacity has physiological underpinnings, though an exact understanding of how conscience functions remains beyond the grasp of psychology and neuroscience. Given the complexity of the human brain and its various systems no clear roadmap for conscience's functioning exists that satisfies every neuroscientist. Even so, the complex thinking patterns, self-reflection, and emotions required for a healthy functioning conscience most likely involve specific aspects of the brain's association areas. Moreover, the human brain possesses a larger proportion of these areas than rats, dogs, monkeys, or any other mammal. See, for example, David G. Myers, *Psychology,* 4th ed. (New York: Worth Publishing, 1995), 59–64, and Donald T. Stuss, "Self, Awareness, and the Frontal Lobes: A Neuropsychological Perspective," in *The Self: Interdisciplinary Approaches,* ed. Jaine Strauss and George R. Goethels (New York: Springer-Verlag, 1991), 255–78.

8. Patrick Glynn, *God: The Evidence* (Rocklin, Calif.: Prima Publishing, 1997), 168–69.

9. Charles Taylor, *The Ethics of Authenticity* (Cambridge, Mass.: Harvard University Press, 1991), 4.

10. My explanation of authenticity is psychological in nature. For a philosophical analysis of authenticity see Charles Taylor, *The Ethics of Authenticity.* I am deeply indebted to Taylor's discussion of culture and authenticity.

11. See Michael J. McCarthy, "Virtual Morality: A New Workplace Quandary," *Wall Street Journal,* October 21, 1999, B1, B4.

12. Robert Coles, "Gatsby at the B School," *New York Times Book Review,* October 25, 1987, 40.

13. I use interchangeably words such as "ethical," "moral," and "good."

14. Norma Haan, Eliane Aerts, and Bruce A. B. Cooper, *On Moral Grounds: The Search for Practical Morality* (New York: New York University Press, 1985), 38.

15. Associated Press, "Boy, 5, Is Killed for Refusing to Steal Candy," *New York Times,* national edition, October 15, 1994, 8.

16. Associated Press, "Voices from Asia," *International Herald Tribune,* May 22, 1995, 4.

17. Quoted in Tom Brokaw, *The Greatest Generation* (New York: Random Houses, 1998), 338.

18. Seth Mydans, "In an Interview Pol Pot Asserts He's No Savage," *New York Times,* national edition, October 23, 1997, 1.

19. Jim Salter, "HIV-Injecting Dad Gets Life Term," *Denver Post,* January 9, 1999, 3A.

20. Charisse Jones, "Racist Guilty in Dragging Death," *USA Today,* February 24, 1999, 1A.

21. "Good Grief," *The Economist,* April 8, 1995, 57.

22. Robert H. Frank, *Passions within Reason: The Strategic Role of the Emotions* (New York: W. W. Norton, 1988).

23. The day I wrote this page I received the *Wall Street Journal,* which in a short piece on its front page reported a national poll by the National Association of Colleges and Employers. It indicated that companies and organizations ranked communication skills as the most important personal quality desired by employers. Other personal qualities cited in the article were: work experience (second); motivation (third); academic credentials (sixth) and *ethics* (tenth)! See *Wall Street Journal,* "Work Week: Ability to Communicate," December 28, 1998, A1.

24. See Carol Hymowitz, "CEOs Set the Tone for How to Handle Questions of Ethics," *Wall Street Journal,* December 22, 1998, B1.

25. Quoted in Robert Coles, *The Moral Life of Children* (Boston: Houghton Mifflin, 1986), 16.

Perspective: Why Conscience?

1. I have disguised the names of all clients in order to insure anonymity.

2. For an excellent discussion of the ego ideal's role in human development see Janine Chasseguet-Smirgel, *The Ego Ideal: A Psychoanalytic Essay on the Malady of the Ideal* (New York: W. W. Norton, 1985).

3. For advances on Freud's narrow view see Eli Sagan, *Freud, Women, and Morality* (New York: Basic Books, 1988) and George E. Vaillant, *The Wisdom of the Ego* (Cambridge, Mass.: Harvard University Press, 1993).

4. See, for example, Nancy Eisenberg and Janet Strayer, eds., *Empathy and Its Development* (New York: Cambridge University Press, 1987), and Daniel K. Lapsley, *Moral Psychology* (Boulder, Colo.: Westview Press, 1996), 166–238.

5. For further discussion see the summary of these and other statistics in Carnegie Council on Adolescent Development, *Great Transitions: Preparing Adolescents for a New Century,* abridged version (Waldorf, Md.: Carnegie Corporation, 1996), 16–17.

6. Julie Stacey, "Ways and Means," *USA Today,* May 19, 1993, 7D.

7. Mary Beth Marklein, "Revealing the Answer to Cheating," *USA Today,* January 5, 2000, 9D.

8. Philip J. Hilts, "Misconduct in Science Is Not Rare, a Survey Finds," *New York Times,* November 12, 1993, 22.

9. "American Opinion: A Quarterly Survey of Politics, Economics, and Values," *Wall Street Journal,* September 16, 1999, A9–A16.

10. Data reported in "Chasing the Value Vote," *USA Today,* international edition, August 7, 1996, 1A.

11. Quoted in Eleanor Smith, "The New Moral Classroom," *Psychology Today* (May 1989): 36.

12. "Special Report: The State of the Union," *Time,* January 30, 1995, 54.

13. Howard Fineman, "Virtuecrats," *Newsweek,* June 13, 1994, 31.

14. Jonathan Alter and Pat Wingert, "The Return to Shame," *Newsweek,* February 6, 1995, 21–25.

15. Quoted in Susanna McBee, "Morality," *U.S. News and World Report,* December 9, 1985, 58.

16. Derek Bok, "Ethics, the University, and Society," *Harvard Magazine* (May–June 1988): 47.

17. An ethics of justice approach is best reflected in the work of Lawrence Kohlberg. See Lawrence Kohlberg, *The Psychology of Moral Development* (San Francisco: Harper & Row, 1984). Psychologist Carol Gilligan champions an ethics of care approach to morality. See Carol Gilligan, *In a Different Voice* (Cambridge, Mass.: Harvard University Press, 1982). Both approaches have more than their share of critics. A well researched summary of the various issues, theories, criticisms, and research in moral psychology can be found in William M. Kurtines and Jacob L. Gewirtz, eds., *Moral Development: An Introduction* (Needham Heights, Mass.: Allyn & Bacon, 1995). See also Charles C. Helwig, "Making Moral Cognition Respectable (Again): A Retrospective Review of Lawrence Kohlberg," *Contemporary Psychology* 42 (1997): 191–95.

18. See Lapsley, *Moral Psychology,* and Kurtines and Gewirtz, *Moral Development.* An exception to the lack of interest in conscience is the work being done by psychiatrists Barbara Stilwell and Matthew Galvin and psychologist Stephen M. Kopta. See, for example, Barbara Stilwell, Matthew Galvin, and S. Mark Kopta, "Conceptualization of Conscience in Normal Children and Adolescents, Ages 5 to 17," *Journal of the American Academy of Child and Adolescent Psychiatry* 30 (1991): 16–21. Of particular interest is their recently published *Right vs. Wrong: Raising a Child with a Conscience* (Bloomington: Indiana University Press, 2000). A thoughtful look at the interplay of emotion

and reason in moral decision making is contained in Sidney Callahan, *In Good Conscience: Reason and Emotion in Moral Decision Making* (San Francisco: HarperCollins, 1991).

19. John T. Noonan, Jr., *The Lustre of Our Country: The American Experience of Religious Freedom* (Berkeley, Calif.: University of California Press, 1998).

20. Gina Kolata, "Boom in Ritalin Sales Raises Ethical Issues," *New York Times,* national edition, May 15, 1996, B8.

21. See "The Future of Medicine," *Time,* January 11, 1999, 42–91.

22. For an insightful article on the "moral confusion" the country experiences around the issue of abortion see Peter Steinfels, "Beliefs: The opinion surveys on abortion do not clearly show a national consensus, and there seems to be much moral, or perhaps verbal, confusion," *New York Times,* national edition, January 24, 1998, A13.

23. James Q. Wilson, *The Moral Sense* (New York: Free Press, 1993), vii.

24. Dan P. McAdams, *The Person: An Introduction to Personality Psychology,* 2d ed. (San Diego: Harcourt Brace, 1994), 3.

25. Albert Bandura, "Social Cognitive Theory of Personality," in *Handbook of Personality: Theory and Research,* 2d ed., ed. Lawrence A. Pervin and Oliver P. John (New York: Guilford Press, 1999), 179.

26. I wish to acknowledge psychiatrists Barbara Stilwell, M.D., and Matthew Galvin, M.D., who introduced me to this technique.

27. Judith S. Beck, *Cognitive Therapy: Basics and Beyond* (New York: Guilford Press, 1995).

28. Some psychologists distinguish between "feelings" and "emotions." Here, however, I use them interchangeably throughout the text.

29. For discussions of psychologists use of "meaning," see Roy F. Baumeister, *Meanings of Life* (New York: Guilford Press, 1991).

30. Jonathan Lear, *Open Minded: Working Out the Logic of the Soul* (Cambridge, Mass.: Harvard University Press, 1998), 24.

31. See Paul Ekman and Richard J. Davidson, eds., *The Nature of Emotion: Fundamental Questions* (New York: Oxford University Press, 1994), and Lawrence Hinman, "Emotion, Morality, and Understanding," in *Moral Dilemmas: Philosophical and Psychological Issues in the Development of Moral Reasoning,* ed. Carol Harding (Chicago: Precedent Publishing, 1985), 57–70.

32. Jerome Kagan, *The Nature of the Child* (New York: Basic Books, 1984), 123.

33. See, for example, Eisenberg and Strayer, *Empathy and Its Development.*

34. Robert Jay Lifton, *The Broken Connection* (New York: Simon & Schuster, 1979), 122.

35. Nico H. Frijda, "The Law of Emotion," *American Psychologist* 43 (1985): 349–58.

36. Haan et al., *On Moral Grounds,* 147.

37. Ibid.

38. Deanna S. Pledge, Richard T. Lapan, P. Paul Heppner, Dennis Kivlighan, and Helen J. Roehlke, "Stability and Severity of Presenting Problems at a Univer-

sity Counseling Center: A Six-Year Analysis," *Professional Psychology: Research and Practice* 29 (1998): 386–89.

Dimension One: Energy

1. Timothy D. Schellhardt, "Company Memo to Stressed-Out Employees: 'Deal with It.'" *Wall Street Journal,* October 2, 1996, B1.

2. Sue Shellenbarger, "Work and Family: These Top Bosses May Signal Move to More Family Time," *Wall Street Journal,* April 30, 1997, B1.

3. Jonathan Kaufman, "At Age Five, Reading, Writing and Rushing," *Wall Street Journal,* February 4, 1997, B1.

4. Dirk Johnson, "A Generation's Anthem: 'Smells Like Teen Pressure,'" *New York Times,* national edition, January 1, 2000, 22.

5. In writing about "psychic energy" I have been influenced by psychologist Mihaly Csikszentmihalyi. See Mihaly Csikszentmihalyi and Reed Larson, *Being Adolescent* (New York: Basic Books, 1984), and Mihaly Csikszentmihalyi, *Flow: The Psychology of Optimal Experience* (New York: Harper & Row, 1990).

6. James J. Gross and Ricardo F. Munoz, "Emotion Regulation and Mental Health," *Clinical Psychology: Science and Practice* 2 (1995): 155.

7. Anthony Storr, *Solitude: A Return to Self* (New York: Ballantine Books, 1989).

8. Hugh McIntosh, "Solitude Provides an Emotional Tune-Up," *APA Monitor* (March 1996): 1, 10.

9. Robert Kraut, Michael Patterson, Vicki Lundmark, Sara Kiesler, Tridas Mukopadhyay, and William Scherlis, "Internet Paradox: A Social Technology That Reduces Social Involvement and Psychological Well-Being?" *American Psychologist* 53 (1998): 1017–31.

10. Peter Jaret, "Special Health Report: The National Sleep Debt," *USA Weekend,* January 3–5, 1997, 4.

11. She writes honestly and eloquently of "the tomorrow trap" in her own life and offers excellent advice. See Sue Shellenbarger, "My Own Mirage," *Wall Street Journal,* December 17, 1999, W1, W16

12. Paul C. Vitz, "Back to Human Dignity: From Modern to Postmodern Psychology," *Intercollegiate Review* 31 (1996): 19. This article is a very readable introduction to chaos theory.

13. Thomas Petzinger, Jr., "How Creativity Can Take Wing at Edge of Chaos," *Wall Street Journal,* October 18, 1996, B1.

14. Albert Ellis, "The Impossibility of Achieving Consistently Good Mental Health," *American Psychologist* 42 (1987): 374.

15. William C. Spohn, Book Review: *Morality of the Heart, America,* November 2, 1991, 322.

16. For a discussion of this debate see Judith Stevens-Long and Michael L. Commons, *Adult Life,* 4th ed. (Mountain View, Calif.: Mayfield, 1992), 305–19. For a popular discussion of findings questioning the existence of "midlife crisis" see Erica Goode, "New Study Finds Middle Age Is Prime of Life," *New York Times,* national edition, February 16, 1999, D6.

17. See Csikszentmihalyi, *Flow.*

18. Dan P. McAdams, *Intimacy* (New York: Doubleday, 1989).

19. Rose Mary Volbrecht, "Friendship: Mutual Apprenticeship in Moral Development," *Journal of Value Inquiry* 24 (1990): 301–14.

20. Laura L. Carstensen, Derek M. Isaacowitz, and Susan T. Charles, "Taking Time Seriously: A Theory of Socioemotional Selectivity," *American Psychologist* 54 (1999): 165–81.

21. Grazyna Kochanska, "Toward a Synthesis of Parental Socialization and Child Temperament in Early Development of Conscience," *Child Development* 64 (1993): 325–47.

22. Richard A. Depue, Paul F. Collings, and Monica Luciana, "A Model of Neurobiology — Environment Interaction in Developmental Psychopathology," in *Frontiers of Developmental Psychopathology*, ed. Mark F. Lenzenweger and Jeffrey J. Haugaard (New York: Oxford University Press, 1996), 48.

23. James J. Gross, "Emotions and Emotion Regulation" in *Handbook of Personality: Theory and Research*, ed. Lawrence A. Pervin and Oliver P. John, 2d ed. (New York: Guilford Press, 1999), 525.

24. See James J. Gross and Ricardo F. Munoz, "Emotion Regulation and Mental Health," *Clinical Psychology: Science and Practice*, 2 (1995): 151–61, and Claire B. Kopp, "Young Children and Their Paths to Self-Regulation," *American Psychological Association, Division 7 Newsletter* (January 1995): 1, 3–6.

25. Gross and Munoz, "Emotion Regulation and Mental Health," 155.

26. A brief but interesting discussion on this issue is found in Michael Marriott, "The Urge to Blurt Plagues Strangers," *New York Times*, national edition, December 30, 1996, B5.

27. Richard R. Bootzin and Joan Ross Acocella, *Abnormal Psychology: Current Perspectives*, 5th ed. (New York: Random House, 1988), 195.

28. Edward P. Sarafino, *Health Psychology: Biopsychosocial Interactions*, 2d ed. (New York: John Wiley, 1994), 95–97.

29. National Institute of Mental Health, *Basic Behavioral Science Research for Mental Health: A National Investment* (Washington, D.C.: U.S. Government Printing Office, 1995), 14–15.

30. Mihaly Csikszentmihalyi, *The Evolving Self: A Psychology for the Third Millennium* (San Francisco: HarperPerennial, 1994), 35.

31. Susan Heitler, *From Conflict to Resolution* (New York: W. W. Norton, 1990).

32. See, for example, Carol Tavris, *Anger: The Misunderstood Emotion* (New York: Simon and Schuster, 1989), and Jeffrey Kottler, *Beyond Blame* (San Francisco: Jossey-Bass, 1994).

33. Nico H. Frijda, "The Laws of Emotion," *American Psychologist* 43 (1988): 354.

34. Anne Colby and William Damon, *Some Do Care: Contemporary Lives of Moral Commitment* (New York: Free Press, 1992), 278.

Dimension Two: Defenses

1. Though many Americans (primarily white middle-class Americans) view the 1950s as a sort of "ideal" period, for some groups statistics tell a different

story. Particularly for minorities, single women, and the poor, it was hardly a tranquil period. See Stephanie Coontz, *The Way We Never Were* (New York: Basic Books, 1992).

2. "American Opinion: A Quarterly Survey of Politics, Economics, and Values," *Wall Street Journal,* December 13, 1996, R4.

3. For the formulation of defenses as discussed in this chapter I rely upon the work of a number of noted researchers and sources. See, for example, American Psychiatric Association, *Diagnostic and Statistical Manual of Mental Disorders, DSM-IV* (Washington, D.C.: American Psychiatric Press, 1994); Mardi J. Horowitz, *Introduction to Psychodynamics: A New Synthesis* (New York: Basic Books, 1988); George E. Vaillant, *Adaptation to Life* (Boston: Little, Brown, 1977); George E. Vaillant, *Ego Mechanisms of Defense: A Guide for Clinicians and Researchers* (Washington, D.C.: American Psychiatric Press, 1992).

4. For "reasons" why we need defenses I rely upon my own clinical experience and George E. Vaillant, *The Wisdom of the Ego* (Cambridge, Mass.: Harvard University Press, 1993). For classification purposes, defenses are described in a variety of ways, e.g., mature, healthy, immature, and neurotic. In order to simplify this terrain I label those defenses that are psychologically adaptive and conducive to moral growth as "healthy" whereas those defenses that impair human and moral development I label as "unhealthy."

5. Barbara M. Stilwell, Matthew R. Galvin, and Stephen M. Kopta, *Right vs. Wrong: Raising a Child with a Conscience* (Bloomington: Indiana University Press, 2000), 9.

6. Ibid.

7. Jonathan Lear, *Open Minded: Working Out the Logic of the Soul* (Cambridge, Mass.: Harvard University Press, 1998), 8.

8. Ibid.

9. Edwin I. Megargee, "Internal Inhibitions and Controls," in *Handbook of Personality Psychology,* ed. Robert Hogan, John Johnson, and Stephen Briggs (San Diego: Academic Press, 1997).

10. Sharon Begley, "Is Everybody Crazy?" *Newsweek,* January 26, 1998, 52.

11. For a critique of the "psychology industry" see Tana Dineen, *Manufacturing Victims: What the Psychology Industry is Doing to People,* 2d ed. (Westmount, Quebec, Canada: Robert Davies Multimedia Publishing, 1998).

12. See, for example, Jerome Kagan, *Three Seductive Ideas* (Cambridge, Mass.: Harvard University Press, 1998), 187.

13. Katharine Q. Seelye, "Concealing a Pregnancy to Avoid Telling Mom," *New York Times,* national Sunday edition, June 15, 1997, Section E, 5.

14. For the insight of the self's burden in the modern world I am indebted to social psychologist Roy Baumeister. See Roy F. Baumeister, *Escaping the Self: Alcoholism, Spirituality, Masochism, and Other Flights from the Burden of Selfhood* (New York: Basic Books, 1991).

15. For an interesting perspective on multiple selves see Kenneth J. Gergen, *The Saturated Self: Dilemmas of Identity in Contemporary Life* (New York: Basic Books, 1991).

16. For a more detailed discussion of human behavior in a computerized world see the special issue of *Monitor on Psychology* (April 2000): 5–65.

17. For the sake of clarity, the "self" (unified whole) is a conscious sense an individual has of himself or herself as an "I" (self-agency) and a "me" (personal attributes). A "self" that is one of many ("multiple selves") is the conscious sense of "who I am" at a specific moment in time. A "role" is a socially defined relationship I have with others (e.g., a son, a parent, a supervisor). In contemporary society we "feel" often as many selves (a self for each role). Though viewing the self as "multiple" might have some advantages, I maintain that to foster moral integrity we must view the self as a unified whole.

18. Quoted in Rob Hiaasen, "A Single Word Pigeonholes Clinton," *Denver Post,* January 14, 1999, 6F

Dimension Three: Empathy

1. Robert D. Hare, *Without Conscience* (New York: Pocket Books, 1993), 44.

2. Ibid., 33.

3. Clifford Krauss, "How Personal Tragedy Can Shape Public Policy," *New York Times,* national edition, May 16, 1993, 16.

4. There exists no consensus on empathy's meaning among psychological researchers. Most would agree, however, that it involves a type of experience in which one understands or feels another's experience. When the emphasis is on *understanding* someone else's perspective, the term "perspective-taking" (a "cognitive" form of empathy) is sometimes applied. My own thinking on empathy has been influenced by the writings of Martin L. Hoffman, one of the preeminent scholars in the field of empathy research, to whom I am deeply indebted. See Martin L. Hoffman, "The Development of Empathy," in *Altruism and Helping Behavior,* ed. J. Philippe Rushton and Richard M. Sorrentino (Hillsdale, N.J.: Lawrence Erlbaum, 1981), 41–63; Martin L. Hoffman, "Empathy, Its Limitations, and Its Role in a Comprehensive Moral Theory," in *Moral Behavior and Moral Development,* ed. William M. Kurtines and Jacob L. Gewirtz (New York: John Wiley, 1984), 283–302; and Martin L. Hoffman, "The Contribution of Empathy to Justice and Moral Judgment," in *Empathy and Its Development,* ed. Nancy Eisenberg and Janet Strayer (New York: Cambridge University Press, 1987), 47–80.

5. Robert J. Lifton, *The Broken Connection* (New York: Simon & Schuster, 1979), 123–24.

6. Many psychologists, including Martin Hoffman, have made this same point.

7. I say "might" because empathy alone does not guarantee that we help someone. For example, while driving down the highway you see a person stranded next to a car whose hood is up. Let's say this same situation had happened to you two weeks previously, and a total stranger stopped and gave you a lift to the nearest gas station. Even though you had benefited from this stranger's generosity and had recalled this incident as you observed the stranded motorist, you do not stop. Why? Numerous reasons might explain your decision (even as

you empathize with the stranded motorist). You could be in a rush to make an appointment. In addition, the time of day, the amount of traffic, the feelings you have (e.g., fear of stopping and talking with a total stranger), or any number of other reasons could lead you to override any empathic inclinations you have to stop and offer assistance. My point is that there are numerous conflicting factors contributing to what you ultimately view as the "right" thing to do. Any number of these factors could override your empathy-induced inclination to respond. Of course, you could also be creative. You might get off at the next exit and stop at a gas station and inform the attendant, or call "911" and inform the operator of the location of the stranded motorist.

Dimension Four: Guilt

1. For a popular discussion of the social trend toward public shaming see Jonathan Alter and Pat Wingert, "The Return of Shame," *Newsweek*, February 6, 1995, 21–25; Pam Belluck, "Forget Prisons: Americans Cry Out for the Pillory," *New York Times*, Sunday national edition, Nation section, October 4, 1998, 5; and Jan Hoffman, "Crime and Punishment: Shame Gains Popularity," *New York Times*, national edition, January 16, 1997, A1, A11.

2. By contrasting the hierarchical and relational models I do not wish to leave the impression that baby boomers place no emphasis on personal fulfillment or satisfying relationships. Most certainly they do. Just ask any happily married baby boomer. Post-baby boomers, likewise, see the need for authority and structure. Just talk to any young parent today about the need for rules and regulations for their children. My point is that the baby boomer generation grew to adulthood in a period that was in many ways unique. Enrollment in higher education surged, the economy expanded dramatically, and America became a global superpower that confronted an identified and feared enemy (communism). It was within this cultural context that the perception of hierarchy initially took on an aura of respectability.

3. Sue Shellenbarger, "Work and Family: These Top Bosses May Signal Move to More Family Time," *Wall Street Journal*, April 30, 1997, B1, and Sue Shellenbarger, "Work and Family: Future Work Policies May Focus on Teens, Trimming Workloads," *Wall Street Journal*, December 30, 1998, B1.

4. For a discussion of how the relational model has influenced the business and corporate understandings of successful leaders see Robert Hogan, Gordon J. Curphy, and Joyce Hogan, "What We Know about Leadership: Effectiveness and Personality," *American Psychologist* 49 (1994): 493–504, and Peter G. Northouse, *Leadership: Theory and Practice* (Thousand Oaks, Calif.: Sage Publications, 1997).

5. See Robert N. Bellah, Richard Madsen, William M. Sullivan, Ann Swidler, and Steven M. Tipton, *Habits of the Heart: Individualism and Commitment in American Life* (Berkeley, Calif.: University of California Press, 1985) and Christopher Lasch, *The Culture of Narcissism* (New York: Norton, 1978).

6. Suein Hwang and Michelle Green, "Restaurants Get Rude!" *Wall Street Journal*, February 26, 1999, W1, W14.

7. Asra Q. Nomani, "In the Skies Today, a Weird New Worry: Sexual Misconduct," *Wall Street Journal*, June 10, 1998, A1, A8.

8. See, for example, Martin L. Hoffman, "Development of Prosocial Motivation: Empathy and Guilt," in *The Development of Prosocial Behavior*, ed. Nancy Eisenberg (New York: Academic Press, 1982), 282–313, and Carolyn Zahn-Waxler and Grazyna Kochanska, "The Origins of Guilt," in *Nebraska Symposium on Motivation 1988: Socioemotional Development*, ed. Ross A. Thompson (Lincoln: University of Nebraska Press, 1990), 183–258.

9. Jerome Kagan, *Three Seductive Ideas* (Cambridge, Mass.: Harvard University Press, 1998), 193.

10. Ibid.

11. For a discussion of these issues see Martin L. Hoffman, "Development of Prosocial Motivation: Empathy and Guilt." See also Carolyn Zahn-Waxler, "From the Enlightenment to the Millennium: Changing Conceptions of the Moral Sentiments," *Developmental Psychologist* (Fall 1998): 1–7.

12. Zahn-Waxler and Kochanska, "The Origins of Guilt," 204.

13. For an excellent discussion of the psychology of forgiveness see Robert D. Enright and Joanna North, eds., *Exploring Forgiveness* (Madison: University of Wisconsin Press, 1998).

Dimension Five: Idealization

1. Martin E. P. Seligman, "President's Column: Striking a Healthy Balance in Ethics," *APA Monitor* (June 1998): 2.

2. Some distinguish between the terms "moral beliefs" and "moral principles." I use them interchangeably to refer to ideas that provide moral guidance for our behaviors.

3. Gary Smith, "Sportsmen of the Year," *Sports Illustrated*, December 21, 1998, 42.

4. Thomas Hargrove and Guido H. Stempel, "Americans Don't Have Heroes, Poll Finds," *Indianapolis Star*, August 14, 1994, D5.

5. June Kronholz, "Political Leaders Aren't Heroes to Youngsters Anymore," *Wall Street Journal*, April 21, 1998, A24.

6. Dennis Kelly, "Teens Want, Can't Find Character in Leaders," *USA Today*, June 18, 1999, 12D.

7. Brent Staples, "Role Models, Bogus and Real," *New York Times*, national edition, June 24, 1994, A26.

8. Rick Reilly, "The Big Hero of Littleton," *Sports Illustrated*, May 3, 1999, 100.

9. Quoted in June Kronholz, "Political Leaders Aren't Heroes to Youngsters Anymore."

10. Quoted in Don Yaeger, "Goodby, Sweetness," *Sports Illustrated*, November 8, 1999, 86.

11. For a philosophical approach to moral imagination see Mark Johnson, *Moral Imagination: Implications of Cognitive Science for Ethics* (Chicago: University of Chicago Press, 1993).

12. Thomas F. Green, "The Formation of Conscience in an Age of Technology," *American Journal of Education* (November 1985): 23.

13. Though I identify moral imagination most closely with the idealization dimension of conscience, this imaginative capacity is interweaved throughout the seven-dimensional model. We noted that to imagine morally requires that we create, converse, and view fresh perspectives. To illustrate, moral imagination surfaces when we invest the psychic energy to converse with friends who offer us "another view" or empathize with others that produce in us new insights about them or help us understand their suffering or situation. The seven-dimensional model of conscience I propose offers a framework for the moral imagination to come alive. Nonetheless, because of the distinctive nature of idealization — its future perspective and its quest for the greater good — moral imagination is best understood within the context of this dimension of conscience.

14. Edward Tivnan, *The Moral Imagination: Confronting the Ethical Issues of Our Day* (New York: Simon and Schuster, 1996), 266.

15. Thomas F. Green, "The Formation of Conscience in an Age of Technology," 24.

16. Charles Taylor, *Sources of the Self: The Making of Modern Identity* (Cambridge, Mass.: Harvard University Press, 1989), 47.

17. Ibid., 44.

18. Ibid., 23. I expand somewhat on Taylor's conception regarding the scope of what constitutes ordinary life.

19. See Eli Sagan, *Freud, Women, and Morality* (New York: Basic Books, 1988).

Dimension Six: Self-Esteem

1. David G. Myers, *The American Paradox* (New Haven: Yale University Press, 2000), 165.

2. See Sharon Begley, "You're OK, I'm Terrific: 'Self-Esteem' Backfires," *Newsweek*, July 13, 1998, 69 and Nancy Hellmich, "Emphasizing Achievement Not Faint Praise," *USA Today*, October 24, 1995, 1D–2D.

3. Hellmich, "Emphasizing Achievement Not Faint Praise," 2D.

4. Randall Edwards, "Is Self-Esteem Really All That Important?" *APA Monitor* (May 1995): 43–44.

5. For a summary of this research see Roy F. Baumeister, ed., *Self-Esteem: The Puzzle of Low Positive Regard* (New York: Plenum, 1993), and Roy F. Baumeister, "Identity, Self-Concept, and Self-Esteem: The Self Lost and Found," in *Handbook of Personality Psychology*, ed. Robert Hogan, John Johnson, and Stephen Briggs (New York: Academic Press, 1997), 687–91.

6. Roy F. Baumeister, Laura Smart, and Joseph M. Boden, "Relation of Threatened Egotism to Violence and Aggression: The Dark Side of High Self-Esteem," *Psychological Review* 103 (1996): 5–33.

7. Ibid., 29.

8. Many psychologists have offered cogent critiques of the self-esteem movement. See, for example, Martin E. P. Seligman, *Learned Optimism: How to Change Your Mind and Your Life* (New York: Simon & Schuster, 1998).

9. "The Powerful Idea of Human Rights," *New York Times,* national edition, December 8, 1999, A30.

10. Charles Taylor, *Sources of the Self: The Making of Modern Identity* (Cambridge, Mass.: Harvard University Press, 1989), 11. Taylor's thinking offers a helpful summary of how respect for the individual in the modern era has come to pass and explains succinctly the pitfalls facing a moral person in the modern era (see 3–90).

11. Ibid., 3–14.

12. For a discussion of various psychological issues related to self-esteem see Richard L. Bednar, M. Gawain Wells, and Scott R. Peterson, *Self-Esteem: Paradoxes and Innovations in Clinical Theory and Practice* (Washington, D.C.: American Psychological Association, 1989).

Dimension Seven: Moral Beliefs

1. Martin E. P. Seligman, "President's Column: The American Way to Blame," *APA Monitor* (July 1998): 2.

2. Ibid.

3. Charles Taylor, *The Ethics of Authenticity* (Cambridge, Mass.: Harvard University Press, 1991), 29.

4. Sidney Callahan, *In Good Conscience: Reason and Emotion in Moral Decision Making* (New York: HarperCollins, 1991), 65.

5. See, for example, Roger Rosenblatt, "Teaching Johnny to Be Good," *New York Times Magazine,* April 30, 1995, 36–41, 50, 60,64, 74. See also Marvin W. Berkowitz, "Integrating Structure and Content in Moral Education " (1997), available at http://www.uic.edu/~lnucci/MoralEd/aotm/article13.html

6. Howard Fineman, "The Virtuecrats," *Newsweek,* June 13, 1994, 33.

7. Jerome Kagan, "The Moral Function of the School," *Daedalus* (Summer 1981): 163.

8. Gerald Grant, "The Character of Education and the Education of Character," *Daedalus* (Summer 1981): 148.

9. Rushworth M. Kidder, *How Good People Make Tough Choices* (New York: William Morrow, 1995), 77–92.

10. O. C. Ferrell and John Fraedrich, *Business Ethics: Ethical Decision Making and Cases,* 2d ed. (Boston: Houghton Mifflin, 1994), 261–66.

11. James Q. Wilson, *The Moral Sense* (New York: Free Press, 1993).

12. Kidder, *How Good People Make Tough Choices,* 92.

13. Jerome Kagan, *The Nature of the Child* (New York: Basic Books, 1984), 152.

14. For a brief look at current trends in spirituality see Matt Murray, "A Faith of One's Own," *Wall Street Journal,* January 1, 2000, R50.

15. The psychologist most responsible for the view that psychology must restore the role of intention to human behavior is Joseph F. Rychlak. He argues this point persuasively in his book *In Defense of Human Consciousness* (Washington, D.C.: American Psychological Association, 1997).

Conclusion: Conscience in Work and Relationship

1. Real-life issues are more likely to reflect people's understanding of everyday morality than abstract, hypothetical dilemmas. See Lawrence J. Walker, Russell C. Pitts, Karl H. Hennig, and M. Kyle Matsuba, "Reasoning about Morality and Real-Life Moral Problems," in *Morality in Everyday Life,* ed. Melanie Killen and Daniel Hart (New York: Cambridge University Press, 1999), 371–407.

2. The most readable and informative discussion on evil I have read as applied to modern American culture is Ron Rosenbaum, "Staring into the Heart of the Heart of Darkness," *New York Times Magazine,* June 4, 1995, 36, 39–41, 43, 50, 58, 61, 72.

3. See, for example, Roy F. Baumeister, *Evil: Inside Human Violence and Cruelty* (New York: W. H. Freeman, 1997), and John M. Darley, "Social Organization for the Production of Evil," *Psychological Inquiry* 3 (1992): 199–218.

4. Darley, "Social Organization for the Production of Evil," 201.

5. Ibid.

6. Ibid., 207.

7. Jerome Kagan, *Three Seductive Ideas* (Cambridge, Mass.: Harvard University Press, 1998), 192.

8. James Q. Wilson, *The Moral Sense* (New York: Free Press, 1993), 251.